THEY SANG FOR NORWAY

MINNESOTA
HISTORICAL
SOCIETY PRESS

They Sang for Norway

OLAF OLESON'S IMMIGRANT CHOIR

Ane-Charlotte Five Aarset

Originally published by Kolofon Forlag, 2012. © Ane-Charlotte Five Aarset.
Translated to English by Roald Aarset based on the original edition, *Utvandreren*.

www.mnhspress.org

The Minnesota Historical Society Press is a member of the Association of
American University Presses.

Manufactured in the United States of America

10 9 8 7 6 5 4 3 2 1

♾ The paper used in this publication meets the minimum requirements of the
American National Standard for Information Sciences—Permanence for Printed
Library Materials, ANSI Z39.48–1984.

International Standard Book Number
ISBN: 978-1-68134-047-0 (paper)
ISBN: 978-1-68134-048-7 (e-book)

Library of Congress Cataloging-in-Publication Data available upon request.

This and other Minnesota Historical Society Press books are available from
popular e-book vendors.

In memory of my father-in-law, Reidar Aarset; he had such a fine singing voice and was a member of the students' choir in Trondheim 1938–42, and I know he would have enjoyed following me in writing this book, as he did with my two previous projects.

The Norwegian Singers' Association of America arranges a three-day *Sangerfest* every other year at a chosen location in the Midwest. The summer of 1912 the festival was held in Fargo, North Dakota. *Grieg Mandskor,* founded by O. M. Oleson in Fort Dodge, Iowa, 1891, is standing under its banner, number ten from left. *Photo by Dewey's Studio, Norwegian Singers' Association of America, Norwegian-American Collection, National Library of Norway*

These singing groups in America embodied the new Norwegian ideals of enlightened progress and freedom with equal standing.

Camilla Haugen Cai, Professor of Music, Kenyon College, Gambier, Ohio, 2001

Contents

Preface

I have always heard about our family's rich uncle in America and about all the money his relatives in Norway expected to inherit. However, the big inheritance from America never came, disappointing many people in my family as well as others. Many Norwegians believe that the more than five hundred thousand emigrants to America during the nineteenth century let their home country down, while those who stayed behind built it up. Through my research for this book I found a different story.

After having written a book about my great-grandfather the "Marksman General" Ola Five—a guerilla leader who played a large role in Norway's liberation from Sweden in 1905—I became curious about his brother "over there." I started gathering information about this brother and others who had emigrated to America before 1900. Through letters, newspapers, magazines, and books I found a treasure trove of information. This information confirmed that Norwegian Americans supported the illegal army Ola Five was building up and also contributed to funding the creation of Norway's first political party, Venstre (Liberal Party). Both the Liberal Party and the guerilla army played important roles in the fight against the Swedish king and his servants in the Norwegian bureaucracy which led to Norway gaining parliamentarianism in 1884. This formed the background for what happened in 1905, the dissolution of the union with Sweden. Once again, Norwegian Americans were ready to help, this time also with weapons in their hands.

Patriotism toward the old homeland was a driving force when immigrant organizations were formed. Special among these were the Norwegian American male choruses—they brought the music of Norway over the ocean.

Ane-Charlotte Five Aarset
Høvik, June 2016

Radicals

They were brothers. One organized guerrillas, the other established male choruses and became a philanthropist. One was "a good Norwegian," the other emigrated to America. Both made an impact on Norway's history. This is the story about the one who left.

On May 7, 1939, a tall, ninety-year-old man welcomed fifty-three members of *Den norske Studentersangforening* (the Norwegian Student Choral Society) to the city of Fort Dodge, Iowa. The singers have sidetracked from their official program with Norwegian crown prince Olav and crown princess Märtha in order to greet the old man. For a short moment, without anybody noticing, he shuts his eyes and lets his mind float back in time:

> . . . to June 19, 1905, when he led an earlier generation of Norwegian student singers through the doors of the White House to meet President Roosevelt. The singers were cultural ambassadors to America at a critical time for Norway.

> . . . to March 18, 1881, when he persuaded Norway's most famous author, Bjørnstjerne Bjørnson, to come to Fort Dodge. While in America, Bjørnson spoke against the pietistic Norwegian American congregations and gathered support for Johan Sverdrup, who was working to establish the Liberal Party, in Norway.

> . . . and further back, to the 1850–60s, when his older brothers were pretending to hold parliamentary elections on their family farm, Østre Five, in Stod (later Kvam), one of the most radical rural districts in the "Red County," Nord-Trøndelag. He himself was happiest when playing in the woods, carving flutes, and listening to the harp-like sounds of the rustling leaves of the aspen trees. Or when the family formed an

orchestra, with his parents and sisters singing, his older brothers playing violin and he accompanying them on the piano.[1]

This story begins on the Five farm, where the main house, built in the traditional style of the region, was situated on a hilltop with its broad front facing the beautiful lake Snåsavatnet. The people from Five were among those who occupied the front seats in the two-hundred-year-old Kvam church. A crucifix kept in the church proved it to be founded on top of an older church from the thirteenth century or earlier, which in its turn had been built on the remains of an old Viking settlement. In the area nearby were found graves, small fortresses, and petroglyphs from that period.

The farmer Ole Larsen Sunde (later Five) and his wife, Olava, born Andersdatter Kirkol, could both follow their line of ancestors back to the beginning of the seventeenth century. Ole Larsen Sunde was a knowledgeable and well-respected man. He came from the farm Nedre Sunnan, in the neighboring parish of Egge. He had acquired Østre Five in 1828. Besides being a farmer, he was a teacher, parish clerk, sexton, founder of *Kvam Sogns Brandassuranseforening* (an insurance institution), member of the first township council, and township treasurer. As treasurer he kept the money in a small wall cabinet in the living room. A "quick trip" to the city, Trondheim, was usually an eight-day undertaking and included travel by boat. The people in Kvam, however, did not feel isolated. Ole Sunde subscribed to newspapers from the capital, and he looked to England to stay updated on potato growing. He was among the first to cross local species of cattle with imported Ayrshire cattle. The result was what became the popular breed known as *rødt trønderfe* (red trønder cattle).

The Five brothers and their friends from the surrounding farms debated the hot topic of the time: the struggle against the rule of appointed government officials. Their slogan was "Power to the people," meaning the farmers, who no longer accepted the heavy taxes imposed on them. As early as the 1830s the author and poet Henrik Wergeland traveled the country speaking of democracy and the power of ordinary people. In addition, a sense of Norway as an independent nation was growing in reaction to the four hundred years of Danish rule over Norway, a role taken over by Sweden in 1814.

The real breakthrough of Norwegian national romanticism came in February of 1849 when the composer and violinist Ole Bull performed in Kristiania (now Oslo) in front of an audience of fifteen hundred people. In the meanwhile, Peter Christen Asbjørnsen, one of Norway's most beloved authors and storytellers, collected Norwegian folktales. He believed these stories were part of the soul of the Norwegian people and would strengthen their feeling of national identity. Visible signs of a nation in the making were emerging: for example, the Royal Palace was completed in 1849, and the university continued to develop. The parliament building was under construction, and in 1868 people in the counties around the city of Trondheim started the first nationwide collection to restore the Nidaros Cathedral to its former glory. St. Olav, the patron saint and "eternal king" of Norway, is said to have been buried where the cathedral now stands. Even as much as three hundred years after the Reformation, many Catholic customs were kept alive out in the rural areas. Boys were given names like Olaf, Oluf, and Ole after St. Olav and Ingebrigt or Engebregt after the last Catholic archbishop Olav Engelbrektsson.

The youngest of five siblings, Oluf (later Olaf) Martin Olsen Five was the family's piano player. The other children were Eilert Andreas, Karoline Jørgine, Ingebrigt, and Ole—or Ola as they usually called him. Olaf also had two half sisters, Ingeborg Marta and Lorense Petrine. They were daughters of Ole Larsen Sunde and his first wife, Inger, born Pedersdatter Haugan. The women in this family were strong and independent. Perhaps they reflected a heritage from the young Viking woman found buried close by. She had with her in her grave weapons, a dog, and tools, suggesting she was more powerful than most women at the time.

Contrary to what was customary among wealthy people in the cities, meals at the Five farm were taken with everybody gathered around the same table, both the Five family and the people hired to work on the farm. Outside, the farmyard and the meadows were covered with wildflowers. In the woods surrounding the farm were blue and white anemones, lilies of the valley, and the largest orchid in Scandinavia, called St. Olav's Bowl by the people in the region. Along the water's edge grew yellow lilies. The lime-rich soil around the lake made the ground fertile and the flora luxuriant. Many different kinds of birds

Olaf's parents, Ole Larsen Sunde (Five) and Olava Andersdatter Kirkol, 1870. Both of them could trace their ancestors back to the early seventeenth century. *Private collection*

nested in the area. Olaf found all of this exciting, and it seems to have influenced him for life.[2]

During the summer the scent of flowering bird cherries filled the air, and when autumn came the orange berries of the mountain ash trees stood out among the green leaves. The roads, lined with flowers, wound their way between the farms, around the hills and soft mountaintops. The boys, wearing shirts made of rough, itchy wool, ran about barefoot far into the autumn. When the days grew shorter, the families gathered around the fireplace after sunset. The women were carding and spinning wool while the men spent time mending tools in preparation for the next farming season. The fireplace was fed with small pieces of pine which gave enough light to work by. The winters could be extremely cold, with dangerous open channels on the ice. The year Olaf was born, a group of men, his father among them, went through the ice. A horse and four men died, but luckily his father survived. The incident inspired the local poet, Ole Øveråsen Litlemarken, to write a popular song which was much sung in the region.[3]

Oluf Martin Olsen Five was born June 29, 1849, at the time of summer when the wildflowers were in full bloom. The sign for this day on the old traditional wooden calendar stick was a key or a flower, the symbol of the apostle Peter. This indicated that it was the day for harvesting herbs. This almost seems like a premonition of Olaf's occupations in adult life—gardener and pharmacist. Later he used the name of Olaf Martin Oleson, sometimes just O. M. Oleson or even the Hon. O. M. Oleson. In addition to his work as gardener and pharmacist, he also became an influential businessman, a patron of the arts, and a politician in the city of Fort Dodge, Iowa, which was sometimes referred to as "Little Chicago." When asked to run for Congress, which could have been the start of a long political career, he turned down the offer. Instead it was song and music, in addition to his business activities, that would make his name known in the Midwest. The many male choruses that were formed by Norwegian Americans became an important cultural link to their old homeland. Thousands of people gathered for concerts on both sides of the Atlantic. Olaf invited both the famous Norwegian author Bjørnstjerne Bjørnson and the internationally known composer Edvard Grieg to participate, but they did not take the invitation seriously.[4]

From Inderøya to the Palace

From their home on the farm in Nord-Trøndelag, Olaf and his brothers and sisters eventually found different places in society. Eilert, the oldest brother, was the natural heir to the farm. He also became a teacher and the local bank manager. He was a key person in many of the activities in the parish and founded what was probably the first liberal youth association in Norway, Stod Youth Association. Ingebrigt became a wood carver and artist. Ola went to the university in Kristiania and was educated as a high school teacher. Quite early he started forming rifle clubs, which over the years to come would develop into a nationwide illegal army. Karoline married the local farmer Henrik Aageson Langhammer and had many children, among them Ole Langhammer, who later became mayor. Olaf dreamt of becoming a gardener, a profession that was in high demand in those days.[1]

Younger sons, not in position to take over the farm, were often encouraged to get an education in horticulture. They were trained by foreign gardeners or by Norwegian gardeners educated abroad. Local garden associations were established to promote the subject. Books and magazines were issued to show how to make an attractive park or garden. In the early 1860s a position as county gardener was set up in Nord-Trøndelag, where gardening had a long-standing tradition. The old monasteries there, Munkeby, Tautra, and Rein, used to have large kitchen gardens, where fruit trees, berries, and herbs were grown.

The first county gardener, the Swede Gustav Landgren, tried to encourage people to eat more vegetables, but with limited success. People did not want to have "grass" in their meat stew. So, instead he turned to planting trees in parks and gardens and creating allées. In the beginning the trees were simply brought out from the woods. However, it soon became a modern trend to import more exotic types of trees.

The gardens more and more became places of beauty and recreation. Large romantic gardens, or landscape gardens as they were called, were popular among the wealthy when Olaf was young. The French Renaissance and Baroque gardens had no appeal in Norway, at least not outside of the cities. Most Norwegians did not want symmetry, straight lines, artistically shaped trees, or anything else reminding them of constraint and pompous architecture. They wanted the English style of landscape park with its attempt to resemble nature.

The design of the landscape parks was inspired by philosophers, poets, and artists who wanted to create paradise on earth. The parks contained clusters of trees, large lawns, graveled paths, creeks, bridges, and pavilions. Benches were scattered about to allow visitors to sit and admire the picturesque view. A variety of flowers were arranged "randomly" in small groups or in large beds to create a carpet of blossoms. The kitchen garden still served its function but was now separated from the rest of the park. Trees commonly found in these parks included lilac, laburnum, jasmine, elder, hazel, linden, and elm. In addition, imported weeping willows and various columnar trees were increasingly being used. To plan, create, and maintain these parks, landscape gardeners were needed, and that was what Olaf wanted to become.

After finishing primary school, where learning parts of the catechism and the Bible by heart seems to have been the main goal, and after being confirmed in the small red church in Kvam, in 1865 Olaf became gardener apprentice under the county gardener Gustav Landgren. There he met another apprentice, Peter Zakariassen Nøvik from Ytterøya, a bit further out on the Trondheimsfjord. Not long after their arrival, Landgren returned to Sweden. It was said to be a love affair with a local married woman that made him decide to leave. He was replaced by Edvard Guldbrandsen from Nes in Romerike. For a year Olaf and Peter traveled with Guldbrandsen from one wealthy family to the next in the region around the Trondheimsfjord, arranging gardens and planting trees and flowers. During the winter months when gardening was not possible, Olaf went home and worked on the farm.[2]

Olaf must have done good work as a gardener. In 1866 he was offered a permanent position by the landowner Herman Løchen on the Sundnes estate on Inderøya, innermost in the Trondheimsfjord. It must have been like entering a fairy tale. The estate is located on top of a small hill with a long allée stretching from the main road up to the

The Sundnes estate, Inderøya, Nord-Trøndelag. Drawn by Henrik Mathiesen, 1889.
Private collection

front yard. The two-story main building has the shape of a horseshoe, its front facing the fjord with a view of the fjord on three sides. Inside are found a banquet hall, fancy stucco work on the ceilings and thirty-two beautifully decorated iron stoves placed in oval niches throughout the building. Eleven chimneys are visible on the roof. The estate was originally an archbishop's residence, but was later used as a military center, a so-called dragoon headquarters, and after that it was in the hands of several landowners before Herman Løchen bought it in 1847.[3]

Olaf's task was to help create a garden according to an outline created by the folklore collector Peter Christen Asbjørnsen. At the time Asbjørnson was director of forestry in the Trøndelag region. He had recently been on a journey to Cairo and had brought back new ideas.

Olaf assisted in the construction of an intricately designed fountain system where the water ran in a closed-circuit arrangement including ponds, caves, wells, creeks, and a lion head spouting water. Weeping willows were planted with their branches touching the water's surface. A sundial was placed on the lawn, and a variety of exotic trees, including fruit trees, were planted along paths throughout the garden. He built greenhouses, benches, and pavilions and planted flowers such as roses, tulips, and grape hyacinths, among many other types. Herman Løchen's children longed to pick the flowers, but this was not allowed.

Løchen was an innovator in Norwegian farming and had developed Sundnes into a model farm of close to four hundred acres. The combined barn and cowshed was approximately two hundred and thirty feet long and housed four hundred cows and oxen. He also built and ran what was probably the country's first industrial dairy, one of the country's two distilleries, a brewery, and a barrel workshop. He experimented with oyster and freshwater fish farming, owned large forests in Snåsa, and ran a steam sawmill in Steinkjer. To help bring products to and from his estate, he established a steamship company and built a private port. He acquired treasures from faraway countries which he put on display both inside and outside his house. In addition to all of this, he was mayor of Inderøy and a member of Parliament representing the district of Nordre Trondhjem.

Unlike the people at the Five farm, the Løchen family and the servants on the estate did not share the same table when meals were served. There were two kitchens, one for the landowner's family and one for the workers.

Just uphill from the farm, where an old Viking settlement once existed, stands the medieval Sakshaug church. It was erected by the same masons who had built the Nidaros cathedral in Trondheim. The Sakshaug church was consecrated by Archbishop Eystein in 1184. Its white walls and high tower were visible to Olaf at Sundnes and to people for miles around. Olaf no longer sat in the front pew as he was used to back home in the Kvam church. He had to find a place in the balcony above the entry together with the cottars from the region.

Herman Løchen, like many other wealthy men, supported several artists, and Sundnes became a center for cultural activities. Jørgen Moe, colleague of folklore collector Asbjørnsen, visited Sundnes, as did the violinist Ole Bull, the painter Adolf Tideman, and the poet Aasmund O. Vinje. Vinje was so taken by the place and the sunset he experienced when sitting on the front steps leading down toward the fjord that he wrote the poem "*Sundnes: Her ser eg fagre fjord og bygder.*" It was printed in *Ferdaminne*, a travelogue covering his many journeys around the country.

Olaf's admiration for Asbjørnsen was not only due to his landscape design. Asbjørnsen, an outstanding scientist, was the author of the six-volume *Naturhistorie for Ungdommen* (History of Nature: An Introduction for Young People). He introduced Darwin and his *Origin of Species* to the Norwegian public through a newspaper article just a few years before Olaf came to Sundnes.

Olaf stayed at Sundnes for two years. He then went to Kristiania, probably because the county gardener post in Nord-Trøndelag was eliminated for financial reasons. Olaf and his friend Peter Nøvik parted ways and did not meet again until twenty-five years later, in Chicago in 1893.

In Kristiania Olaf got a job with the gardener Peter Lorange, just opposite the Royal Palace. Lorange, a gracious and sociable man, was often called the palace gardener. He came from Fredrikshald (now Halden) and had a university degree, Ingenieur Agricol de l'Etat Gembloux, from the university in Ghent, Belgium. After his return to Norway he established a large nursery located at Ruseløkka in Kristiania. Although not far from the palace, it was an area of small wooden houses and narrow streets that attracted many different kinds of people. Nicknames for the area included Algerie and Robbers' Alley. Lorange's business was of course aimed at the wealthier residents of the capital. He

Olaf Martin Olsen Five, circa 1869, when employed by the gardener Peter Lorange in Kristiania. Photographer: Lindegaard, No 12, Kongens Gade, Christiania. *Private collection*

imported trees, flowers, and other plants from Holland, Belgium, and England. For the next two years Olaf helped Lorange build the Royal Palace's own nursery. The park around the palace was designed in the natural landscape style, which reminded him of Sundnes. Except for the graveled palace square with flowers arranged in the middle and an allée leading up to it, the main impression was of a large park with paths winding their way between trees and ponds and over small hilltops with benches scattered throughout.[4]

Lorange later acquired the large Store Stabæk estate in Bærum, six miles west of Kristiania. He settled there as a landowner, ran the farm, and sold flowers from the estate's nursery. A few years later the Ruseløkka area, including Lorange's old nursery, was torn down and redeveloped. Olaf decided not to follow Lorange to Store Stabæk. He thought he had enough practical experience and wanted to continue his education at the University of Leipzig. This was one of Europe's oldest universities and was well known for its botanical garden, formerly a monastery garden that boasted around ten thousand species of plants, among them many different herbs. Olaf's father had set aside enough money for Olaf to pursue his education there. However, one of Olaf's older brothers had left for America a few years earlier, and this would turn out to be a bigger temptation.

Ole Rynning's *True Account of America*

When the American Civil War ended in 1865 and slavery was abolished, a wave of emigration from Norway started. The first year, four emigrant ships left from Trondheim. As the rush of emigrants from the county of Nord-Trøndelag grew, *The Queen* took off from Ytterøya every second week. The first stop was Newcastle. From there the passengers were transported by railway to Liverpool, where once a week a steamship left for either New York or Quebec, Canada.[1]

In the spring of 1866, just after Olaf started as an apprentice, his twenty-five-year-old brother Ingebrigt traveled to America. Ingebrigt may have felt that he did not have enough opportunity to develop as an artist, or maybe he did not have any success finding a sweetheart while he worked as cabinetmaker for Morten Elden on the Elda farm in Namdalseid. Two of his brothers had better luck. Ola was engaged to Charlotte Elden, one of the daughters of the farmer Morten Elden, and Eilert had married her elder sister Ingeborg Henrikka.

On the Elda farm the Five brothers found kindred spirits. During Christmas parties and other family gatherings, humorously called *Collegium politicum,* radical and "dangerous"

Olaf's older brother Ingebrigt Olsen Five traveled to America in the spring of 1866. Photographer: N. J. Fjeldsæth, Trondheim, 1866. *Private collection*

ideas were discussed. Morten Elden, the head of the family, was a proud man. He felt equal to the old Viking chiefs and he wanted to see an end to the time when farmers were just tenants and commoners. He also wanted Erik Pontoppidan's pietistic catechism removed from primary school and from the preparation for confirmation. People from the inner part of the county were well known for speaking up for freedom and independence, whether in politics or religion. When Christianity was imposed on the Norwegian people about a thousand years earlier, many from the region gathered their pagan items and fled to Iceland, bringing their old traditions with them.

The first organized emigration from Norway to America took place from Rogaland in 1825 with the sloop *Restaurationen*. It was, however, Ole Rynning from Snåsa in Nord-Trøndelag who wrote the first Norwegian book about America. It was published in 1838 under the title *Sanfærdig Beretning om Amerika til Oplysning og Nytte for Bonde og Menigmand, forfattet af en Norsk, som kom derover i Juni Maaned 1837* (True Account of America for the Information and Help of Peasant and Commoner. Written by a Norwegian who arrived there in the month of June, 1837). It was commonly known as *Amerikaboken* (The America Book).

Ole Rynning, son of a pastor, was a tutor in Snåsa and a close friend and classmate of the liberal agitator and poet Henrik Wergeland. He quarreled with his father when he wanted to marry a girl from a lower social class. At the age of twenty-seven he went to Bergen and boarded the bark *Ægir*, aiming for America. The plan was to come back and fetch his fiancée as soon as he had acquired some land. From New York Rynning took a boat up the Hudson River. Eventually he made his way to Chicago, "The Capital of the Midwest." From there he went with an expedition south to Beaver Creek, where they acquired land for free. Ole Rynning, however, contracted malaria. While he lay sick, he wrote his book; he died half a year later. No one knows where his grave lies. His manuscript, however, was taken care of and brought back to Norway.

With this book Ole Rynning hoped to help poor young farmers or workers achieve a better life on the other side of the Atlantic. "The prairies are a great boon to the settlers," he wrote. Only thirty-nine pages long, his book nevertheless provided useful information and a realistic but also inviting description of the "Promised Land." A quarter of a century before the Civil War he opposed slavery, which he noticed the southern states were in favor of. He called it "An ugly contrast to this freedom and equality which justly constitute the pride of the Americans." He predicted that this contradiction would end either in a bloody war or in America being split in two. Many copies of the book were printed. It was widely available and helped keep the dream of America alive. At the time it was said that only the Bible was more read in Norway. The book was so popular that many learned to read just in order to see for themselves what Rynning had written. Ole Rynning's father, however, used the pulpit to rail against this growing emigration fever, but his preaching only fanned the flames. The original manuscript is said to have had a chapter about religious practices in Norway. This chapter was removed by a parish pastor, as in it Ole Rynning had accused the Norwegian clergy of intolerance by not promoting social reforms and education.

Before Rynning's book was published in 1839, about eighty thousand Norwegians had emigrated to America. By the end of the century the number had increased to more than five hundred thousand. This surge in emigration, constituting a substantial portion of the Norwegian population, can be read as a vote of no confidence in the future in Norway. Although Norway was not among the poorest countries in Europe, still, Norwegians left in hope of a better life in America. Many disliked the powerful officialdom and state church, both of which agitated against emigration. Already in 1837 the bishop Jacob Neuman published a pamphlet, "A Word of Admonition to the Peasants ... Who Desire to Emigrate." In this pamphlet he quotes David's advice to his people from the Bible: "Stay in the land and support yourself honestly." Neumann, being among the more liberal clerics, accepted that people from the higher social classes, students, and merchants might travel abroad to study, carry on trade, and prosper. Farmers, on the other hand, should remain where they belonged and in the social class to which they were born. This idea was in opposition to the liberal American attitude that anyone could achieve success through their own hard work.[2]

The poet Henrik Wergeland also warned against emigration, which he described as "the bleeding of our homeland." The Norwegian author and cultural leader Bjørnstjerne Bjørnson was of the same opinion, while the cosmopolitan violinist Ole Bull was among those who regarded the United States as the land of opportunity. Although a young nation, the United States wanted to show the world it was a land with appreciation for culture and invited great European musicians and composers to visit. Ole Bull was one of them. He performed all over America with his *hardingfele*, the special violin from Hardanger, to wildly enthusiastic audiences. His popularity made it possible for him to charge whatever he wished for his concerts. People flocked to his performances, and it is said that he made women faint when he entered the stage. He always had folk tunes in his repertoire. The audience felt he gave them a touch of Norway, a great comfort to those who longed for the old country. Ole Bull bought a piece of land in Pennsylvania and called it Oleana—the New Norway—with the intention of parceling it out into lots for Norwegian immigrants. The project failed quite soon, however, due to lack of a railway connection and soil that was not suited to farming.

Establishing Fort Dodge

A longing for travel and adventure together with strong hopes for the future drove many into leaving Norway in the 1800s, much as it had for the Vikings centuries earlier. Olaf's elder brother Ingebrigt Olsen Five was not scared off by Ole Bull's failure with his Oleana project. He waved farewell to his family as he left. His first stop was England. From there he sailed to Quebec, Canada, and then continued by train to Sault Ste. Marie on the east end of Lake Superior. There a large immigration port had been arranged for those not wanting to enter the United States as long as the Civil War raged. Through a series of locks the boats could enter Lake Michigan and sail all the way to Chicago. From Chicago the railroad brought Ingebrigt as far west as Iowa Falls. He probably had to walk the last stretch before coming to the small town of Fort Dodge, Iowa. The final leg took him three days. A stagecoach would have brought him there in two days, but at a high price, not to mention an uncomfortable ride on the bumpy trails. Most of Iowa, originally part of the vast Sioux Indian territory, was still uncultivated land with buffalo, mountain lions, elk, black bears, and wolves roaming the area.

It is likely that Ingebrigt chose Iowa as his destination because of Hans Barlien, "an able farmer and skilled mechanic." He came from Overhalla, not far from Ingebrigt's home, and in 1840 he founded the first Norwegian settlement in Iowa, located in Sugar Creek, Lee County. He came to America in 1837, the same year as Ole Rynning. Barlien had been the first farmer to represent Nord-Trøndelag as a member of Parliament. There he spoke against the establishment but met strong opposition. He did not fare much better at home. His wife left him, and he decided to go to America.[1]

Norwegians must have come to Fort Dodge before 1855, as the first Norwegian congregation was already established by then. This congregation was connected to the Episcopal Church, which had some similarities to Catholicism. The first Norwegians in Fort Dodge whose names we know are the blacksmith Ole Peterson and his wife Olena from Skedsmo, just north of Kristiania, and their three children, a baby daughter Olena and two sons, Jacob and Fredrick. The family arrived in Fort Dodge in 1865, the year before Ingebrigt. They moved a bit further on along the Old Cavalry Road and settled in Moorland. Swedes, Englishmen, Irishmen, and Germans also found their way to the Fort Dodge and Moorland region.

Everywhere he looked, Ingebrigt could see the flat, treeless landscape of the prairie. It resembled the ocean on a fine day. The winters were harsh, but in the summer a wide variety of flowers, such as wild roses, clover, oxeye daisies, blue anemones, bird's-foot trefoils, and lilies spread across the prairie. There were large forested areas along the Des Moines River, which ran from north to south before joining the Mississippi. The areas along Soldier Creek and Lizard Creek were also wooded.

In Fort Dodge, at that time a young town of a few hundred people, Ingebrigt intended to make a living as an artist. He changed his family

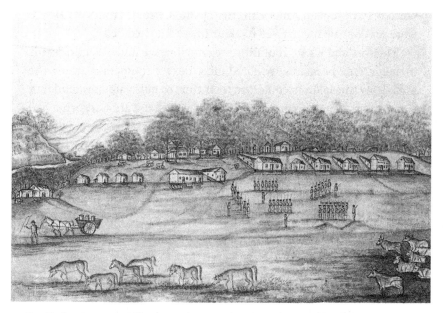

Fort Dodge, June 1852. Military post for a squadron from the US Sixth Infantry. Drawn by William Williams, later the town's mayor. *Webster County Historical Society*

name to Oleson. Fort Dodge had grown into a town around the military post of Fort Clarke, which had been built in 1850 to protect farmers in the region from the Santee Sioux Indians. About eighty soldiers had been sent from Fort Snelling in Minnesota to set up the fort. They traveled by steamship down the Des Moines River, and at the Lizard Creek outlet they found a suitable location. The area offered timber, building stones, and coal. Later Fort Clarke was renamed Fort Dodge in honor of Colonel Henry Dodge, who had served as governor of Wisconsin Territory, which for a time included Iowa.[2]

The newcomers around Fort Dodge had avoided confrontations with the Native Americans. However, in 1852, a chief of the Wahpekute band of the Dakota was killed by a drunken white whiskey trader. The murdered man's brother, Inkpaduta, who lived just outside the town, was a sociable person and well respected by both the soldiers and civilians. He wanted the killer punished by the Fort Dodge authorities. Instead, the sheriff placed the head of Inkpaduta's brother on a pole. Five years later Inkpaduta had his revenge when conflict arose in the northwestern part of Iowa where white people had settled around Spirit Lake, a sacred place for the Indians. The confrontation ended with forty European Americans being killed. People from Fort Dodge were sent to help but arrived too late. Inkpaduta had fled.[3]

The fort and its surroundings regained peace and quiet after this incident. One occasionally could meet beaver trappers roaming the area. Now the soldiers could use their time to cultivate new land. But a new temptation was growing. Gold! The rush toward California had started, and soon about a third of the soldiers deserted. Just a couple of years later the remaining soldiers were sent further north to establish Fort Ridgely in Minnesota, in an area where Dakota Indians and Euro-Americans were challenging each other. Fort Dodge was sold to private investors. The first store opened in 1855, and the town started developing around the main street where a few small workshops were located. An office was established where people could purchase land in the region. Overnight prices increased from $1.25 to twelve dollars per acre, and speculators soon made a fortune.

The town was still in a remote part of the United States, however, and was hard to reach. Goods to and from had to be transported by horse and wagon from Des Moines or Oskaloosa—a two- to three-weeks' journey, providing no accidents occurred. When the Civil War broke out, most of the real estate speculation and trade ceased. The need to transport soldiers led to the rapid building of railroads. Many small towns benefited from this as they became much more accessible.

Many American towns were founded much like Fort Dodge was. Around ninety military posts had been built to accommodate soldiers. Their task was to protect the transportation of mail and newcomers from attacks by Native Americans. The forts, in turn, attracted traders and farmers, and the Midwest gradually became populated by Euro-Americans converting Native American hunting grounds into cultivated land.

About 20 million immigrants from all corners of Europe swept over the prairie—hunters, trappers, carpenters, gold miners, adventurers, gamblers, gunslingers, cavalry soldiers, cowboys, saloon hostesses, businessmen, craftsmen, mercenaries, teachers, preachers, missionaries, and farmers. Most of them came in search of wealth, and they took advantage of nature's abundance. The buffalo, the Native Americans' most important source of food, were slaughtered. Of the 3.7 million buffalo cut down in the period 1821–74, only 150,000 were taken by the Native Americans.[4]

Churches, Choruses, and Homes

Ingebrigt and the other emigrants had a limited amount of space for luggage when crossing the ocean, yet a songbook was normally included. Singing and music were almost as important as food and drink at celebrations or social gatherings. Many of the men had been members of a local chorus back home. These choruses played an important role in the growing nationalistic movement and the forming of Norway as a nation, and many Norwegian songs written in the nineteenth century had a national romantic content. The choral groups were often the first associations to be founded in local communities and provided a place where people could gather and exchange ideas. The first chorus in Ingebrigt and Olaf's home area was founded when they were still children.

Behrens Mandssange (Behrens' Songs for Male Chorus) was one of the most popular song booklets among the immigrants. J. D. Behrens, who in Norway was sometimes referred to as the "Chief of the Singers," had collected and printed about five hundred songs. He also cofounded three choruses in Kristiania. *Den norske Studentersangforening* was established in 1845, and gave its first performance at the funeral of the great poet Henrik Wergeland. Later *Håndverkernes Sangforening* (the Craftsmen's Chorus) and *Handelsstandens Sangforening* (the Mercantile Association's Chorus) were formed. The *Trøndernes Mandskor* (Trøndernes Male Chorus), founded in 1858, is also among the oldest in Norway. It is said that the first national choral festival was held in Bergen in 1863. There was a long tradition of choral singing at European universities. European choruses were organized according to social class, a structure that was not followed when American choruses were formed.

Nearly every Norwegian settlement in America had a male chorus. A writer in the Chicago newspaper *Vinland* reported that "The first two things they did when they formed a new community were build a church and start a male chorus. Then they built their homes."[1]

The choruses were made up of small groups of men, regardless of social class, age, or income. They were workers, store clerks, and businessmen, who changed clothes after work, fetched their songbooks, and hurried to the assembly hall to practice singing for a couple of hours. Rehearsals took place whether times were good or bad. Many of the immigrants were poor and lonely, and singing offered an opportunity to forget their problems and let their thoughts float back to the Norwegian mountains. The choruses were invited to perform at gatherings such as weddings and funerals. Their repertoire included Norwegian folk songs, popular songs that most of them remembered from childhood, or romantic songs filled with longing.[2]

The same year that Ingebrigt came to Fort Dodge, Emil Berg from Trøndelag arrived in Chicago. Berg soon became known for his fine tenor voice. He is probably the first Scandinavian to form a large male chorus. His chorus was named *Nora*, and had a proper director, as well as singers filling all of the positions, including first and second tenor and first and second bass. There was no doubt some pressure on the Norwegians to achieve this as German immigrants had established their large chorus several years earlier. Soon after, Hauman G. Haugen from Kristiania started the *Normanna Sangkor* in La Crosse, Wisconsin. La Crosse was one of the most important stops for the immigrants on their way westward. The city soon saw additional choruses, with Norwegian names such as *Luren* and *Gauken*. Other choruses also got Norwegian names, including *Fram, Viking, Odin, Bjarne, Grieg, Bjørnson, Kierulf, Norønna, Bjørgvin, Dovre, Nordkap, Varde,* and *Norges Ekko*.[3]

Many newspapers written in Norwegian were established in America. Some of them actually had editions as large as some newspapers in Norway. In addition, the Norwegians soon started forming their own congregations as America had no state church. To keep an eye on the Norwegians, many pastors came to America, among them Bernt Julius Muus, a nephew of Ole Rynning, author of the *True Account of America*. Muus was a conservative man and soon became a powerful leader of St. Olaf College in Northfield, Minnesota. He and his fellow pastors from Norway led congregations that belonged to *Den norske Synode* (the Norwegian Synod), faithful to orthodox Lutheran dogma and confession. The synod established several seminaries and colleges in America where the children of farmers could receive the same education as sons of the upper classes in Kristiania. Norwegian children in America went to public schools, but the churches offered additional education in Sunday schools and summer schools, where the children received instruction in both religion and Norwegian.

Many emigrated pastors and laymen had liberal religious views and were in favor of a more democratic Norwegian church, setting the scene for a religious fight among the Norwegians in America. Norwegians, Swedes, and Danes formed separate congregations even in small towns. Three years after Ingebrigt came to Fort Dodge, eighteen Norwegians founded a Lutheran congregation there. Two small Lutheran churches had already been built, but services in these churches were carried out in English or Swedish.[4]

Only a Dollar in His Pocket

Ingebrigt's letters back to Norway seem to have tempted Olaf to a point where he decided to go to America instead of Leipzig. On May 13, 1870, "Olaf Olsen Five, gardener, 20 years of age," as his travel documents said, boarded SS *Sweden* in Kristiania. Unlike some emigrants, he did not leave because of poverty or religion. He traveled to America to seek challenges for his abilities, to explore opportunities, and to develop himself further.[1]

His destination was listed as Iowa Falls, which was as far as the railroad went when Ingebrigt arrived. Ten of the other passengers on the SS *Sweden*, mostly farmers from Ullensaker, a few miles north of Kristiania, were also headed for Iowa Falls. One of them was Niels Halvorsen Hilton, possibly the uncle of Conrad Nicholson Hilton, founder of the Hilton hotels. Their first stop must have been Edinburgh or Glasgow, Scotland. Both cities had railroad connections to Liverpool, England, where Olaf boarded a steamship, either SS *Moravian* or SS *Nova Scotian*, on May 19. Both ships reached Quebec on May 30. From there Olaf followed the same route his brother Ingebrigt had taken four years earlier by crossing the Great Lakes to Chicago.

One year after Olaf arrived in Chicago, the city was destroyed by an enormous fire. One-third of the buildings were turned to ashes. The city was soon rebuilt using steel and concrete, and the architects and city planners were granted much freedom in planning and design. Before leaving Chicago, Olaf spent most of his money, all of fifty cents, on a nice green tie. He then found his seat on the train which now went all the way to Fort Dodge. Ingebrigt was shocked when he met Olaf at the station and saw his green tie. Green was the color of Ireland; people might think Olaf Irish and therefore Catholic! Reluctantly and with poorly concealed regret Olaf took off his tie.

Olaf came to Fort Dodge with one dollar in his pocket. It seems his father was not willing to support his stay in America, as he would have

Two Norwegian brothers in America, Olaf (left) and Ingebrigt Olesen (right). Fort Dodge, Iowa, circa 1871. *Private collection*

supported Olaf at the university in Leipzig. Olaf had not discussed his plans with his brother. He seems to have arrived with an open mind. At the railway station, Olaf could not take his eyes off the brakeman, as he connected and disconnected the railroad cars and elegantly swung himself up the ladder, waved his hands, and made the whole train move and then stop. This might be an exciting occupation, Olaf thought.[2]

Fort Dodge was called "the mineral city" because the region had large resources of coal, gypsum, gravel, and clay, all of which needed to be transported to market. When Olaf arrived, Fort Dodge had just recently obtained railway connection to Chicago, as well as important junctions at Sioux City and Des Moines. The railroad reaching Fort Dodge had a vital impact on the city's development. Business activity, and thereby the city itself, expanded rapidly. The population had passed three thousand, making it one of the larger towns in Iowa. Goods that had to be transported further west still had to be carried by horse and wagon.

Ingebrigt did not share Olaf's enthusiasm for work on the railroad. Instead, he helped his brother get a job as an ox driver on a farm near North Lizard Creek, just outside of town. His job was clearing new land. Two men were needed, one to drive the oxen and one to operate the plow. The soil was hard, so although Olaf and his partner sharpened the plow often and put all their weight and strength to it, they only got between two and four inches deep. They managed to clear seven to eight acres a day, however. The oxen were good natured, and Olaf thought they learned to understand Norwegian faster than he managed to learn English. Even though he struggled a bit with the language, he seems to have felt at home in his new country, both on the flower-covered prairies and the wooded banks of the Des Moines River. The vegetation was rich, the winters cold, and the summers hot—almost like his home place, Kvam, in Norway. He was not used to the thunderstorms and tornados, which regularly swept over the prairie, but they did not scare him. After two years of clearing land, he accepted a position at a drugstore owned by James Swain, one of the most successful storekeepers in Fort Dodge. This decision would change Olaf's life forever.

The Singers' Associations

Olaf soon realized that buying, selling, and keeping contact with customers appealed to him. He also found that pharmacy and botany, which he had been interested in all his life, had much in common. As long ago as the Renaissance period, gardeners had run pharmacies, and pharmacists had planted gardens to grow herbs and plants for medicinal use. In addition to introducing Olaf to pharmacy, James Swain brought him into liberal and intellectual circles, similar to those back home in Kvam. Swain's wife, Adeline M. Swain, was a feminist and suffragette. She provided lessons in botany and became one of the pioneers in the State Historical Society of Iowa.

The city of Fort Dodge continued to grow, populated mainly by Swedes, Germans, and Irish. Many of the immigrants discovered that life in their new country was not as easy as they had imagined. The work was demanding, pay was low, and a normal working day could be sixteen hours. In 1872, the year Olaf began working for James Swain, about a hundred thousand workers in New York went on strike for shorter working days. The strike lasted for three months and resulted in the workers obtaining eight-hour days and a nationwide laborer's union being established. Olaf, having grown up in a family with liberal views, thought he had come to the right place and decided to stay in America. He changed his name from Oluf Martin Olsen Five to Olaf Martin Oleson. His new friends in America called him Martin, while in Norway he was still known as Oluf.

Norwegian music was starting to be heard in America. In 1872 Norwegian male choruses began in earnest. On April 18 the violinist Ole Bull gave a concert in Chicago, and the *Nordmennenes Sangforening* (Norwegian Singers' Association) paraded with Norwegian flags outside the concert hall. On May 17, Norway's Constitution Day, the *Normanna* chorus from La Crosse performed at a concert in Madison, Wisconsin, to help finance the construction of a Scandinavian library. Later in the summer Norwegian singers in Chicago arranged a celebration of the thousand-year anniversary of Norway being united into one kingdom through the victory of Harald Hårfagre in the battle at Hafrsfjord. A chorus of 120 men sang *Sønner av Norge* and the national anthem, *Ja, vi elsker*. Under Norwegian banners and flags and with rifle salutes they marched through the streets of Chicago ahead of nine other Norwegian organizations, followed by twenty carriages filled with women in their best dresses.[1]

This musical festival was the largest gathering of Norwegians in America thus far, and *Nordmennenes Sangforening* was the main Norwegian American organization in Chicago for many years. By arranging concerts and bazaars, they built up funds which were used in part to help indigent Norwegians in Chicago. The association was the first Norwegian organization in America to establish their own health insurance and funeral fund. They also built a library which soon contained several hundred volumes. Over time *Nordmennenes Sangforening* obtained such a good reputation that anyone who did not belong was not considered to be "a good Norwegian." Their financial strength grew until they were even able to send money to Norway. Among the first contributions was $400 to people in the county of Finnmark who were suffering after a dramatic storm in 1882 when the roof of the Talvik church was blown away.

Besides Norwegian folk songs, the choruses increasingly added to their repertoire patriotic and heroic songs like *Landkjenning*, text by Bjørnstjerne Bjørnson, music by Edvard Grieg; *Norge, Norge!* composed by Johan Selmer; and *Olav Tryggvason*, composed by F. A. Reissiger. These songs told of Norway's former glory which Norwegians longed to see restored. Even though all the chorus members were Norwegians, the director might be a Swede or a Dane. The choruses often came together for celebrations. Their songbooks, like *National- og Selskabs-Sange med Musik*, published for the first time in 1875, and *Sangbog for Mandskor* by John Dahle, were repeatedly printed in new editions.

The choral associations were nonpolitical and broad minded and represented a sanctuary for many Norwegians in America. Associations in the United States in the nineteenth century otherwise consisted mostly of lodges and unions. The Norwegians felt the need for alternatives and formed youth clubs, skiing clubs, gymnastic societies, and literary societies. Some of them were quite elitist, like *Det Norske Selskab* (the Norwegian Society), with mainly academic members, and others were pietistic, like those church groups where singing and dancing were prohibited. The farmers normally found their place in the latter. In addition there were prohibitionist organizations. The choral societies were for all, that is to say, all men. Women were eventually welcome as soloists at the festivals.

Olaf was fond of both singing and dancing, but he was a teetotaler. He had probably seen many tragic fates due to drunkenness back in Norway. In 1874 he established his first singing group in Fort Dodge. It was a quartet with his brother Ingebrigt and two friends, Knud Berven and James Fremming, as members. "Whenever we had time and opportunity we came together and practiced four-part singing the best we could. We spent many happy hours that way," Olaf reminisced in an interview in *Sanger-Hilsen* (the periodical for the Norwegian choral societies).[2]

Their first performance took place in 1875 when they participated in the comedy *Ervingen* by the Norwegian poet Ivar Aasen. It is the first play written in *landsmål*, a version of Norwegian based on rural dialects. The play is an intrigue spun around a love affair and the right of an heir to a farm. Among other things, Olaf said that

Besides the quartet mentioned, Mr. E. Ovren and Nils Suckow participated. As we did not find any girls willing to take part in this play, Knud Berven and James Fremming had to act as the women "Inga" and "Gunil"—and they played the roles brilliantly. The audience, coming from far and near, filled the largest hall in town to its brim. Many had to stand throughout the performance as all seats were taken.

The editor of the city newspaper and others not familiar with the Norwegian language had hired a Norwegian farmer to explain what was happening on stage and to give notice when to applaud. They were seated in the center of the hall, the best place to observe and hear the six actors' performance.

Unfortunately, the Norwegian farmer had drunk a little too much, and he was not able to guide his American friends with correct timing. It developed into great merriment, not only for the performers but for the whole audience as all roared with laughter.

Olaf was regarded as a sociable person and was well respected both by the singers and by the people of Fort Dodge. It seems, however, that it was only his closest family who knew him well. He seldom agreed to interviews, and there are few public pictures of him. He grew to become a powerful businessman, had correspondence with many people, and wrote articles in newspapers and periodicals. However, we know few personal details about him. What we do know is that he was very energetic and engaged in a variety of activities, just like his brother Ola back in Norway.

About the same time as Olaf formed his quartet, Ola founded his first rifle club in Nord-Trøndelag. It was named *Mjølner* after the hammer of the Norse god, Thor—the hammer that always found its target when thrown. Ola feared, as did many other Norwegians of the time, that decades of peace had weakened their ability to handle weapons. Shooting clubs were for officers, merchants, and professors and were mainly located in the cities. *Mjølner*, however, was the start of a grassroots movement called *Folkevæpningen* (the People's Arms Association). These clubs gradually changed from a focus on defense and instead became an instrument in the struggle for independence from Sweden.

Bjørnstjerne Bjørnson took an active role in this struggle by using the power of his pen. He was one of the prime architects of modern Norway and agitated for universal suffrage and greater democracy, as well as for Norway to be a nation on equal terms with Sweden and

Olaf's brother Ola Five, who started the People's Arms Association in Norway in 1882. *Private collection* other European countries. Norway had achieved a liberal constitution in 1814, formed on the same principles as the French and American constitutions, based on freedom, equality, and brotherhood. Bjørnson encouraged people to take advantage of their constitutional rights.[3]

America was also experiencing a political change. In 1873 a worldwide depression, "the Panic of 1873," began as a consequence of a crash in railroad and land speculation. A banking crisis followed, leading to collapse in the financial system. World trade stagnated, the stock market crashed, and mass layoffs followed. The Republicans were blamed, and the Democrats started to gain influence in the northern states. Up until then, the Democrats' foothold had been in the southern states. The conflicts from the Civil War were not forgotten, but the Republicans, who had dominated since the war, started to move in a conservative direction. At the same time, the Democrats started absorbing social-liberal ideas and supporting small enterprises and entrepreneurs against the large trusts that had been formed. This shift inspired Olaf to take part in political discussions. He was among the few Norwegians at that time who voted for the Democrats and among the even fewer who accepted political positions in the party, as he did some years later. The roots of his political engagement are likely to be found in his upbringing in the "Red County." But above all else he wanted to have a university degree so he could start his own pharmacy.

Get Rich with Pharmacy

Through his work with the businessman James Swain, Olaf learned that pharmacy was lucrative and had great future prospects. Pharmacy was a young profession in America, in contrast to continental Europe, where already from the 1230s a university degree was required to be a pharmacist and where one was not allowed to be both physician and pharmacist. The United States, on the other hand, followed the British system far into the nineteenth century, allowing anyone to sell medicines, doctors as well as ordinary storekeepers.

Pharmacy as a discipline was undergoing great changes. Up until this time, plants or parts of plants had been the main source of medicines. In 1805 the first pure substance from plants was isolated and extracted, morphine from the opium plant. This innovation led to the isolation of a wide variety of substances from plants and herbs, which created challenges for pharmacists. It's one thing to be able to recognize a plant or part of a plant, but it's quite another to distinguish one white powder from another. Chemistry soon became the most important subject within pharmacy. The ability to isolate substances made it possible to develop new types of medicine in the form of tablets or as liquid for injection. As pharmacists needed to improve their technical knowledge, colleges and universities were established to teach these subjects. No specific education was necessary to run a pharmacy or drugstore. However, several states required a special examination and registration for pharmacists.[1]

Olaf was one of many who wanted to learn more about this profession, and by 1875 he had set aside enough money for further education. He was accepted to the College of Pharmacy in Pennsylvania, the first pharmaceutical college in the United States, established in 1821. There he developed a close friendship with Silas Mainville Burroughs, son of a wealthy family. Silas did not find Olaf's housing adequate, and invited him to live in his apartment. He also treated Olaf to nice dinners, giving Olaf his first taste of luxury, which he later in life could afford for himself. Silas was a kind and extroverted person, but their friendship was first and foremost founded on shared social-liberal attitudes. Even though they both became powerful employers, they maintained an active engagement in social issues and shared the assets they created with employees and the local community. It's not known whether they met each other again after leaving college, but they most certainly had contact and kept an eye on each other's career. Silas and his family were struck by a tragic accident twenty-five years later, leading Olaf to make a vital personal decision.[2]

Life as a student was carefree. In his spare time Silas worked at the John Wyeth & Brother's pharmacy, while Olaf worked with Dr. D. J. R. Stevenson on the corner of Twelfth and Callowhill Street in Philadelphia. Besides being a doctor, Stevenson prepared herbs by hand, packaged them in small boxes, and sold them to pharmacies. Stevenson also had great success with a certain type of make-up. Monday was the busiest day of the week as many came to him with black eyes or other marks on their faces after too much partying on the weekend. His remedy was a thick coat of skin-colored paint applied artfully with a brush. Olaf, however, was more interested in mixing medicines and writing prescriptions despite the doctor reminding him that the facial treatments produced higher profit.

The professors at Philadelphia College inspired their students, were open to questions, and were willing to let the older students try lecturing. On one occasion, when a professor in chemistry was out sick for some weeks, Olaf was given responsibility for the laboratory activities. The younger students said later that they were very pleased with Olaf's instruction in chemistry.

In Philadelphia, Olaf was treading on historical ground. The city was often called the cradle of the nation, as it was there that the Declaration of Independence had been signed in July of 1776. While at the college, Olaf had the opportunity to visit the Centennial Exposition in Philadelphia, where America demonstrated its position as the new industrial power. At the same time the city was the host for the United States Centennial. The event was officially called the International Exhibition of Arts, Manufactures and Products of the Soil and Mine. It was the first world's fair to be held in America. Thirty-seven nations participated with thirty thousand exhibitors and about 10 million visitors. For comparison, the population of the United States at the time was about 47 million.

Olaf witnessed electric lights and the telephone for the first time in his life at the exhibition. He understood that these innovations were potential moneymakers, and not many years later he was engaged in the founding of both Fort Dodge Electric and Power Company and Fort Dodge Telephone Company. He chose five as his private telephone number, probably as a compensation for having dropped Five as his family name. But first he took his exams in pharmacy, for which he was awarded two gold medals: one for best student of the year, the other for obtaining top grades in all disciplines. This had happened only once before in the history of the fifty-six-year-old college. In Norway, his brother Ola had done equally well in his exams in science and mathematics at the University in Kristiania.

During the world exposition, for the first time in his life Olaf entered a department store. This store was Wanamakers, and its owner, John Wanamaker, was a pioneer in marketing and is known as the father of modern advertising. He was the first to introduce price tags. Previously, prices had been set through bargaining. As a Christian, Wanamaker believed that everyone was equal before God and therefore should also be presented with equal prices. He offered quality products with a money-back guarantee. He gained people's trust, and his business thrived. To keep a steady flow of goods, he arranged summer and winter sales. Olaf took notice of all of this.

The need for a wide variety of skilled labor continued to increase. Industry expanded steadily, and the American economy thrived. The pharmaceutical business, in which Olaf was now engaged, was part of this expansion.

SUDDARDS & FENNEMORE.   N° 820 ARCH ST PHILADA.

Olaf as a student at the Philadelphia College of Pharmacy, March 1877. Photographer: Suddards & Fennmore, No 820 Arch Street, Philadelphia. *Private collection*

Omaha and Leadville

During Olaf's stay in Philadelphia, Ingebrigt moved south from Fort Dodge to Des Moines. There he married Minnie C. Hedlund, who was ten years younger than Ingebrigt, and was an immigrant from Sweden. Ingebrigt and Minnie then moved to Cheyenne, Wyoming, which was located in cattle country and was sometimes called "the magic city of the plains."

Minnie and Ingebrigt had two children, Helen and Oliver Elwood. Ingebrigt was not able to support his family as an artist so he also worked as a painter. In 1879 a silver rush developed in Leadville, Colorado, which soon became the largest silver camp in the world. Tens of thousands of immigrants came to make their fortune, Ingebrigt and his family among them. Ingebrigt, however, had no success. The small family was instead struck by tragedy. Only four years after their marriage, Minnie died of smallpox.

A smallpox epidemic had spread worldwide, and close to 300 million people died. Many thought of this illness as God's punishment. In Europe, vaccination against smallpox had begun around 1800. This was also the case in Nord-Trøndelag, largely thanks to the pastor in Overhalla and the radical politician Hans Barlien. According to the church registers in Kvam, as early as 1808 all confirmands were vaccinated. Ingebrigt and Olaf must have felt safe. Minnie, however, was not vaccinated. She died at the age of twenty-six, leaving Ingebrigt alone with a three-year-old son and a one-and-a-half-year-old daughter.

The same year that Minnie died, Ingebrigt and Olaf received news of their mother's death. They also heard that a financial crisis had rocked northern Norway. Herman Løchen at Sundnes had gone bankrupt and the estate was sold. The Sakshaug church had been "beheaded," meaning the steeple had been torn down, the church sold at an auction, and the rest of the ruins given to the Association for Historical Monuments.

While Ingebrigt had tried to take a shortcut to wealth in the silver mines, Olaf became a millionaire the hard way. His fortune later got an extra boost through marriages with two rich women.

After graduation from college in 1877, Olaf looked at the future with great optimism. He returned to Fort Dodge and started a pharmacy with a partner. After a while he let his partner run the business and went to Omaha, Nebraska. At the time, Omaha was the fastest-growing city in the United States. He took a job as a clerk in the Cheney & Meservey pharmacy, located on Farnam Street. He soon became partner and manager and ended up buying the company, renaming it Cheney & Oleson Drug Store. Omaha lay on the banks of the Missouri River and functioned as a gateway to the West. A double-tracked railway went straight through the city, making it a hub for transportation and commerce. The place swarmed with stock speculators and day laborers. The inhabitants included people from many places: Native Americans, African Americans, Asians, Czechs, Germans, Greeks, Irish, Italians, Russian Jews, Mexicans, and Scandinavians, mostly Danes and Swedes. Olaf found fellow singers among the Scandinavians. He joined Otto Wolff's Danish singers' association, *Droslen*—an elite chorus, according to Olaf.[1]

A few years later Olaf came back to Iowa and Fort Dodge. He was instrumental in setting up the Commission of Pharmacy, a state board that certified pharmacists and established operating procedures for pharmacies in Iowa. He was himself a member of the board. His new drugstore in Fort Dodge, on the corner of Central Avenue and Seventh Street, was named Cheney & Oleson, like the one in Omaha, but later he renamed it Oleson Drug Co. His business involved both retail and wholesale. He soon found a wide range of customers among the pharmacists in Iowa, and he began to set aside money so he could invest in property in Fort Dodge. At the time, Fort Dodge was still a young city where cows could roam freely in the streets.[2]

Olaf's college friend, Silas Mainville Burroughs, went to London as an agent for John Wyeth & Brother. Soon Silas established his own company in London, Burroughs & Company, to import medicines to Great Britain from the United States. In the years 1880–84, he traveled the world and built the basic structure of what was later to be GlaxoSmithKline, the world's second-largest pharmaceutical company. His first employer, John Wyeth & Brother in Philadelphia, also grew to become one of the world's largest pharmaceutical companies.

Olaf became a rich and powerful man in Iowa through his business dealings in pharmacy and real estate. Many years after his death it became clear that his pharmaceutical business had become part of a large international company and represented a fortune of several million dollars. That is when expectations of a large inheritance from the rich uncle in America started growing.

Old Remedies

Olaf and Ingebrigt's father, Ole Larsen Sunde, did not seem very impressed by pharmacy as an occupation for Olaf. About the time Olaf left for America, his father wrote in a notebook that he used to record information about the farm (*Agerbrugsbog*) that to obtain healing one did not necessarily need a doctor or pharmaceuticals. On the contrary, much of what was already found in the pantry or just outside the house could be used. In a chapter called "Home and Travel Pharmacy," we find

It is not common knowledge that many of the best remedies may be found in most homes. When travelling or at home we think ourselves helpless without a pharmacy nearby. We ask for medicine to be sent from miles away and critical time passes before help arrives. What we do not know is that we have the same or at least similar remedies in our homes that could have saved a person's life.

Every household, be it large or small, may be regarded as a pharmacy. All the things we use in daily life for nourishment may be used in time of need as pharmaceuticals. It is therefore our duty to spread this knowledge, not in order to educate quacks, but to help people find home remedies. In some cases half an hour may be the difference between life and death, and a remedy might be close at hand, but still we do not see it because we are so used to thinking that our only help is to be found at a pharmacy. Many doctors deserve reproach for this belief. Below are listed the home remedies that may be found everywhere, even on the poorest farms.

Examples of advice recorded by Ole Larsen Sunde include:

SUGAR. When the blood, for one reason or the other, is concentrated in the head, there is nothing better than to immediately drink a glass of water (not too cold) with a good portion of sugar dissolved. This is also useful when one has a fever or any fierce disease, but it has an especially good effect after being struck by fright, annoyance or anger, in which case it will help dampen the thereby agitated bile. It will help when having a cold, hoarse throat or dry coughing. It also helps cleanse the stomach and the intestines.

VINEGAR should be taken in large quantities for all sorts of poisoning by anesthetic substances, such as opium and poisonous plants or when one has eaten poisonous mushrooms or mussels. A cloth soaked in vinegar should be placed on the head and the chest as well. In cases of fainting, vinegar put to one's nose and washing temples, face, hands and feet with vinegar are of much better help than any smelling salts. When one has a high fever or heavy hemorrhage, one should drink water mixed with vinegar.

SOAP, ASHES, LYE AND MILK may be used in cases of arsenic poisoning.

LINSEED OIL, EGGWHITES, AND CREAM, all mixed to an ointment should be used on burns.

RAW, UNPEELED POTATOES mashed to a paste will also be helpful on burns.

FOOTBATH. Salt and two spoons of mustard seeds mixed in some lukewarm water is an excellent remedy against headache, dizziness, buzzing in the ears, cases of deafness, tightness in the chest, asthma, backache, stomach cramps, colic; also to be used after a cold and after sudden flowing of blood to the head and chest, and at non-appearance of the Ladies monthly.

MUSTARD, HORSERADISH AND PEPPER. Excellent ingredients for making a Mustard plaster, which is one of the fastest working remedies when suffering from one of the maladies, mentioned under FOOTBATH, . . . yes, it can in many cases, like stroke and chest pains, save one's life. It is prepared this way: Two spoons of fine mustard seeds, one spoonful of crushed horseradish and the same amount of sourdough with some vinegar added are mixed together to make a plaster which is smeared out on a piece of canvas the size of a hand. This is then applied on the arm or the calf. It should not stay on longer than until the patient feels an intense burning. When the plaster is removed, the remaining particles should be washed off with warm water. If a severe inflammation or pain develops, the best way to reduce this is to rub in some cream or freshly churned butter. Should the case require immediate help one can simply bind some crushed horseradish against the skin and within a few minutes a feeling of intense burning will occur.

WINE, BRANDY. Wine is the best means for improving one's strength and state of mind and may in cases of great weakness, exhaustion, sadness and fainting be used to regain strength. Also, people frozen stiff or close to drowning or suffocation may be given some wine if they are about to pass out. If not able to drink, their hands, feet and face may be washed with wine. For external bruises and blows washing with wine is a very good treatment; for children who are in a decline, it is good advice to wash the whole body with warm wine.

CHAMOMILE, ELDERBERRY FLOWERS, CURLED MINT, PEPPERMINT. These plants should be grown in every farmer's garden, dried and kept in every household, or at least be available in every village, as they are useful for a variety of purposes.[1]

Much of what Olaf's father had written in his notebook was copied from what he had read in the newspaper *Dagbladet*, and was part of an attempt to educate ordinary people at the time.

Bjørnstjerne Bjørnson and Kristofer Janson in the Midwest

While Olaf's future looked bright, times were getting worse in Norway, and dissatisfaction was growing among the people. The conservatives, who were in power, believed that politics was not for the common people. As a counterweight, a variety of independent social-liberal organizations were formed to enlighten and educate people. These groups included organizations for farmers, women, young people, laymen, laborers, and various discussion groups. Meetings were often held at the folk high schools. Several of these organizations merged into party-like associations having on their agenda topics such as universal suffrage, women's emancipation, and democratization of the state church. These left-wing groups were particularly strong in Olaf's home county.

The author Bjørnstjerne Bjørnson was a dedicated liberal. He accused the Norwegian church of being narrow-minded and pietistic. He wanted Norway to be a country on equal footing with the rest of Europe and was a strong supporter of a pure Norwegian flag. The Norwegian flag at the time had the Swedish flag incorporated into one corner. This mixed Norwegian and Swedish flag was referred to as "the herring salad." King Oscar of Sweden and Norway was furious with this agitator and was afraid that a Norwegian uprising could blow the Swedish-Norwegian union to pieces.[1]

Through letters from his brother Ola, the rifle club leader, Olaf was fully updated on the situation in Norway. Together with the rest of his fellow Norwegians in America he eagerly read the news from Norway in Norwegian American newspapers. An important event occurred when Bjørnson's close friend Kristofer Janson, the liberal author, teacher, and theologian, went on a lecture tour in the Midwest in 1879–80. Together with Bjørnson, Henrik Ibsen, and Jonas Lie, Janson was one of the four great authors of the time in Norway. His position in the top four was later taken by Alexander Kielland. Janson was well received in America, where he spoke to the farmers in *landsmål*, the Norwegian language that was based on rural dialects. In his lectures he spoke about both folktales and the social and political issues of the day. People flocked to his lectures in great numbers, and the press praised him to the skies.[2]

As Kristofer Janson became familiar with Norwegians in the Midwest, he began to criticize them for isolating themselves in their own communities and for holding fast to outdated Norwegian traditions. In addition, Janson became very taken with Unitarianism, a religious movement that was growing in America. Its values were based not so much on dogma, but on common sense and personal experience. He began to speak against the pastors in the Norwegian Synod. He pointed out that the synod pastors had defended slavery, opposed public schools, held fundamentalist religious views, and did not want members of their congregations to participate in ordinary American social life.

As a consequence, not only the Norwegian Synod and the farmers, most of them frequent churchgoers, but also much of the Norwegian American press turned their backs on him and regarded him as the worst of scoundrels. A few, however, listened to what Janson had to say. Among them was the small Lutheran congregation in Fort Dodge that withdrew from the Norwegian Synod the same year.

Kristofer Janson returned to Norway, but would come back to America some years later. He had supporters who wanted him to establish Unitarian churches in America. One of them was professor Rasmus B. Anderson, a second-generation immigrant well known in cultural circles.

In the winter of 1880–81, while Janson was back in Norway, Bjørnson himself paid the Norwegians in America a visit. This took place just after he had delivered a speech at the funeral of the violinist Ole Bull in Bergen. Norway's first international "pop star" was dead. Bjørnson traveled the Midwest, meeting Norwegians and delivering lectures. His mission was to earn enough income to support the running of his farm Aulestad in Norway and to help Johan Sverdrup build up the liberal party in opposition to the ruling conservatives.

Members of *Nordmennenes Sangforening* were among the first to pay homage to Bjørnson as they gathered outside his hotel in Chicago and sang. He held his first lecture there, on the topic "The Political Crisis in the Scandinavian Countries." A record number of eighteen hundred listeners attended. Not even Ole Bull had enjoyed such a large audience. Ole Bull's young widow, Sara, had invited Bjørnson to America, but his friendship with her ended when he discovered that she just wanted to show him off in high society. He did not want to be an object on display. Instead, he wanted to meet the Norwegians out on the prairie. So Sara was replaced by Rasmus B. Anderson, who then organized Bjørnson's tour, as he had done for Kristofer Janson.

Bjørnson did not manage to gather as many funds from his lectures and speeches as he had hoped. This freethinker was opposed by many of the pastors because he told the immigrants that there were better ways to read the Bible than those prescribed by Pontoppidan. On several occasions he was denied the use of churches for his presentations, although the churches were often the only halls available for public assemblies. In letters back to his wife, Karoline, he complained:

St. Paul, Minn., January 17, 1881: . . . The pastors keep their sheep assembled; the ones who show up are the apostates; there are a lot of them here. But, had the believers been my audience, I could have kept going for a year and become rich. Everywhere it is the best ones that are the apostates, those with the best heads, those who are best educated and those who have accomplished the most in material terms. It is altogether a matter of intellect. . . . In Fargo, the farthest I have been, and almost as far as the land has been cultivated, you find Norwegians everywhere. My latest lecture was diametrically opposed to the pastors, who were sitting there making notes, and I thought, now I'll give you something to write about! Never in my life have I given a better speech. The hall was in an uproar, and when I ended, a full-throated Hurra! roared out. . . . From Fargo I issued an invitation to help Sverdrup; now we'll just have to wait and see![3]

Bjørnson wrote that he put his trust in the next generation of Norwegian Americans, who went to public schools and learned to read and write English, "thus giving access to English language newspapers and periodicals and public discussions,—and with that, the end of faith."

Olaf followed Bjørnson to several of the places he visited, among them Albert Lea in Minnesota and Des Moines in Iowa. Olaf also persuaded him to come to Fort Dodge to hold a lecture. Bjørnson wrote home:

Fort Dodge Iowa, March 19, 1881: . . . I lectured one day (after having travelled 18 miles) for 4—four—hours, two presentations. The pastor had gone out of his way to speak against me at the same time and it made me so angry that I decided I would give my speech free of charge—and I was allowed to use a church where the congregation does not believe in the Bible. There was a full house and everyone paid close attention. This is a life and death fight. But I also find gratitude here, as I am doing what has been longed for in the older communities. . . . The snowstorms have robbed me of at least 2000 *speciedaler*. It is the worst winter even the old people have experienced and it never seems to end. I am returning with not much more than 4000 *speciedaler*! I could cry over this poor outcome after so much effort.[4]

Bjørnson stayed weather-bound in Fort Dodge for some days and visited Olaf at least three times. After Bjørnson returned to Norway, Olaf received a letter in which Bjørnson thanked him for all the pleasant time they had spent together. They surely must have discussed politics and social conditions. Olaf later told his friend Waldemar Ager that he had asked Bjørnson if drinking and drunkenness was still as bad a problem in Norway as it was when he lived there. Bjørnson answered slowly, after a long pause: "Well, yes, it is maybe a little bit better, but progress is slow."[5]

The political situation in Norway was coming to a head. The Liberals in Parliament started planning impeachment against the government, which for some time had declined to implement several of Parliament's decisions. Liberal politicians wanted to take away the king's right to an absolute veto. King Oscar had made use of the veto on three occasions. One was his denial of funds to the rifle clubs, or the "army of the Liberals," as the volunteer marksmen under Ola Five's leadership were often called. The king regarded the rifle clubs as an irregular rebel army.

Bjørnson, safely back in Norway, gave a speech at the unveiling of a statue of Henrik Wergeland in the center of Kristiania on May 17, 1881. In this speech he said he was talking to Norwegians on both sides of the Atlantic. He praised Henrik Wergeland as the Nation's Greatest Son, who stood up for freedom, democracy, and independence for Norway. The day was a great public celebration and developed into a political mass meeting. Kristofer Janson followed up on this when he gave a lecture at a gathering of rifle clubs in Gjøvik about the French revolution and the new social classes emerging in Norway.

In the meantime, plans were being made for Kristofer Janson to return to America, become a Unitarian minister, and set up a congregation in Minneapolis. Before he left, however, he instructed Rasmus B. Anderson to keep quiet and help prevent these plans from becoming public knowledge. He feared that the pastors would scare people away before he had even started his mission. Only "three energetic but discreet men" in three different cities were to be informed. The cities were Minneapolis, Minnesota, where many Norwegians lived; Fort Dodge, which had just a few but very friendly and loyal Norwegians; and a city Anderson himself was to pick out. In each city the selected person should in turn contact others he thought would support the congregation financially. Olaf and his like-minded acquaintances in Fort Dodge contributed $112.[6]

Kristofer Janson stayed in America for eleven turbulent years. The Unitarians and those who belonged to the Norwegian Synod were not on speaking terms, even when they came from the same place in Norway. The Norwegian American newspaper *Budstikken*, in contrast to the other Norwegian American newspapers, supported Olaf's party, the Democrats, displayed social-liberal attitudes, and took an independent stand in the Norwegian American church dispute. The editor, Luth Jæger, originally from Arendal in Norway, was one of the few who defended Janson: "He is not in America to destroy the Synod, but to promote religious tolerance and intellectual freedom."

When he left America, Kristofer Janson proclaimed that "The old idolatry of Bible quotations, the self-contradictory doctrine of the

Trinity, the blood-stained doctrine of atonement and the notion of eternal hell were superbly dismissed."

Back in Norway, Janson joined the poet Arne Garborg in his work to liberalize Norwegian religious attitudes while Ola Five intensified his work to arm the nation through the rifle clubs, now a nationwide movement beyond the king's control. This movement attracted people from all social classes. Seven of its leaders were members of Parliament, others were sheriffs, officers, farmers, storekeepers, lawyers, pastors, and teachers, like Ola himself. Hagbert Berner, editor of the newspaper *Dagbladet*, as well as the poet Arne Garborg also joined the organization. Gatherings of marksmen were arranged, with music and banners. "Best to be prepared" one of the banners read, as suggested by the poet Ivar Aasen. Bjørnstjerne Bjørnson addressed Ola as "Mon General." And in 1881, Ola encouraged Bjørnson to write a song dedicated to the Norwegian rifle clubs. It was called "the Marksmen's Marseillais" and was soon printed in Norwegian American newspapers.[7]

Uproar from Norway Reaches across the Atlantic

In America protests against low pay and bad working conditions for labor intensified, and on September 5, 1882, ten thousand workers marched in the streets of New York City. During that same year the liberal movement in Norway won a majority and was able to start impeachment against the government. There were rumors that King Oscar would perform a coup d'état if the Norwegian government lost the case. There were also rumors that the "people's army," with Olaf's brother in front, would call for a revolution if the king actually did so. The authorities feared the marksmen groups would plunder the military's weapon and ammunition depots and implemented strong security measures in response.[1]

The Norwegian American newspaper *Budstikken* followed the court case and the military movements closely. Olaf and the other immigrants were able to read long articles reprinted from the Norwegian newspapers *Verdens Gang* and *Dagbladet*, both of which supported the liberals. An article entitled "Norwegians in the West and the Struggle in Norway" reported, "The uproar from the political struggle back home reaches across the Atlantic and the conflict is being followed by our countrymen here." Nicolai Grevstad, the former editor of *Dagbladet* who had recently emigrated to America, traveled around the Midwest and spoke about the impeachment case.[2]

The Norwegian church took sides in the political conflict and chose to support the monarchy as the radical uprising was considered to be incompatible with Christianity. From pulpits all over Norway the liberals and their politics were condemned with the warning that the structure of society was threatened. The political goal, it was claimed, was to "destroy the power Christianity has had up until now on the everyday lives of our people." The church claimed the impeachment was a national sin and that on Judgment Day those advocating it would be sentenced to the torment of hell where there is "weeping and gnashing of teeth."[3]

The leaders of the Norwegian Synod in America also took a stand against the uprising, but Norwegian Americans in general were in favor of Norwegian self-government. The immigrants thought the conflict could not be resolved without blood being spilled. They were also convinced that Norway would become a republic. In the meantime, Johan Sverdrup and the Norwegian liberals needed funding to establish a party organization and Ola Five's rifle clubs needed money to buy weapons and ammunition. Money, however, was scarce among people in Norway, so when the government decided not to support the rifle clubs, the local savings banks all over the country offered loans to the marksmen. Many Norwegians in America had placed some of their savings in their local Norwegian savings bank, so cash was available.

The Norwegian liberals tried to make people pay a symbolic membership fee, but the amount they received was insignificant. The situation trigged the Norwegians in the Midwest to organize a large fund-raising campaign. This campaign started in Minneapolis in 1883 after Luth Jæger, the editor of *Budstikken*, gave a Norwegian Constitution Day speech to the liberal association *Fram*. This speech was printed in *Budstikken* on May 30. In it, Jæger said that Norway's "one hundred year long sleep" now was over:

> To us, who have become used to a government for the people, by the people and of the people, it seems curious that a nation, having a constitution based on such a democratic foundation as the Norwegian, is not able to carry through its principles in all particulars, is not able to govern as it will. . . .
>
> They have a parliament that makes laws, but a government that refuses to abide by them.
>
> If it was up to us over here, such a government would not last long, but they are treading carefully and slowly over there. . . .
>
> We feel resentment seeing the will of the people being defied again and again and find it difficult to understand how they still can reach out a hand for reconciliation. . . .
>
> Love for the old fatherland and its people, to whom

we are connected by so many and heartfelt ties, survives
Americanization.... And last but not least, we, as residents in
a free, self-governed country, have the obligation to keep up
with the fight for political freedom and national independence
where ever it takes place in the world . . . especially when it con-
cerns our friends and family, our own flesh and blood!

Do we think that the Irish in America should calmly and
indifferently watch their countrymen living in poverty and
turn their backs on the struggle to shake free from domination
by the detested English? . . .

Our voice, however, is not heard above the noise of the
waves breaking against the Norwegian coast—so let our
letters convey the message, let them urge, incite, excite, scorn,
threaten, if needed....

The right of people to self-determination is at stake. The
path towards political development, that gained such high
hopes on May 17, is being blocked. Absolutism lurks behind the
sparkling facade of the throne and the king's cabinet....

As a reminder of the seriousness of the moment, a telegram
arrived just today threatening retaliation by the king if the
Norwegian people do not cowardly and dishonestly cave in.
A civil war is regarded as a possible consequence of the measures the king in that case intends to take.

We can hardly interpret the distress signal the Conservatives have sent to call on help from their fellow partisans in
Europe in any other way than that these very same Conservatives actually want a revolution, want a coup d'état and now
with threats to that effect are trying to get their way.

In France, a situation like the one that has prevailed in Norway for so long would have found its solution on the barricades
long ago. The people in Norway should not shy away from such
a solution . . . and we in America must then do what we can to
help the people of our fatherland to victory.[4]

Jæger ended his speech by mentioning "the battle line of farmers now
forming a color guard at the Parliament." He was referring to the rifle
clubs of volunteer marksmen Bjørnson had encouraged in his song.

The Norwegian Americans were ready to support a fight for national independence in Norway, and they agreed to help fund Ola Five's rifle clubs so they could buy weapons and ammunition. The association *Fram* led the way, hoping to acquire enough money to send three hundred rifles to Norway. The newspaper *Folkebladet* in Minneapolis followed up: "Let us contribute 7–8,000 dollars for rifles to the rifle clubs in Norway." The editor, Sven Oftedal, who was also a professor of theology, accepted such rebellious and unreligious articles in the paper. The paper *Skandinaven,* published in Chicago, added that "With 7–8,000 dollars you do not get far; more is needed. The Liberal party in Norway is large, but poor. The Conservatives have the money and the power. With the huge number of Norwegians in this country, it should be possible to collect a sizeable sum, now that old Norway's freedom and independence is at stake."[5]

For Olaf personally this was a dramatic year. The authorities counterattacked by having his brother Ola court-martialed for encouraging the uprising. Their father died at age eighty-seven in his home in Kvam. That same year Ingebrigt, who was only forty years old, died of small-

pox, three years after his wife Minnie had died of the same cause. Maybe Ingebrigt had not been vaccinated after all? All the other siblings, Olaf, Eilert, Ola, and Henrikka were to have long and eventful lives.

Ingebrigt's two children, Oliver and Helen, six and four years old, were suddenly orphans. Minnie's sister, Anna, took care of them

Olaf's niece and nephew, Helen and Oliver Oleson, several years after their parents died. *Private collection* to start with. Oliver and Helen were separated from each other after a few years and only met occasionally until they finally ended up in the same retirement home in Fort Dodge. We do not know Oliver's story very well. We do know that he married Ida Melvina Simpkins and lived, among other places, in Sioux City and Hardin, Iowa, and Hennepin County and Lakefield in Minnesota. Olaf wanted Oliver to work in pharmacy, but Oliver did not carry out Olaf's wishes. Helen, on the other hand, brought a lot of pleasure into Olaf's life. He regarded her as his own daughter, but he did not adopt her, perhaps because he was not married at the time. Helen went to St. Katherine's Boarding School in Davenport before she moved to Fort Dodge, where she worked as an accountant.

The Norwegian-American Liberal Society

In January 1884, Norway's first political party, *Venstre* (the Liberal Party), was founded in Kristiania. At the same time, *Den Norsk-Amerikanske Venstreforening* (the Norwegian-American Liberal Society) was established in Minneapolis. About two hundred people were gathered, with theology professor Sven Oftedal acting as chairman. The intention was to collect money to support the cause of the Liberal Party in Norway. Many argued that the money should be earmarked for Ola Five's rifle clubs. Among them were influential Norwegians in America such as Kristofer Janson, Judge Andreas Ueland, editor Luth Jæger, and Nicolai Grevstad. Others, however, feared that supporting the rifle clubs and the Liberals would harm the cause of liberation in Norway. They pointed out that "the Conservatives are comparing us with the Irish-Americans who are sending dynamite to England to blow public offices to pieces." It was finally decided that the money from the Norwegian-American Liberal Society should be sent to the Liberal Party in Norway for it to determine the best use for the money.[1]

Judge Andreas Ueland was elected chairman, Nicolai Grevstad vice chairman, and Luth Jæger secretary. The charter included:

The Norwegian-American Liberal Society's objective is to work for a closer relationship between the Norwegians in America and the Liberal Party in Norway, now represented by the majority in the Parliament headed by Johan Sverdrup, and from time to time with appropriate means, support the Norwegian people in their struggle for freedom and self-government.... The money collected by the Society shall, as often as the Board decides, be offered to the Norwegian Parliament's Liberal Union. If a donor requires that his contribution be used for a specific purpose, the Norwegian Parliament's Liberal Party shall be informed of such when the money is sent.[2]

At the same time the paper *Budstikken* in Minneapolis argued against reactionary theologians in Norway who condemned the Liberal Party and reassured the Norwegians that "Where ever one travels among fellow countrymen here, one is always assured that if Norway's freedom and independence are threatened with violence, the Norwegians here will be ready to help with men and money."[3]

Other Norwegian American newspapers also supported the cause:

The freedom and independence of our old fatherland are at stake.

Threats against its constitution are reaching us . . . and we would be poor sons of a freedom loving people and even poorer citizens of America if we watched this with indifference.[4]

Several local liberal organizations were established in the United States to undertake fund-raising. Among them was *Norske Kvinner i Minneapolis* (Norwegian Women in Minneapolis), which encouraged other women throughout the United States to do the same. The organization *Norden* set up its own fund-raising committee. Norwegian American newspapers printed lists of names of individuals and their contributions, ranging from ten cents to sixty dollars. For example, professors at Milton College in Wisconsin donated twenty-five dollars and included a note from Rev. Hvistendal saying that "We are first of all sending this. But *Budstikken* can inform the Conservative Party on behalf of many of us that, if needed, we will come ourselves, and I for my part am preparing for the right to do so."[5]

Olaf seems to have chosen to keep a low profile, maybe because his brother played such an active role in the struggle. They kept in close contact, however, and Ola was managing Olaf's financial interests in Norway.

On February 27, 1884, the impeachment sentence was passed. All members of the Norwegian government were sentenced to leave office. But not until March 11 did the king accept the result and ask the Conservative prime minister Selmer to step down. The king then formed a reconciliation ministry which failed. What would happen now? Was the king planning a coup d'état? The cannon on Akershus Fortress were ready to fire. So were the gunboats in Horten. And if this happened, would the rifle clubs' army start a revolution? Rumor had it that the marksmen, with Ola Five in front, were marching toward the capital.[6]

Fund-raising in America intensified, and the Norwegian singers in America arranged concerts for the benefit of the Liberal Party. *Luren* was one of the choruses that collected money and sent it directly to the marksmen's organization. Large-scale meetings and arrangements were held around the country. Knut Hamsun was one of the promoters. He was in America to try to establish himself as an author. He failed in that, and ended up working for Kristofer Janson as a secretary and assistant. In May 1884 Hamsun delivered a speech at a meeting in Peterson Hall in Minneapolis, which was reported in *Budstikken*: "The podium was covered in red cloth with a golden lion encircled by green leaves embroidered on the front facing the hall. A large Norwegian flag was mounted behind the podium and above this there was ... an excellent picture of Johan Sverdrup, arranged as the central decoration. Underneath there was a picture of old Ueland with busts of Bjørnstjerne Bjørnson and Henrik Ibsen on each side. Above the picture of Sverdrup one could read the quote: 'Norway's time for solemn celebration has arrived. The hall of Parliament is now open.' "[7]

This arrangement lasted for five days. Bazaars, a lottery, and food stands brought in $459.55.

A good part of the money collected in America was sent directly to Ola Five's army. The donations, large and small, came from both individuals and organizations. The saving banks had their hands full converting all these "Five-money" to Norwegian currency. We don't know how much money actually came in, as the marksmen's main office burned down and the archives with it. It is reasonable to conclude that not all donations were registered since much of the organization's activities were secret. It is fair to assume, though, that the sums were substantial.[8]

The Norwegians in America established their own volunteer rifle clubs organized along the Norwegian model. Among these were the Norwegian Rifle Club *Norden* in New York, the Norwegian Sharp Shooter's Society in Chicago, and the Norwegian Rifle Club in Minnesota, which also had its own male chorus. The club members drilled regularly dressed in the uniform of the Norwegian Cavalry, and it attracted attention in many American cities when two to three hundred men marched through the streets in Norwegian uniforms, waving both American and Norwegian flags.[9]

It turned out that King Oscar had no support in Sweden for his uncompromising policy. Swedes felt that the union would be better served if the king went along with the Liberal Party to avoid fanning the flames of the Norwegian nationalistic and republican movements. On July 2, 1884, Johan Sverdrup, leader of the Liberal Party, was made prime minister; Norway had obtained parliamentarianism. Ola Five's court-martial was dropped and the volunteer rifle clubs he headed were given regular financial support by Parliament. The Liberal Party wanted to use the rifle clubs as a model for creating a Home Guard.

Several Norwegian American newspapers from 1884 and books about the history of the Norwegians in America have given some indication of how much money was sent to the Liberal Party. In Norway little attention has been paid to the amount of money sent from America. The Norwegian historian Leiv Mjeldheim, however, found that these donations were crucial for the party's growth in its first years. In writing his history of the Liberal Party from the 1880s to 1905, he went through the party's accounts, which he found in the diaries of Anton Qvam from Nord-Trøndelag. Qvam was the party leader after Johan Sverdrup became prime minister. These accounts show that the Norwegian Americans sent over 7,000 Norwegian kroner (about $90–100,000 today) as gifts to the party. Other income, from Norwegian members and donors, amounted to just over 200 Norwegian kroner (about $4,000 today). Income in the next year was about the same, contributed mostly by Norwegian Americans. In the following years the amounts dropped dramatically.[10]

Norwegians in America felt that their effort had been important. That the donations more or less stopped was possibly a reaction to a lack of gratitude from Norway. One of the Liberal associations in Nord-Trøndelag, for example, concluded that it was fine that men and women who could afford it "offered a little extra for the sake of freedom," but the money from America was not enough to ensure it, "not to speak of the fact that it is strange and dishonorable that our struggle for freedom shall be achieved with foreign money."[11]

Leiv Mjeldheim, however, points out that the money crossing the

Atlantic formed the financial basis for the party's early and vital period: "Yes, there was even a surplus enough for the liberal associations
in Norway to subsist on for a couple of years, at least to 1888."

One can safely say that it was the Norwegian Americans who built
the Liberal Party financially and enabled it to gain control of the government. Norwegians have never acknowledged the help they received
from America. Some Norwegians might have been envious of their
relatives who became rich "over there," and at the same time some
gloated over those who did not succeed, much like sibling rivalry—
competition and envy. This seems not to have been the case between
Olaf and Ola, who stayed close friends all their lives and wrote letters to
each other about once a month. This regular exchange of letters meant
that they never had to bid each other a final farewell. Unfortunately,
these letters were not preserved. Their friendship may have flourished
because they both were successful in their chosen fields. They also had
the good fortune of being safely anchored in happy marriages.

Olaf saw the situation in Norway calming down for the time being.
His brother Ola had many irons in the fire, now of the peaceful kind.
He agitated for a state pension arrangement and took part in founding a steamship company operating on the lake Snåsavatnet, a savings
bank, a dairy, and a telegraph company and later also newspapers and
the Norwegian theater and *Det Norske Teatret*. Ola did not, however,
stop rifle training. Along with the rest of the rifle club leaders and the
radical section of the Liberal Party he wanted a complete separation
from Sweden and for Norway to be a republic so that the people could
elect their own head of state, as in France and the United States. On
recommendations from Ola, Olaf bought shares both in the steamship
company and in Norsk Hydro, later to become one of the largest and
most successful companies in Norway. He collected dividends from
these investments for many years.

The Americans were also experiencing political changes. After
twenty years with the Republicans in power, the Democrats won the
election of 1884 and Grover Cleveland became president. The Democrats had gradually become more radical, with a strong foothold in the
cities, among factory workers and labor unions. Most Norwegians in
America, however, lived in rural areas, where they remained loyal to
their party, the Republicans.

In Chicago the struggle for workers' rights intensified. The Norwegian radical Marcus Thrane was prominent among the city's socialists. A strike started on May 1, 1886, and the struggle climaxed when a riot broke out at the Haymarket in Chicago on May 4, ending with mass arrests and several deaths. As a result, May 1 became an international workers' holiday, though not in the United States, where this day represented socialism and anarchism. In 1884 the first Monday in September was designated as Labor Day in the United States, to pay tribute to working men and women. The labor movement spread from New York and Chicago further into the Midwest. For example, a Norwegian labor union in La Crosse invited Viggo Ullmann, a prominent feminist, liberal politician, and supporter of rifle clubs, to come to America and give speeches. Even though the labor struggles led to some disturbances in the United States, the general picture was one of peace and quiet.[12]

Music Rings Out in Chicago

Despite the tense situation between Norway and Sweden, the Norwegian, Swedish, and Danish immigrants in America cooperated at this time. Most of them regarded themselves as Scandinavians with a common culture, and felt overshadowed when German immigrants arranged a large choral festival in Brooklyn in 1885 that gained much attention. As a counterweight and an attempt to promote Scandinavian culture, Olaf encouraged all Nordic male choruses in America to come together for an annual Scandinavian choral festival. Assisting him were the Danish businessman C. M. Machold in Philadelphia and the law student Olaf Ray. Ray, whose name was originally Olaf Edward Olsen Ree, came from Levanger, north of Trondheim, to Chicago, where he joined *Nordmennenes Sangforening*. In January 1886, Olaf wrote in the paper *Budstikken*, suggesting that

Would it not be a good idea for Minneapolis to invite all Scandinavian choral societies to a festival next summer, exact time to be decided later? There are many good singers among the Norwegians in the western states, but they have never had the opportunity to attend a large arrangement of this kind, and their talents are hidden. A festival would most certainly stimulate Scandinavian singing in this country, and that is needed so it will not die out. That would be a great loss, as there are no other nations that can boast such fine music, suited for male voices, as the Scandinavian countries. That they have as good singers as any has been proven several times at festivals in Europe, when performing before the most critical of audiences. It would be rewarding for the individual singers to make such a trip, as most of them are workers occupied day in and day out with their routine business, without much time for recreation. A vacation of this kind would be encouraging in more ways than one. However, if this is to happen, it must be communicated soon, in order for the various societies to have time to prepare. It is desirable, maybe even necessary, to have some songs selected for all choruses to practice, so they all could participate in a single chorus. In addition each society could have its own songs. To cover most of the travelling costs, they could arrange concerts during the winter. If the audience is aware of the purpose of the concert, they should be able to get a full house, and collect a goodly sum of money.

If this undertaking should succeed (which it should, without doubt, if it is taken seriously), the next gathering could take place in Chicago, St. Paul, Omaha, Kansas City or any other large place where there are enough Scandinavians who are interested in this matter. This way the singers would have a goal to work for, which would act as a strong driving force. As an example, look at the great German choral festivals, that are arranged every summer. They started out small. Even though we are not as numerous as the Germans, we can have successful festivals with music performances second to none that would make the Scandinavians proud. Other opinions about this suggestion would be much appreciated.[1]

As a consequence of this initiative, *De Forenede Skandinaviske Sangere af Amerika* (the United Scandinavian Singers of America) was founded with the Dane C. M. Machold as president and the Norwegian O. Tønnesen, leader of *Den norske Sangerforening* in New York, as vice president. The first large Scandinavian festival was held in Philadelphia the year after. The festival lasted for three days, and a joint chorus of 128 men gave the main concert for an audience of two thousand people. Each individual chorus had its own concert. There were solo performances, speeches, parades, and parties. Eight choruses participated, but only two were Norwegian, *Den Norske Sangforening* from New York and *Nordmennenes Sangforening* from Chicago. Encouraged by Bjørnson, the singers from Chicago raised the pure Norwegian flag, the one without the union symbol in the corner, while singing about the old Norwegian Viking Olav Tryggvason. The participants all agreed that the festival had been a success, and they felt they had reached a milestone on the Scandinavians' path of progress in this country.

The next festival was held in Chicago in 1889. Twenty-six choruses and six hundred singers, two-thirds of them Norwegians, participated. The festival started with rehearsals, followed by concerts, parades through the city, picnics in the parks, sports arrangements, and parties. This was the beginning of a tradition that continues to this day at the festivals that are arranged every other year.[2]

More Male Choruses Are Formed

Around 1890 there were about 55 million European immigrants or descendants of European immigrants in America. The Norwegians were well integrated in the political and financial affairs of the nation, especially in the Midwest. Their love for singing helped spread Norwegian culture.

Olaf was interested in how to increase the influence of the growing number of Norwegians in America. He also paid close attention to developments in Norway, where the Liberals wanted a Norwegian foreign minister and for Norwegian interests to be represented abroad in their own consulates. The issue of the consulates remained a cause of disagreement between Norway and Sweden and also between the Liberals and the Conservatives in Norway until 1905, when Norway gained its sovereignty.

The conflict between Norway and Sweden also led to disagreements between the Norwegian and Swedish singers in America. Their relationship had so far been good, and together they even managed to organize the largest music festival that had ever been arranged in the United States. This took place in Minneapolis in the summer of 1891. Unfortunately, the seed was sown here for the conflict that would later split the United Scandinavian Singers of America.

The festival started out well. A choir of nine hundred men sang *Landkjenning* by Bjørnstjerne Bjørnson and Edvard Grieg as part of the opening ceremony. Three sold-out concerts were held in Normanna Hall, the main hall of *Nordmennenes Sangforening* in Minneapolis. Several female soloists performed. Among these was Aagot Lunde from Boston, who sang *Sæterjentens søndag* accompanied by Ole Bull's young widow, Sara. In addition, individual choruses had their own performances. Finally, they all marched through the city singing *Ret som ørnen stiger*, waving a beautiful new banner that had been given by a rich Swedish businessman. When the donor soon after made several negative comments about Norway in the newspapers, Olaf and the other Norwegian singers found it beneath their dignity to continue singing under a Swedish banner.

As a consequence, the Norwegians decided to assemble all their choruses in a separate singers' association, and the following year Olaf and some of his friends established *Den Norske Sangerforbund i Amerika* (the Norwegian Singers' Association of America). Their objective was to promote Norwegian music and to encourage Norwegian singers and composers. Olaf helped finance the start-up and volunteered as treasurer. At the same time, Norwegians and Danes founded *Det Nordvestlige Norsk-Danske Sangerforbund* (the Northwestern Norwegian-Danish Singers' Association), which was comprised of sixty-four choruses. The president was Gabriel Bie Ravndal of Sioux Falls, an immigrant from Soknedal in Rogaland, Norway.

The first Danish-Norwegian music festival was arranged in Sioux Falls in July 1892. Olaf attended with a new and larger chorus from Fort Dodge, *Grieg Mandskor* (Grieg Male Chorus), where he himself was the

H. L. OFTEDAHL, *President*
4956 W. Ferdinand St., Chicago

TH. F. HAMANN, *Corresponding Secretary*
4009 Harriet Ave., Minneapolis, Minn.

A. O. SATRANG, *Treasurer*
State Bank of Chicago

THE NORWEGIAN SINGERS' ASSOCIATION OF AMERICA

FOUNDED SEPT. 21, 1892
Incorporated under the State Laws of South Dakota as an Educational Society

GRAND OFFICERS
O. M. OLESON *Honorary President*, Fort Dodge
H. L. OFTEDAHL, *President*, Chicago
A. C. FLOAN, *Vice-President-at-Large*, St. Paul
TH. F. HAMANN, *Corresponding Sec'y*, Minneapolis
MARTIN BERGH, *Recording Sec'y*, Sioux Falls
A. O. SATRANG, *Treasurer*, Chicago
A. W. MYHRE, *Grand Marshal*, Minneapolis
SIGV. HUSEBY, *Ass't Grand Marshal*, Chicago
FRED WICK, *Director-in-Chief*, Sioux City
I. N. SODAHL, *Ass't Director-in-Chief*, Duluth

STATE VICE-PRESIDENTS
Illinois—HARALD HANSEN, Chicago
Iowa—CHRIST DAHL, Sioux City
Minnesota—AXEL RUSKE, Duluth
North Dakota—J. O. ENGESATHER, Petersburg
South Dakota—CARL MANNERUD, Sioux Falls
Wisconsin—H. P. PETERSON, Superior

"SANGER-HILSEN," Official Paper
One Dollar Per Year
Published from Office of Corresponding Secretary

The Norwegian Singers' Association of America was established in 1892. Olaf's letterhead, 1926. *Private collection* director and sang second bass. Their silk banner was embroidered with a golden harp encircled by flowers. Among the first members to join the chorus were Carl C. Haugen, M. M. Dahl, and Lars Ranes. Carl C. Haugen was a barber with his shop on the premises of the First National Bank, where Olaf had his office as vice president. Ranes was employed by Olaf as an accountant at the Oleson Drug Store. Ranes had come to America intending to make enough money to open a dry goods store in his hometown of Ålesund on the west coast of Norway. *Grieg Mandskor* had up to twenty-eight members during its best years and participated in every festival to come.[1]

Olaf had his hands full as both director and leader of the group, according to *Sanger-Hilsen,* the periodical of the Norwegian Singers' Association of America:

> The director must require correct breathing, correct articulation, correct resonance, and handling of register from the singers. The ABC of vocal training, on which all singing is based, contains no hidden tricks, only the natural use of the voice in choral singing, often by individual humming practice—vocal practicing. Each and every person can learn to develop a technically correct tone in his singing. That is called tone development or vocal training.[2]

Olaf Helps Establish a Church

By 1891 Fort Dodge had grown to a city of close to five thousand people. Most of the immigrants in the city were Germans, English, Irish, and Swedes, with only thirty-eight Norwegians. Even though they were few, Olaf and his fellow Norwegians decided they did not want to have their services held in the Swedish church any longer. As in Norway, the Norwegians in America wanted to make their own decisions in clubs, on committees, and in church life. They started planning their own church, and wanted it to be named St. Olaf Norwegian Lutheran Church. The church took its name from the medieval King Olav, who had many Catholic churches named after him in Europe, and who was known as the patron saint and eternal king of Norway.

Until the church was built, the small Norwegian congregation received help from the Rev. Knute Bergeson Birkeland, originally from Hosanger in Hordaland, Norway. He lived in Badger, Iowa, and came regularly to preach in Norwegian in the Swedish church. The congregation had limited resources at their disposal, so to start with they searched for a suitable location for the church southwest of the city, where working people lived and land was inexpensive. But Olaf said no, they should not operate on a limited budget. His engagement was not based on an extraordinary religious interest or a lack of English skills. He did not need the services and the hymn singing to be carried out in Norwegian. His intention was rather to show that the Norwegians also had a proud tradition in the construction of churches. He bought a piece of land in the center of the city, on the corner of Fourth Street and First Avenue South. There he wanted to have a large, solid church made of stone, not just a small wooden structure as the Swedes had. He probably had the old Sakshaug church close to the Sundnes estate in Nord-Trøndelag in mind. He engaged an architect and guaranteed the building expenses. He then encouraged every member of the congregation to pay twenty-five cents per week until the church was in place. This did not take many years. At the same time, Olaf started planning what was to become the centerpiece of his own business empire.[1]

Olaf was now forty-two years old and a powerful man in Fort Dodge. The railroad made it possible for him to order his pharmaceutical products in large quantities. He hired sales agents who visited all the drugstores in the western part of Iowa. Through them he introduced products most people had not seen before, both because there had been little demand for them and because prices were so high. It was said that he had available almost fifty thousand different pharmaceutical remedies which could cure nearly any disease. Buying in quantity, he paid less for the products than his competitors and was able to keep prices low for his customers. He then decided to expand his business by bringing in and selling other types of products, leading to the need for a new and larger store.[2]

To help him with the office work he engaged the eighteen-year-old Thorvold S. Larsen, who had just recently come to America from Moss, Norway. A friend had suggested him, and Olaf, responding that in America there would always be positions available for able men, hired him at once. It became the start of a lifelong friendship, and in the years to come they would build up a large business together.

In addition to starting businesses and creating employment in Fort Dodge, Olaf encouraged young people to pursue an education. In his spare time he taught at the Tobin Business College, which accepted both male and female students, and he offered gold and silver medals for the best achievements. He probably remembered how proud he had been when he received distinction at the college in Philadelphia.[3]

The United States was again hosting a world exposition in the summer of 1893, this time in Chicago. The Norwegian composer Edvard Grieg was invited to conduct at the opening ceremony of the Norwegian pavilion, but he did not accept, thus greatly disappointing the Norwegian American singers who attended as a chorus of one hundred men. Grieg had over the years received many invitations from America. Unlike Ole Bull, he never made the trip.

During the exhibition Olaf almost certainly met his old friend and colleague from the Sundnes estate, Peter Zachariasen Nøvik. Nøvik had come from Norway to participate in a horticultural congress that took place in conjunction with the exhibition. He also went on a tour to study American horticulture. He was impressed by the methods used in growing roses and apples and by how Americans preserved and dried fruit. When he returned to Norway, he was offered the position as Norway's first state gardener.[4]

This world's fair was called the Columbian Exposition to commemorate Columbus and the four hundredth anniversary of his "discovery" of America. It was the Norwegians, however, who stole people's attention, according to Norwegian newspapers. An exact replica of the Viking ship *Gogstadskipet*, named *Viking*, had sailed across the Atlantic in stormy weather. It traveled up the Hudson River, crossed the Great Lakes, and dropped anchor in Chicago on July 12, 1893. By this deed, Captain Magnus Andersen and his crew demonstrated that the Norwegian Leif Eiriksson had made the "discovery" five hundred years earlier than Columbus.

The Norwegian pavilion covered a large area, displaying Norwegian skis, skates, silversmith work, photographs, and aquavit. A replica of a stave church was erected to demonstrate Norwegian building tradition. The church had been prefabricated in Orkdal, Sør-Trøndelag, and was richly decorated with carvings. It was later moved to Little Norway in Wisconsin. The Viking ship is still in existence and is on display just outside of Chicago.[5]

The large Norwegian presence at the exhibition strengthened the ties between America and Norway. One effect was that donations and financial gifts by postal orders to Norway that year amounted to 2.2 million Norwegian kroner, or about $400,000. In addition money was sent via banks or in letters to private persons and associations.[6]

Until the 1890s, most of the emigrated Norwegians thought of themselves as Norwegians. As the second-generation immigrants grew in number, it gradually became more common to use the term Norwegian American.

Olaf Declines to Run for Congress

Olaf was not a typical Norwegian immigrant. He was not part of the large group of Norwegian Americans, mostly farmers, who lived in small Norwegian American communities where they maintained the Norwegian language and cultural traditions and attended the local Norwegian church. Neither did he join the small group of the highly educated Norwegian immigrants who became American overnight and who no longer took part in Norwegian activities. Instead, Olaf became one of those immigrants who lived with several identities. He seems to have had a pragmatic attitude, on one hand maintaining his Norwegian language and culture and on the other hand learning English and doing business with others, be they Irish, Catholics, or political opponents.

Olaf was not content with only running his own business and taking part in the decision-making in the Norwegian church in Fort Dodge. He also wanted to have his voice heard more widely in the state of Iowa. His long business experience gave him enough confidence to enter the political arena as one of the progressive politicians in the Midwest. He wanted to take part in changing political life. He had seen enough of shady deals, corruption, and politicians buying votes. He was a supporter of democratic humanism rather than puritanical intolerance in an America that had opened its arms to all types of immigrants. He wanted to work for the welfare of all, not only for himself or his own interests.

The Democrat Grover Cleveland was elected president again in 1892 after having lost the 1888 election. Olaf's friend Rasmus B. Anderson, a Norwegian American, was hoping to become vice president, but was not nominated. Even in Iowa, a typical agricultural state, the Democrats improved their position, and Olaf was elected to the state senate as the first Scandinavian and the first Democrat to represent Webster and Calhoun Counties. That same year, his brother Ola was elected alternate member of the Norwegian Parliament, representing the Liberal Party of Nord-Trøndelag.[1]

Democrats in the United States had many similarities to the Liberals in Norway. Conditions in the two countries, however, were quite different. Norwegians wanted independence, but they feared a Swedish invasion. Americans did not fear invasion and began instead to look abroad, to begin building a world power. The first step was to use warships to annex Hawaii, due to its strategic location and its economic importance in whaling and sugar plantations. Most Democrats opposed this imperialistic approach.

The Democrats attracted people from the working class in the larger cities, especially Irish and Germans. They resented the power of the large trusts and wanted tariffs and subsidies removed to create fair competition for smaller companies. The Democrats also disliked the immigration of cheap labor that was used by owners of large industries to suppress the labor unions.

The Republicans appealed to the upper classes and received their main support from industrialists and businessmen along the East Coast, but also to a large extent from farmers in the Midwest and pietistic Protestants. The lines dividing the Republicans and the Democrats coincided closely with the lines distinguishing various religious attitudes. The view on alcohol also played an important role. The Methodists and the Scandinavian Lutherans sympathized with the Republicans, and they considered the drinking of alcohol as a sin. The Catholics and the Democrats, however, opposed prohibition and thought politicians should stay away from such moral questions.

In 1894 Olaf was reelected as the only Democrat to represent Webster and Calhoun Counties in the Iowa State Senate. The United States was now entering a new period of depression. Three million people lost their jobs, and the Democrats were blamed. The Republicans became the leading party in Iowa, as in most of the Midwest. It would take forty years before a Democrat again was elected from Olaf's district. His main political opponent, but also a good friend in Fort Dodge, the lawyer Jonathan P. Dolliver, who later became a state senator, was reported to have said, "Iowa will go Democratic when Hell goes Methodist."[2]

In 1896 the Republicans won power and William McKinley was elected president. Many Democrats went over to the Republican party, among them Olaf's friend Rasmus B. Anderson. The decimated group of Iowa Democrats did not give up, however, and asked Olaf to run for office in Washington. Olaf declined. Had he not, and had he won the election, he would have been the only Norwegian-born Democrat to sit in the US House of Representatives until at least 1925, and he would have been joined by the legendary Norwegian American Republican and lawyer Knute Nelson from Voss, Norway. Nelson was the first Scandinavian to take a seat in the US Senate. Olaf's reason for not accepting the nomination has not been recorded. Maybe he felt the Republicans had too strong a hand, or maybe he saw that his political engagement consumed so much of his time that there was not enough left for his other interests.[3]

When Olaf came to America, he brought with him his interest in and experience with botany. These interests and practical experiences were planted in good soil in the Midwest. He also carried with him skills and attitudes acquired from birth and upbringing. His liberal ideas found rocky soil in the strongly conservative Midwest, where he was in the minority. And finally, he carried with him a large portion of curiosity and energy, which seems to have been a family trait.

Both he and his brother Ola looked far beyond the fences surrounding the farm, and they both managed to transform their social engagement into political activities. This brought them to the forefront of the new political movements. Olaf found practical outlets for his social interests rather than continuing his political career. Ola also gave up active political work after having served two terms as a member of Parliament, most likely because compromises and long and tedious proceedings did not agree with his temperament.

Department Store, Church, and Matrimony

Olaf invested much effort in the development of Fort Dodge and in making the small Norwegian community visible in the city. By the mid-1890s, Fort Dodge had grown to about six thousand inhabitants. In September 1894, the St. Olaf Norwegian Lutheran Church in Fort Dodge was consecrated. Its high steeple made it visible from far away, and several hundred guests from Eau Claire, Chippewa Falls, Eagle Grove, Ruthven, Badger, and other places were invited to the ceremony. When Olaf started playing the organ, the first service in the new church began.[1]

St. Olaf Norwegian Lutheran Church in Fort Dodge. Constructed with financial support from Olaf in 1894. *Webster County Historical Society*

By acquiring land and guaranteeing the construction cost, Olaf had made it possible for the Norwegian congregation to have its own church building as well as a place to meet for social events. The church had an office, a kitchen, restrooms, and a large meeting room in the basement where banquets could be held. No other church in Fort Dodge had anything like this.

The small congregation had to share its pastor with other Norwegian congregations in Iowa. It was not until 1902 that they got their own pastor, J. T. Bursett. Construction costs amounted to close to $10,000, of which Olaf paid about one-third out of his own pocket. He continued to handle the congregation's financial affairs and was their treasurer for twenty-five years. His old friend and fellow member of *Grieg Mandskor*, the barber Carl C. Haugen, functioned as secretary for forty-five years. A few years after construction of the church, the congregation bought two acres of land northwest of the city to use as the church's cemetery.

The same year the church was consecrated, Olaf opened the doors to the Oleson Block, Iowa's most elegant building, according to the *Fort Dodge Messenger*. The interior was such that they called it "a perfect pharmacy palace." Olaf wanted Fort Dodge to have a building so magnificent and beautiful that people would pause as they passed by, stopping to take in the view. The city had grown to about ten thousand inhabitants, so there were many potential admirers. With towers, spires, large arched windows, and balconies, the 32 by 160–foot brick building was said to have a Romanesque style with a touch of Renaissance. Olaf had engaged the architect Charles A. Dunham, who also had designed the church, and chose the corner of Eighth Street and Central Avenue for its location, right in the middle of the city's shopping district.[2]

The pharmacy had entrances from both streets. The large building also housed departments where one could buy books, stationery, wallpaper, window glass, paint, and oil, among other things. Everything was systemized and arranged nicely down to the final detail, as the local newspaper reported, and "Daylight flowed into the room where the ladies could sit down and study interior decor." The new trend in wallpaper was the so-called Morris design, with lush blooms, branches, and birds. The English designer William Morris had an interest in

The Oleson Block, with the Oleson Drug Store on the first floor, on the corner of Eighth Street and Central Avenue, Fort Dodge. Architect: Charles A. Dunham. *Private collection*

bringing art and craft that was affordable and introduced wallpaper with designs that counterbalanced the sumptuous Victorian style.

The Oleson Block also became the headquarters for students. During September each year, long lines of young people waited to buy books and stationery for the coming semesters. "Iowa's most beautiful soda fountain" inside the building also attracted a lot of people. On hot summer days it offered thirsty passers-by refreshing fruit juice. The

Olaf, second from left, outside his department store. *Private collection*

Oleson Block was a palace for consumers, making the necessary act of shopping into an event. To encourage his customers to return, Olaf practiced what he had learned from Wanamaker's in Philadelphia. He kept prices for high-quality goods low, and he ran summer and winter sales to maintain a high volume of trade.

In the center of the building was a round office from which all departments could be seen. Olaf, however, had his office in the innermost part of the building, and he ran all his businesses from there. He had one of the fifty-two telephones in the city, and used it to carry out his business. A wide staircase led up to the second floor. Here there was a large covered veranda with granite columns and a wrought-iron fence, a nice place to sit on a hot summer day and, according to the local press, "when the smoke from the fragrant Havana curls upwards, dreams of future enterprises, wealth and happiness can be indulged in with supreme comfort as well as elegance." Inside were twelve offices and several large halls, among them the Grieg Hall where the *Grieg Mandskor* practiced. The third floor offered apartments and lounges. The building was state of the art, with restrooms, gas heat, and electric lights.

There was an elevator used to bring goods up from the basement to the various departments.

Olaf was owner and president of the Oleson Drug Company. His next in command was Thorvold S. Larsen, with the title secretary.

Olaf was a forty-six-year-old bachelor when the church and department store were opened, and people believed he would probably stay single for the rest of his life. He said himself he had been so engaged with his businesses that there had been no time for courting. But in February 1895 he received information that made him sit back and think seriously about his own life. His friend from the Philadelphia College of Pharmacy, Silas Mainville Burroughs, had died of pneumonia at age forty-eight. There were no remedies for the disease at that time. Burroughs left behind a widow and several young children. Only a few months after the sad message, Olaf married Lucy Merrit Deming. She was forty-four years old and recently divorced. The reason for her divorce is not known. Olaf and Lucy's marriage was happy for the few years it lasted.[3]

Olaf's pharmacy was first named Cheney & Oleson's and later the Oleson Drug Company. *Kvam Historielag*

Lucy was characterized as a vivacious and popular lady of high society, but also one who involved herself in the community's social issues. She was the only child of a prominent and broad-minded banker in Fort Dodge, John Harris Deming. Her mother was Maryette Belcher. John Deming had been central in the development of Fort Dodge, lending money at low interest and encouraging both men and women of all classes to get an education. When Olaf and Lucy married, Deming was old and sick, and the pair decided to live in the fashionable Deming House at 1602 First Avenue North so Lucy could take care of her parents.

Lucy had a wide network of contacts and many friends, and Olaf was drawn into the city's social life. She was, among other things, a member of the Fort Dodge Chapter of the Daughters of the American Revolution. The objective of this organization is to promote patriotism and to maintain the historical places, monuments, and memories of the past. This was also to become one of Olaf's interests. He helped found the Webster County Historical Society, becoming a member of the board. One of the first challenges for the organization was to plan the sixty-fifth anniversary in 1906 of the construction of Fort Dodge by US troops.

Lucy and Olaf had no children. But Olaf felt responsible for his niece and nephew, Helen and Oliver, and Lucy had her hands full helping her sick parents.

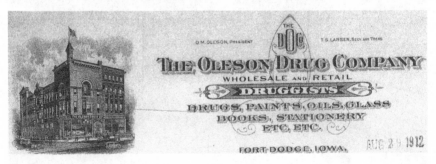

Letterhead for the Oleson Drug Company. *Private collection*

Olaf Contacts Bjørnson and Grieg

Olaf must have felt at his peak both in private life and in business. To crown his achievements he wanted the chorus he led to have its own song, written by Bjørnson and composed by Grieg. Grieg was, like Bjørnson, politically radical and composed many tunes based on Norwegian folk songs. He also wrote many songs for male voice on request. Olaf sat down and wrote a letter to Bjørnson. They had not seen each other since Bjørnson had to delay his departure from Fort Dodge due to bad weather fifteen years earlier, but Olaf addressed him as an old friend, so they may have written to each other in the meantime.

Fort Dodge, Feb. 14, 1896.

Mr. Bjørnstjerne Bjørnson.

Thank you for our unforgettable last meeting, Bjørnson! Yes, it has been a long time since you were here and made such a deep impression on us all! We have a 5 year old male chorus with 16 members. Its name is "Grieg Mandskor." I have been and still am its leader and we are making good progress, so, not just for our fellow countrymen, but also for the Americans, we have several times shown what great material Norway has had in the areas of poetry and music. What we would wish is exactly this: If you could be so goodhearted and write a song for our organization, send it to Ed. Grieg so he can compose the music? The reason for writing to you, is that I am not personally acquainted with Grieg, though I know his magnificent music intimately. I know it is a lot to ask for; but if you find this inconvenient, do not be afraid to say no—but if you could see how just a few lines from you in the form of a poem would inspire us all, I believe you would hardly say no to our request. Hoping you will find time and opportunity to send us a few lines, I remain respectfully yours,

O. M. Oleson

I apologize for taking the liberty to write to you, but it is a sincere heart's desire, as the chorus is very dear to me and it is doing its best to show the highest and noblest in our

Olaf's letter to Bjørnson, February 14, 1896. *Manuscript Collection, National Library of Norway* nation. You will, I guess, remember me—I am still at the same pharmacy—I was pivotal in bringing you to Fort Dodge—I travelled to Albert Lea in Minnesota, as well as to Des Moines, Iowa, to listen to you. I will never forget these memories as long as I live, and they are among my most pleasant.

Much obliged,
O. M. Olesen[1]

Quite soon Olaf received a note from Bjørnson saying, "Yes, I will try." By February 29 Bjørnson had the poem "Norwegian Tones" ready and sent it to Grieg together with a rather sarcastic letter.

Grieg immediately wrote music to the poem, calling it *Impromptu til Grieg Mandskor i Fort Dodge, Iowa, U.S of A.*, and sent it to Bjørnson with an equally sarcastic letter.

Impromptu til Griegs Mandskor. Text by Bjørnson, music by Grieg, 1896. *Bergen Public Library, the Grieg Archives*

Olaf received the poem and the music together with a small card on which was written: "Well, cordial greeting from Bjørnstjerne Bjørnson, Munich, 2,29,96. Over!" The other side read: "and from Edward Grieg, Leipzig, Thalstrasse 10." Olaf heard no more from Bjørnson or Grieg.[2]

"The song was appreciated and is still very much appreciated by Oleson and the members of the organization," reported *Sanger-Hilsen* in its periodical distributed to the members of the Norwegian Singers' Association of America. It seems to be only locally in Fort Dodge that the song was performed. It was never part of the association's repertoire, most likely because both text and music have a foolish character, according to Camilla Haugen Cai, music professor at Kenyon College, Gambier, Ohio. She has written two articles about the contact Olaf had with Bjørnson and Grieg.[3]

Cai suggests that Grieg, coming from a high society family in Bergen, Norway, may have looked down on Olaf, an emigrant and son of a farmer. It may also be that Bjørnson, through his action, wanted to avenge the massive criticism he had received from many Norwegians in the Midwest. Cai says, however, that Grieg could have gained much by maintaining contact with Olaf. American publishers made a lot of money selling Grieg's music, while Grieg received nothing because there was no royalty agreement between Norway and the United States at that time. Grieg complained about this situation and asked people in America to help him. Olaf could have helped as he had many influential contacts within banking and finance. Much might have been different if Grieg had accepted the invitation to conduct at the opening ceremony of the world exposition three years earlier. Olaf and Grieg would then have met, and as Cai has written, "If only Grieg and Bjørnson had understood. These singing groups in America embodied the new Norwegian ideals of enlightened progress and freedom with equal standing. Lost was the opportunity for cultural exchange that would have enriched them all."[4]

Besides promoting Norwegian culture with their performances, the Norwegian singers in America also took an active role in erecting monuments. As an example, *Nordmennenes Sangforening* in Minneapolis decided to raise a monument in honor of Ole Bull. To raise money for this, a concert was held where Ole Bull's young widow, Sara, played the piano and her son the violin. Soon after, a sum of about $8,000 was available and the sculptor Jakob Fjelde from Ålesund,

Norway, was hired. Four thousand people were present at the unveiling of the monument; never had so many Norwegian Americans been assembled in one place. The statue was placed in Loring Park in Minneapolis, which served as the natural gathering place for Norwegian Americans when celebrating May 17, Norway's Constitution Day.

The Norwegian singers also showed compassion for those back in Norway. On October 13–14, 1899, a hurricane swept over the small fishing communities of Røvær, Frøya, Kristiansund, Smøla, and Hitra and 137 sailors drowned. In December of that same year a fund-raising concert was held in Chicago and $1,100 donated by the audience was sent to the local authorities in Norway. A few years later, when the Norwegian Americans in Chicago learned that the city of Ålesund had burned down, they collected $550 to help.[5]

Members of the Norwegian choruses looked forward to the large festivals. In the summer of 1896 a large Scandinavian festival, or in reality a Danish-Norwegian festival, was arranged in "The Danish Omaha," as it was called in one of the songs. The singers chose the Danish building Washington Hall as their headquarters. In Rusers Park the military had put up tents to accommodate the singers. Omaha, where

Cover of the program for the Scandinavian Festival in Grand Forks, North Dakota, 1904. *Norwegian-American Collection, National Library of Norway*

Grieg Mandskor participated in the Scandinavian *Sangerfest* in Grand Forks, North Dakota, 1904. Olaf is sitting in the middle in the second row. *Webster County Historical Society*

Olaf had established his first pharmacy, had grown to a large city of about a hundred thousand inhabitants. In 1898 Omaha hosted the Trans-Mississippi and International Exposition, attracting 2.8 million visitors. Exhibitors from the Midwest displayed products from agriculture, livestock, art, and industry. An Indian Congress was arranged in the city at the same time. Five hundred representatives from thirty-five tribes had come to Omaha. The idea behind the Indian Congress was to showcase Indian regalia and traditions. But visitors wanted to see war dances and cowboy and Indian reenactments. The imprisoned Indian leader Geronimo was on display, and Buffalo Bill put on a Wild West Show. Some people found this unseemly, just eight years after the massacre at Wounded Knee.[6]

The first completely Norwegian festival in America was held in Duluth, Minnesota, in August 1898. A. C. Floan was president and John Dahle, professor at Luther College, was the main director. Two years later the festival was arranged in Chicago with Emil Biørn directing a chorus of one hundred singers. Biørn, who was both an artist and a musician, had come from Kristiania in Norway to Chicago where he joined the *Bjørgvin* Singing Society and became one of the most well-known Norwegian American directors.

In 1904 a Danish-Norwegian song festival was arranged, this time in Grand Forks, North Dakota. In reality the festival was mainly a Norwegian event. F. L. K. Hassel, originally from Biri, Norway, and a member of the chorus *Bjarne* in Grand Forks, was president of the Norwegian Singers' Association of America. Olaf was treasurer. Jens H. Flaaten, originally from Kristiansand, Norway, lived in Duluth and led the Normanna Singing Society. He was the head of the concert arrangements. It must have been a large undertaking, with a festival committee of one hundred. Several subcommittees assisted, among them a reception committee of thirty men led by the city's mayor. There was also a ladies committee. The program brochure had a picture of each chorus with a short introduction, a new standard for the festivals that followed.

Three of Olaf's nephews traveled with him to festivals. Bjarne, Torleif, and Martin, all sons of Olaf's oldest brother, Eilert, had emigrated to America. All three were educated in Norway, one as an engineer, another as a jeweler, and the third within agriculture. One may assume that Olaf's success was the main reason for their decision to leave Norway. Martin returned to Norway after a few years, while Bjarne and Torleif changed their family name to Fieve and settled down in Stevens Point, Wisconsin, and Minneapolis, Minnesota, respectively. Their oldest brother, Oscar, who inherited the Five farm in Kvam, died while trying to save another person from drowning. After this accident, their father, Eilert, sold the farm out of the family and moved to Steinkjer.

War Drums Beat

While the Norwegians in the United States gradually became more prominent in their new country, they were disappointed when Norway gave in to Sweden in the consulate affair. This was lamented in Norwegian American newspapers from coast to coast. Norwegian Americans found the retreat made by their fellow countrymen humiliating. But Olaf knew that his brother would never give in. Ola started training his marksmen in military discipline and nighttime guerilla warfare in unknown terrain. He felt sure the situation would soon become serious. They practiced with the recently developed Krag-Jørgensen rifle by shooting against various targets. In Nord-Trøndelag the target resembled a Swedish officer. Ola Five's men changed their name to *Det frivillige Skyttervesen* (the Volunteer Marksmen), and Ola remained their leader.[1]

While the Liberals and the Volunteer Marksmen wanted Norway to become an independent state, the United States was becoming a world power. The Civil War and the Indian Wars were history, the economic situation seemed stable, and industrial productivity had greatly increased during the period 1860–90. A substantial part of the country's capital was controlled by multimillionaires and companies that dominated in industries such as steel, oil, and railroads. The domestic market soon offered little room for expansion, and the search for new markets began. America had so far not followed the European countries in their race for colonies in Africa and Asia. Expanding westward within its own borders had been the main focus.

The United States wanted maritime control to make sure American goods could be transported safely worldwide and without encountering customs barriers. Spain's dominant position at sea was a threat. The Spaniards ruled Cuba and the Philippines, both strategic locations. The Americans started building up their navy and in a few years warships, cruisers, gunboats, and torpedo boats were constructed. The coastal defense was fortified with cannon and forts. But to ensure the safety of the fleet, it was necessary to control the Caribbean. The United States had already obtained a monopoly by building the Panama Canal and securing a piece of land on each side of the canal so that ships could sail safely between the West Coast and the East Coast. The canal made it possible to avoid the dangerous Cape Horn, where in the past so many ships had been lost.

To support its fleet, the United States needed footholds outside of America. In addition, American citizens and their interests abroad needed protection. Cuba, where Americans owned large sugar plantations and steel factories, stood out as a natural target. Spain ruled Cuba with an iron fist, and Cuban uprisings were regularly suppressed. The United States found this instability to be a threat against American interests in Cuba. Consequently, in 1898 politicians, big industrialists, and newspapers joined forces in an effort to sway public opinion toward a war against Spain. The Republican senator John Mellen Thurston from Omaha informed the people that "War with Spain would increase the business and earnings of every American railroad, it would increase the output of every American factory, it would stimulate every branch of industry and domestic commerce."[2]

In 1898 the United States went to war with Spain in Cuba. The war lasted for one hundred days and ended with a totally defeated Spanish fleet. The Americans withdrew from Cuba but kept the Guantanamo base. A year later the United States invaded the Philippines. The main objective was to quell an uprising, but American soldiers remained mired there for sixteen years.[3]

Most Democrats did not approve of invading the Philippines. And when news about the fighting reached America, including stories about Philippine women and children being massacred, about torture and concentration camps, many Americans protested, among them Mark Twain. He saw the basic American ideas of democracy being betrayed, as the Philippines were not allowed to decide their own destiny when the Spaniards were finally thrown out. He wrote, "I'm sure I wish I could see what we were getting out of it, and all it means to us as a nation."[4]

The most prominent Norwegian American politician, Republican senator Knute Nelson, wholeheartedly supported imperialism, including the annexation of Hawaii and the invasion of the Philippines. About Olaf's reaction had he been elected to Congress we can only speculate.

Olaf's American Landscape Park

It may very well be that Olaf did not care much about America's foreign affairs. He was probably more concerned about Norway's destiny. But his primary interest lay with the people, the businesses, and the landscape in and around Fort Dodge. In 1903 he took part in forming the city's mercantile association, which included all kinds of businesses. The objective was to strengthen the city's welfare and make it attractive for other businesses to open there. One of the first things the association did was to make sure the city got a proper hotel, the Crawford.

In his spare time Olaf would take his fishing rod down from the wall, saddle his horse, and ride out into the fields surrounding the city, where the landscape was rapidly changing. Almost all the wild prairie around Fort Dodge, once covered with flowers, had disappeared. In fact, all of Iowa had been transformed into an agricultural region, most of it owned by European immigrants. In a little more than sixty years the territory once owned by Native Americans had been plowed under, and with that mountain lions, bison, and black bears had disappeared. Even beaver and otter moved on as rivers were rerouted, canals were built, and large trees along the dried-out creeks cut down. For shade, people planted new trees around their houses.

Some of the original vegetation could be found here and there, and Olaf wanted to preserve these places as a reminder of what it once had looked like. He remembered how rich and full of variety the flora around Fort Dodge had been. He thought this was due to the several feet of gypsum that could be found under the thin soil. He remembered the natural setting around the lake Snåsavatnet in Kvam, where the lime-rich soil gave a similar effect. Olaf paid his businesses less attention for a couple of years and, together with M. P. Somes and C. H. Churchill, started to systematically collect plants from a wide area of Webster County. The plants were listed with their Latin name and grouped according to their species with a note telling where they were found and whether they were common or rare. All the plants were dried and pressed and made a large herbarium, a library of plants, with about 850 samples to begin with. Olaf presented their work to the Iowa Academy of Science, where he was accepted as a member. He founded the Webster Botanical Club, which kept his herbarium. It was called the Oleson Collection and in the end contained about twenty-three thousand plants.

Together with M. P. Somes, Olaf published the study "A Flora of Webster County, Iowa." It was used as a textbook at Iowa State College (now Iowa State University), where he occasionally gave lectures in botany. He corresponded with several botanists all over the United States, exchanging plants, books, and scientific reports. Many of his fellow botanists were also bacteriologists doing research on fungi and microbes that caused stomach infections and other diseases. In 1917 scientists started working with these substances to find out if it was possible to develop medicine from them. In 1928 one scientist succeeded in producing penicillin. But it was not until the 1950s that penicillin was taken into common use and helped people with serious illnesses such as pneumonia. Olaf argued strongly for an international code for botanic terminology, as it was difficult to find consensus for an American one. Olaf suggested the Vienna Code, which finally was chosen, but not until 2004.[1]

While Olaf wandered out on what was left of the prairie, people in Fort Dodge saw "skyscrapers" as high as five stories being erected, inspired by the look of Chicago. The State Bank building, located at 629 Central Avenue and regarded as an enormous project at the time, stood ready for use in 1908. Fort Dodge had finally become a real city, if not a large one.

In 1903 a bridge was constructed across the Des Moines River in Fort Dodge. With a length of almost half a mile, it was Iowa's second-largest railroad bridge and an engineering triumph. From then on thirty-five trains carried passengers and goods to and from the city on a daily basis. The city, having grown to about twelve thousand, did not have adequate housing for ordinary people. The Oleson Land Company, which Olaf, as president, ran together with other prominent Fort Dodge businessmen, bought a large farm just southeast of the city. The farm covered an area larger than the city itself. Olaf was certain the city would keep on growing and wanted to build a suburb to accommodate the expansion. The authorities in Fort Dodge did not believe in the project and offered no support. The Oleson Land Company constructed roads, brought water and electricity to the area, built two schools, and extended the streetcar line.

To assist people with modest income and no savings in buying a house of their own, Olaf created a down-payment system. The *Fort Dodge Messenger* published an advertisement explaining that the properties would cost $200, but by paying five dollars cash and a weekly fee of fifty cents the first year, seventy-five cents the next, and finally a dollar per week until $200 had been paid, one could buy a lot—provided one accepted within thirty days. The lots would double in value within three to four years, the ad promised.

The area the Oleson Land Company had bought became an attractive residential district and after some years was incorporated into the city. It also became an area for recreation. In the middle of what was originally the farm, Olaf had found his paradise—an untouched stretch of forest of about seventy-five acres with groves, glades, small valleys and hill tops, a creek, and a small lake. In the spring the ground was covered with flowers that reminded him of the white anemones back home in Kvam. Oak trees, hickory, elm, ash, linden, and aspen stretched their branches over his head. He decided the area should remain untouched and no building should take place there. He wanted to save it as a place for children to pick flowers such as white and red clover, bird's-foot trefoil, large harebells, oxeye daisies, and lilies, just as he had done around the Five farm as a child. The flowers should be for everyone to enjoy, not just the adults, as had been the case on the Sundnes estate.[2]

Advertisement for the Oleson Land Company in the *Fort Dodge Messenger*, May 27, 1905. *Private collection*

This was to become Olaf's American landscape park. The natural beauty was already there. He just needed a gardener to arrange some paths between the groves, take down a few trees to make the Des Moines River visible, and have a couple of small bridges built. Olaf tried to include the trees in a meaningful way. Some had a majestic position, others offered shade for visitors, and still others marked the outskirts of the

In Oleson Park, Olaf built a music pavilion where the *Grieg Mandskor* held concerts. *Private collection*

Seats and benches were arranged on the grass in Oleson Park during concerts.
Private collection

park. In a large, open area close to the entrance he had a music pavilion built, plus a small zoo, a children's playground, and a fountain where
people could cool off on hot summer days. Paths crossed the grassy areas
and led into the woods through small clearings with flowers, down steep
slopes to the creek, over a bridge, and up the other side, passing large
trees and fallen trunks left to rot and give life to new vegetation.

Olaf's idea was to have a park with easy access from several parts of
the new suburb. He wanted children to have a place to meet and play
which could be reached without having to walk along the streets near
the park. He set up a nursery just outside the park where people could
learn gardening skills and buy trees and flowers and, if they wanted,
plant them in the park. Thus all could contribute in forming the park
and have a sense of ownership in it.

Olaf bought the whole park from the Oleson Land Company and
donated it to the city. He offered a detailed description of his ideas for
the park. He did not include many restrictions for the authorities of
Fort Dodge, other than that the park was for the people of the city, that
an elected group of three persons should administer it, and that they
should do it out of love for the park and not to earn money.[3]

Olaf Supports Norwegian American Writers

In his thinking Olaf was both a pioneer and a conservationist. The latter was best expressed in the way he sought to preserve nature through landscape parks. His pioneer spirit was manifested in all his business activities. His involvement in song and music combined these two characteristics. Through singing he kept Norwegian culture alive. Forming the singers' organizations filled him with creative zest. Olaf was also one who quite early encouraged Norwegian American authors to describe the life of Norwegian immigrants in order to prevent their history from being forgotten. He offered a yearly prize in literature through *Det Norske Selskab i Amerika* (the Norwegian Society in America). From the first year of its existence, 1903, and until at least 1936 he gave fifty dollars, later one hundred dollars, to the best literary work. A key person behind the Norwegian Society in America was the newspaperman Waldemar Ager from Fredrikstad, Norway, who lived in Eau Claire, Wisconsin. He was also the first to be awarded a prize by Olaf, who praised his natural presentation of the life of Norwegians abroad: "It does one good to read these stories, and they do not leave a bad taste in one's mouth. . . . My award is not large, but I hope that it will give a little encouragement to a novice, who might have barely enough to live on."[1]

Like Olaf, Waldemar Ager was a liberal person. He was, among other things, interested in workers' and women's rights, and he became a prolific Norwegian American writer. Ager encouraged immigrants to maintain their Norwegian culture. He promoted a multicultural society and opposed the melting pot idea that was being pushed by American authorities. Among the Norwegian American writers to receive the award were O. M. Buslett, Per Strømme, Julius B. Baumann, Johannes B. Wist, Thor Helgesen, Dorthea Dahl, Sigurd Folkestad, Kristian Prestgard, and Ola Særvold.[2]

Olaf was disappointed to see that the Norwegian Americans did not support the writers by buying their books, saying, "Let us hope that we, as time passes, will treasure these products, made in America." Olaf also saw that an increasing number of immigrants focused on the future and wanted to become Americans rather than maintaining their Norwegian traditions and language. In 1903 he had to accept that even the congregation of St. Olaf Norwegian Lutheran Church decided that, if he wished to, the pastor could use English in the service.

Lucy Dies

While Olaf was occupied with his many undertakings, Lucy took care of her father until he died. The effort wore her out, but she thought her father would not receive adequate treatment at the local hospital, which had no facilities for caring for the elderly. A few months after her father died, Lucy became ill and Olaf brought her to the mountains in Colorado, hoping the fresh air would do her good. After they returned, Lucy died of pneumonia on August 13, 1904. None of Olaf's fifty thousand remedies could have helped her, and penicillin was not yet available. Olaf and Lucy had been married for only nine years. His mother-in-law moved to a nursing home, while he decided to stay in the Deming house, which must have felt large and empty with Olaf as the only resident.

Lucy left Olaf an inheritance from her father that amounted to between a quarter and half a million dollars. She was buried next to her father in the large and beautiful Oakland Cemetery just north of the city. Olaf asked for the burial plot for the Deming family to be expanded to include the Oleson family.

Like most people in those days, Lucy died at home. Despite a large and modern pharmacy and a hospital, the city had only one doctor visiting patients at home. The Sisters of Mercy Hospital, built only three years before Lucy died, was run by Catholic nurses, but it accepted patients of all faiths. The nurses were self-taught, however, and the seriously ill had to be sent to Des Moines or Sioux City. The hospital was in a building known as the Haskell House, located on the corner of First Avenue North and Fifth Street, where there earlier had been both a stagecoach station and a school. The first floor could accommodate eighteen patients. The kitchen was in the basement, while the second floor housed the infirmary and the operating room. There was only one bathroom available to serve both staff and patients, so the risk of contagion was high. The staff slept in the waiting room.[1]

The Deming and Oleson plot at the Oakland Cemetery, Fort Dodge, 2010.
Private collection

While it was understood that the hospital needed a new and more suitable building, it did not seem possible for the Catholics, the Protestants, and the authorities to cooperate. A couple of years after Lucy's death, the city was struck by typhoid fever, a serious infectious disease spread due to poor hygiene. Many died and several houses and shops were closed in fear of an epidemic. The hospital could not care for all of those who were ill, and many were brought to the veterinarian's barn, soon nicknamed "the plague house." The need for a new hospital was acute. Again the Catholic Sisters of Mercy took the initiative and said that if the city could raise $25,000 and provide the land, the Sisters should be able to come up with a similar amount. The authorities still hesitated. Then the city's mercantile association, which Olaf had helped establish, cut through the secular and religious conflicts and accepted the challenge. Olaf, together with two other private persons, put up a personal guarantee for the $25,000, while encouraging others to contribute to a dedicated fund.

Olaf was elected to the hospital board, which engaged one of the Catholic nurses to take care of the finances. A lot along Seventeenth Street was acquired and construction began. A year later, the St. Joseph Mercy Hospital was ready, equipped with sixty beds, but the cost was higher than anticipated. Olaf offered an additional $20,000.

The work with the hospital had taken Olaf's mind away from the loss of Lucy. And now another event worth looking forward to emerged. *Den norske Studentersangforening* (the Norwegian Student Choral Society) was coming to America, and Olaf was one of the hosts.

The Norwegian Student Choral Society Tours America

In May and June 1905, a chorus of forty-five men from the Norwegian Student Choral Society made a concert tour across Norwegian America. At this time Norway's military defense was fully armed and set in a state of emergency. Mines were spread across the Kristianiafjord, and Ola Five and his forty thousand volunteer marksmen were carrying out field maneuvers and preparing themselves for a guerilla war if the Swedes decided to invade.[1]

The concert tour unintentionally turned into a political tour. Though the singers protested this interpretation, the Swedish papers wrote, "Yes, they were sent with a political intention," and Swedish Americans agreed with this assessment. The press followed the Norwegian singers every hour, day in and day out.

Ever since 1878, when the student singers in Kristiania together with the Swedish Uppsala students held a concert in Paris, France, some of the Norwegian student singers had dreamed of a concert tour across the Atlantic. Many thought it just "a wild fantasy, a pious wish that nobody seriously thought possible to make come true." But in 1903 the idea surfaced again, and the Norwegian singers turned to the student chorus in Lund, Sweden, asking if they wanted to make a joint tour. The answer was that the Swedes had no principal objections, but they had already made their own arrangements for a tour in America in 1904. The Norwegians decided to travel on their own, and a group of wealthy people in Kristiania soon guaranteed a large sum of money to cover the cost. The chairman of the chorus was Heinrich Thomsen, and the director was O. A. Grøndahl. Soloists were Johannes Berg-Hansen and Rolf Hammer. Before the tour started, they rehearsed the following programs:

Program I
Johan Selmer: *Norge, Norge!*
Kierulf: *Solvirkning*
Heise: *Skjemtevise*
Grøndahl: *Unge Magnus*, soloist: Berg-Hansen
Kjerulf: *Brudefærden*
Sigurd Lie: *Vaar*
Belmann: *Hvila ved denne källa*
Reissiger: *Olav Tryggvason*
Folk song: *Den store hvide flok*, soloist: Berg-Hansen
Folk song: *Ho Guro*
Møbring: *Sof i ro!* soloist: Hammer

Program II
Ole Olsen: *I Jotunheimen*
Sigurd Lie: *Per spillemand*
Belmann: *Joachim uti Babylon*
Heise: *Skjemtevise*
Reissiger: *En sangers bøn*
Svendsen: *Aftenröster*
Reissiger: *Høstandagt*
Folk song: *Den store, hvide flok*, soloist: Hammer
Grøndahl: *O, var jeg med dem i følge!*
Olaf Paulus: *Vestenveir*
Folk song: *Baanlaat*, soloist: Hammer and Berg-Hansen
Reissiger: *Olav Tryggvason*

To create some publicity and attract support for the singers' tour, the chairman had invited the Swedish crown prince to be the patron of the Norwegian Student Choral Society, and this was announced in the program leaflet, without consulting the chorus. Most of its members found the dedication to be royal snobbery. Before leaving for America, the chorus held three concerts in Kristiania, receiving fine reviews and money for their journey. Swedes in Chicago sent a message by way of the newspaper *Aftenposten*, saying, "Tell them that here in America there is no mountain range between Norwegians and Swedes."

The Norwegian student singers were treated as the sole ambassadors from Norway to the United States at a time when Norway's destiny was at stake. The official American attitude was that Norway should stay in union with Sweden, because a weakened Sweden would make Russia's position more powerful. The situation was also carefully watched by the other European countries. Many feared that an independent Norway could alter the already fragile balance of power in Europe. It could also trigger nationalistic agitation in other countries, especially in Finland, which at that time was part of the empire of the Russian tsar, and in the patchwork Austro-Hungarian Empire, where the Czechs, the Hungarians, and the Croatians were considered unmanageable. The Great Powers did not want an armed conflict between Norway and Sweden. Russia was already at war with Japan and did not want another war close to its borders. And Great Britain and Germany made it clear they would not support a Swedish invasion of Norway.

The Norwegian student singers came ashore in New York and celebrated Norwegian Constitution Day, May 17, before beginning their tour, a journey with concerts in twenty cities. They started out via Niagara Falls to Chicago. Arriving at Park Row Station, they were received by five hundred Norwegian Americans singing Grieg's "Song of Welcome" and an overwhelming amount of flowers. At the hotel entrance, all singers, both guests and locals, gathered and sang *Ja, vi elsker*, the Norwegian national anthem. Concerts, excursions, and parties followed.

Nicolai A. Grevstad, the editor of Chicago's largest Norwegian American newspaper, *Skandinaven*, gave the principal speech at the banquet, saying, "Now, that our relatives from the old farm have come to visit us, we should show them around a bit in our new places out here in the West." Not to brag, as he said, he wished to report that three Norwegians had been elected governors in their respective states, and a fourth was soon to come. A dozen Norwegians were, or had been, sitting in the House of Representatives, one was a US senator, and two represented the country as diplomats abroad.

And the Norwegians in America were numerous, he emphasized. The more than five hundred thousand immigrants had grown to close to 1.5 million counting their children born in America. So, more than a third of all Norwegians lived in America. Most of them were farmers, and there were "thousands of Norwegian cotters' sons who now own their own farms here in America."

He continued reeling off facts. There were three thousand Norwegian congregations with over eleven hundred Norwegian pastors

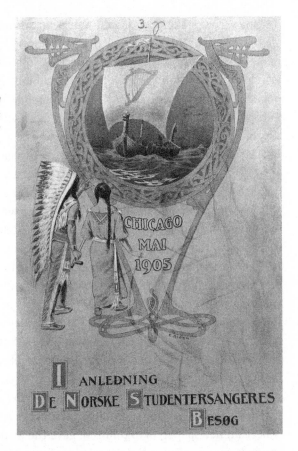

In Chicago, the visit by the Norwegian student singers in May 1905 was greatly anticipated. *Den norske Studenter-sangforening, National Library of Norway's Music Collection*

in two thousand Norwegian churches. There were seven Norwegian seminaries and eighteen schools offering higher education. Furthermore, the Norwegians had built more than a dozen hospitals in addition to old people's homes and orphanages. And, Grevstad continued, "We believe it would please our common mother . . . that she can be proud of her children in America. . . . It is true that only a few of them are to be found in the poorhouse or in jail."

What he did not say, however, was that a relatively high percentage of Norwegian immigrants, compared to immigrants from other countries, were patients in insane asylums. Neither did he mention that Norwegian women were to be found among the prostitutes in larger cities like Chicago, and that many Norwegians became addicted to alcohol in the struggle for a living. This was a night for celebration:

"While living in this country, the Norwegians have become Americans, not just in name, but in their view of life, in their souls and in their minds.... But they carry the picture of mother Norway in their hearts ... they have preserved her treasury of songs and hymns in all its purity. The melodies born in the mountains follow us, raise us up and give us strength in all that we do."

Grevstad thought the Norwegians had something to learn from the Americans: "We hope that work will soon be given a place of honor in our homeland, and that the Norwegians will learn to work as hard as the Norwegians in America can and do."

Referring to the tense situation between Norway and Sweden, he said that "we are pleased to see that the Norwegian people now are unified in trying to achieve the goal set by the men at Eidsvoll ... and we are certain a solution will be found without breaking the union."

From Chicago the Norwegian student singers continued their journey across the prairie, and Olaf traveled with them all the way. In Wisconsin, they visited Madison, Eau Claire, Superior, and La Crosse. In Minnesota, they went by way of Minneapolis, St. Paul, Northfield,

POLITICS TALKED AT THE BANQUET

Senator Nelson and Others Discuss Differences Between Sweden and Norway.

The Norwegian-Swedish political differences bobbed up at the banquet given last evening in honor of the Christiania students at the Odin club.

Newspapers noted the political discussions during the Norwegian Student Choral Society tour of America, May 1905. *Den norske Studenter-sangforening, National Library of Norway's Music Collection*

Red Wing, Duluth, and Crookston. In North Dakota, they traveled to Grand Forks, Devils Lake, and Fargo. They went to Sioux Falls in South Dakota, and to Sioux City, Fort Dodge, Mason City, and Decorah in Iowa. Every place they visited had a committee that organized concerts and banquets. The committees were usually representatives from the local Norwegian male chorus in addition to the most prominent people of the city. In Decorah and Northfield, Luther College and St. Olaf College, respectively, did the organizing.

Everywhere they went the Norwegian singers were met with ovations and rave reviews. The tour was also covered extensively by the press in Norway, and the Americans asked themselves, "Where do we find an American school that can boast of such a love of art and which has reached such a height in music?"

The chorus received gifts and trophies during what was called "the victory march" across America: silk banners, silver bowls, a crystal punch bowl, various photos of the local choruses, a model of the first Norwegian church in America, ten laurel wreaths, and a live bear.

At the beginning of the tour, many Swedes came to listen and Swedish newspapers wrote nice reviews. However, one of the Norwegian student singers, Ludvig Saxe, wrote in his diary that the condition between Swedes and Norwegians was as tense "here as at home, even

From a newspaper published during the Norwegian Student Choral Society tour, 1905. *Den norske Studentersangforening,* National Library of Norway's Music Collection

TALK OF WAR IS RIFE IN NORWAY

Rumor That Swedish Troops Have Already Chosen Mobilization Point.

though the nice speeches try to assure of the opposite." In Grand Forks a veteran from the Spanish-American war, the lawyer and colonel E. Smith-Petersen, who was toastmaster at the banquet, said:

> We have admired the patriotism and eagerness for independence that exist over there and that, in these troubled days, fill the hearts of the Norwegian people so that differences between Conservatives and Liberals are completely erased....
>
> And the message you should bring with you from us, your American brothers, is that we hope the Norwegian people will be faithful to their traditions and not back away a hairsbreadth from their rights, *even if the union with Sweden should shatter.* Patrick Henry, an American patriot, said, "Give me liberty or give me death." We hope that the Norwegians will fight to the last drop of blood for their rights; as it would be much better if Norway were forever erased from the map of the world, rather than let itself be subdued in this matter, which concerns its honor, its glory, its freedom, and its independence. And you must relay that if the signal flames are lit from mountain top to mountain top, if the war drums call people to arms, Viking blood still runs hot in the veins of the Norwegian Americans.

On June 7 the *Fargo Forum* headline shouted: NORWAY TODAY DISSOLVED THE UNION WITH SWEDEN. The Norwegian Parliament had voted and now intensive political negotiations started.

The Norwegian student singers celebrated the day by visiting the stone monument commemorating Bjørnstjerne Bjørnson in Fargo. The next day they went to Sioux Falls, and during a break between the many speeches at the banquet the Norwegian Minnehaha Male Chorus delivered a song, composed by Alfred Paulsen, "with a patriotic and militaristic text by Per Sivle, that suited the mood of the day very well."

The Norwegian student singers celebrated. Shouts of "Long live Norway, long live freedom.... We do not want a king, we shall be a republic, long live the republic" resounded through the halls of the Hotel Garretson, according to the *Sioux City Journal* of June 10. The newspaper also reported that the students threatened to strike if the management did not remove the Swedish song "Listen to us, Svea" from the program.

This change was not enough for the Norwegian student singers, however; they also removed the listing of the Swedish crown prince as patron of the tour from the program and pasted in *Ja, vi elsker*, the Norwegian national anthem, with an English translation.

From newspapers published during the Norwegian Student Choral Society tour, 1905. *Den norske Studenter-sangforening, National Library of Norway's Music Collection*

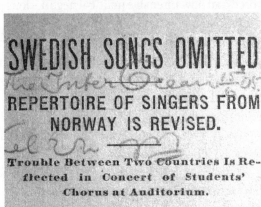

Norwegian Independence Celebrated at the Oleson Drug Store

Animated by the victory in Norway, the Norwegian student singers arrived in Fort Dodge, where Olaf had decorated the Oleson Block with large banners in the Norwegian colors and rented the Crawford Hotel for the occasion. This is how the meeting with Olaf was described in a book about the Norwegian Student Singers' concert tour through Norwegian America during May and June of 1905:

> On Saturday the 10th of June at 9:15, our journey continued
> by train to Fort Dodge, where we arrived at 3 o'clock. We were

The Oleson Block, Fort Dodge, festively decorated in the summer of 1905. *Webster County Historical Society*

received by an old acquaintance, the pharmacist Mr. Oleson, who lives in this small, beautiful city. Oleson had already met us in Minneapolis and followed us from city to city nearly all the time and listened to almost all the concerts; it was like we were meeting an old friend from Norway, when we saw him again. Oleson had prepared everything in the best way; the hotel was ready for us, arranged down to the smallest details. On each singer's bedside table he had placed an envelope containing 10 postcards with pictures showing the nicest parts of the city, including "the Oleson Park." The oldest singers were accommodated in the Crawford Hotel, which they afterwards called the best hotel in the world. They gave this rating to their host in writing. He should be especially proud of this, since an older singer, who had been to America earlier, had a lot of previous experience and exorbitant expectations in this regard.

The singers were to stay in this idyllic place until the next day and during this time had only to present one concert and attend one banquet.

The concert took place in the theater and was one of our best performances during the tour. We had a full house. After the concert the usual occurance took place outside the theater. The singers met and shook hands with the audience coming out, and received greetings to be brought back to old Norway. This nice practice seemed to us even nicer in the beautiful city of Fort Dodge, where so many lovely young women had attended the concert. . . .

After the concert, Oleson and *Grieg Mandskor* invited us to a banquet, which was held in the Oleson Drug Store. We will never forget this party, even though not one speech was delivered. Oleson had, as mentioned, been with us during most of the tour and knew what we already had endured of eloquence; this party, therefore, is one of our nicest memories. The missing speeches were compensated for many times over by singing; quartets were formed on the spot, and competition made the performances even better. And it was far into the wee hours before the last singers crossed the streets of Fort Dodge.[1]

A Tribute to Norway

On June 13, 1905, the Norwegian student singers were back in Chicago. That afternoon they gathered with five hundred other Norwegians in the banker Paul O. Stensland's yard in Irving Park. Stensland, whose name was originally Paul Olson, was one of Chicago's most prominent Norwegian businessmen, and this gathering was seen as one of the most important events in Norwegian American history in Chicago. Hundreds of lights were scattered around the yard, and high above the Norwegian flag waved. The Norwegian singers entertained, and Stensland's daughter-in-law, Grace Nelson Stensland, sang a solo with "political enthusiasm." The idea behind the gathering was to collect signatures on a petition drive to encourage President Theodore Roosevelt to acknowledge Norway's independence.[1]

The next day the student singers held their farewell concert at Carnegie Hall in Chicago, but "Since the Swedes went on strike due to the political circumstances, we had only 3,000 people in the audience. To make up for that a number of encores were demanded."

In Norway, *Verdens Gang* reported that "the atmosphere during the last concert was quite emotional, and the applause seemed never to end when we sang the Norwegian national anthem."[2]

On June 17, ten days after the union between Norway and Sweden was dissolved with the "7th of June Resolution," a mass meeting was arranged in Chicago, where four thousand Norwegian Americans celebrated Norway's new status. Patriotic speeches and congratulations were given. Messages were telegraphed to the Norwegian government and Parliament, assuring them of material help, if there was any need. A request for diplomatic recognition of Norway's independence was sent to President Roosevelt. Similar requests were sent in the thousands from Norwegian American politicians, businesses, and institutions.

The mass meeting in Chicago was arranged by the Norwegian National League, an umbrella organization for all Norwegian associations and clubs. Many of Olaf's friends had taken part in forming this league, including his singing colleague Julius Jæger and the businessman Birger Osland from Stavanger, Norway. A few months later the league planned a closed meeting to decide how best to assist Norway. In the meantime, several new help organizations were established, and Birger Osland in the Norwegian National League said that "many young Norwegian immigrants were ready to return to enlist in the military forces in case of war with Sweden."[3]

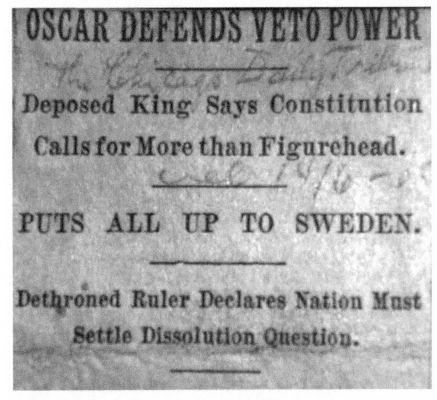

From a newspaper published during the Norwegian Student Choral Society tour, 1905. *Den norske Studentersangforening, National Library of Norway's Music Collection*

The Norwegian Chorus Meets
President Roosevelt

The Norwegian student singers' tour of triumph reached its peak when Olaf arranged for them to meet President Theodore Roosevelt—something the Swedish singers had not achieved when they were in Washington the year before.[1]

It was Olaf's friend in Fort Dodge, the Republican senator Jonathan Prentiss Dolliver, who helped make the meeting possible. Dolliver, who earlier had maintained that Olaf's political party, the Democrats, would never gain a foothold in Iowa, had been widely expected to be nominated to run for vice president of the United States. However, Roosevelt, who had distinguished himself during the war with Spain, was nominated instead. At the next election Roosevelt was elected president.

On Monday, June 19, 1905, the Norwegian student singers were received by President Roosevelt, who was in the middle of peace negotiations between Japan and Russia. The president gave each and every singer a hearty handshake and said, "It is a special pleasure for me to greet you gentlemen from Norway. We do have many Norwegians in America who have become American citizens, but I have to tell you that we can never have too many Norwegians here. I would gladly see all Norwegians, and your whole country as well, move to America. Although I do not speak your language, you could easily test me in the old Norwegian sagas. In any case, I know by heart the poem about St. Olaf, written by the American poet Longfellow."[2]

The Norwegian singers sang both the Norwegian and the American national anthems. The president applauded enthusiastically and said he appreciated their visit and would welcome them back. This concert is believed to be the first held in the White House. During the concert an armed Swede was stopped nearby. However, it turned out that he had just returned from a hunting trip.

The Norwegian students returned to Norway, and Olaf was later

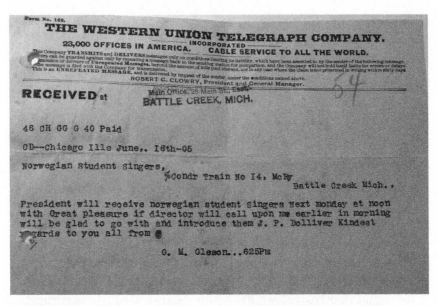

Telegram from Olaf to the student singers confirming that President Roosevelt will receive them in the White House. *Den norske Studentersangforening, National Library of Norway's Music Collection*

honored with the title Commander of the Order of Norwegian Student Singers for his contribution to the singers' tour.

The political negotiations between Norway and Sweden lasted for months. On September 13, from Karlstad, Sweden, the Swedish minister of justice wrote to the Swedish prime minister and said that war against Norway was necessary. The same day the Norwegian authorities issued a mobilization order. Norwegian warships blocked

From a Norwegian newspaper published during the Norwegian Student Choral Society tour, 1905. *Den norske Studentersangforening, National Library of Norway's Music Collection*

THEY SANG FOR NORWAY, CHEERED FOR HER FREE

National Sentiment Stirred at a Students' Concert Here.

PRESIDENT TO RECEIVE THEM

Lone Swede There with a Gun, but He Checked It—Came from Hunting.

From a newspaper published during the Norwegian Student Choral Society tour, 1905. *Den norske Studentersangforening, National Library of Norway's Music Collection*

the Kristianiafjord, and torpedo boats were sent to defend the cities of Trondheim and Bergen. A total of twenty-three thousand soldiers were ordered to watch the borders. They set up their tents, arranged defense lines, dug ditches, and called in Ola Five's forty thousand volunteer marksmen. The marksmen were to operate in small guerilla-like groups, to delay the Swedes in their advance toward Kristiania and Trondheim.[3]

At the same time a committee of the Norwegian National League in America held a secret meeting, led by chairman John Andersen, editor of *Skandinaven*, who was originally from Voss, Norway, and its secretary, Olaf's good friend Birger Osland. The idea was to establish a rescue organization to provide material assistance to Norway. They formed a committee which was to be prepared to organize branches all over the United States that could be set up on short notice. To avoid unnecessary irritation among the Swedes in America, committee members decided not to publish any information about their plan. While it was legal for Americans of foreign origin to offer support to noncombatants, widows, and orphans in their original home country in cases of war, it is also possible that keeping the committee's work secret was vital because the material help they had promised included both money and weapons.[4]

The Swedish military authorities, who had spies in Norway, feared that a long guerilla war would stretch into the winter of 1905–06. The parties finally came to a political solution and not a single shot was fired. Since war was avoided, Ola Five's volunteer marksmen's contribution to the peace process was later forgotten. On October 26, 1905, King Oscar II abdicated as king of Norway, and three days later the United States recognized Norway as an independent nation.

The secret Norwegian American groups were dissolved. But the Norwegian Americans had stood up for Norway, both morally and financially. According to the Norwegian newspaper *Aftenposten*'s rough estimate, made in 1906, about 20 million Norwegian kroner, some $5 million, was sent as gifts through postal orders and transmittals to banks and emigrant offices in Norway in 1905. At about the same time the Norwegian Americans started planning to raise funds for a gift to the old country in connection with the 1914 centennial of Norway's constitution.[5]

Now that Norway was finally freed from Swedish rule, many Norwegians in America were surprised to see that Norway did not abandon the monarchy and the state church. The Norwegian Americans did, however, send a delegation to King Haakon's crowning ceremony in Nidaros Cathedral the following year. Among the representatives was the St. Olaf College Band from Northfield, Minnesota. They were the first American student band to visit Norway. King Haakon received the Norwegian American delegation at *Stiftsgården*, the royal residence in Trondheim, and assured them that he was "fully aware of and thankful for the powerful moral support the Norwegian Americans had offered Norway during the crisis the previous year."[6]

The relationship between the singers of Norway and America grew stronger after 1905, and many Norwegian American choruses planned trips to Norway. A tour to Norway was, to these choruses, "the highest and most glorious goal one could have." The distance between Norway and America was not too wide for a "bridge of song" to be built between them, it was said. But it seemed a long way from dream to reality.

Dovre Sangforening was the first to make the trip. In the summer of 1907 they held a concert in the Tivoli Garden in Kristiania. From there they traveled along the coast, visiting thirty-six cities and holding forty-four concerts, until the tour ended in the city of Steinkjer in Nord-Trøndelag.[7]

The National Trønderlag of America

"Stop the Norwegians!" "Stop the Germans!" "We do not want fifty-percent Americans. We want one-hundred-percent Americans." This sort of thing was heard more and more often throughout the country. People should be converted to American patriots. Even though President Roosevelt had welcomed the Norwegian student singers in the most pleasant way, he did not approve of Norwegians and other immigrants isolating themselves in enclaves. Norwegian Americans did not let this attitude stop them in their effort to preserve the Norwegian language. For example, in 1906 there were 2,639 Norwegian congregations and only twenty-one of them used English. Cultural traditions were sustained. In Norway, Bjørnstjerne Bjørnson made a plea. "The independence process in 1905 has brought the Norwegian people together as one family in an unprecedented way. The need for a lasting bond between the people at home and the emigrants is now strong on each side. A federation should be established based on this," he wrote in an appeal in the Norwegian business paper *Farmand* in 1906. This federation was supposed to include "countrymen all over the world"— not just those across the Atlantic, but also those who had emigrated to Africa, Asia, and Australia. "Because, if we include them all, we will be twice the number!" he emphasized.[1]

In his appeal Bjørnson was joined by 146 other prominent Norwegian women and men, including the polar explorer Roald Amundsen, the composer Edvard Grieg, member of Parliament Carl Berner, the artist Erik Werenskiold, professor J. E. Sars, chairman of the Norwegian Volunteer Women's Medical Service Fredrikke M. Qvam, chairman of the Norwegian Association for Women's Right to Vote Gina Krogh, and Olaf's brother Ola Five, the Marksman General.

Nordmanns-Forbundet (formerly known as the Norse Federation and now called Norwegians Worldwide) was established on June 21, 1907, with the objective to promote Norwegian culture and interests abroad. Its statutes said that any respectable member, man or woman, whether an emigrant or just traveling abroad, is entitled to help from the federation if needed. In many ways the Norse Federation became an extension of the Ministry of Foreign Affairs. With president of the Parliament Carl Berner as chairman, its link to official Norway was consolidated. Olaf signed up as a lifetime member. One of the first things the federation did was to give the Americans a statue of Henrik Wergeland, sculpted by Gustav Vigeland. The statue was unveiled a year later in Island Park in Fargo, North Dakota, with the city's Norwegian male chorus singing the Norwegian national anthem. A few years later, a bust of the Norwegian poet Ivar Aasen was erected in Moorhead, Minnesota.[2]

Norwegian Americans wanted to build a connection with Norway beyond the Norse Federation and started forming *bygdelag,* groups of people who came from the same district in Norway. *Valdres Samband* was the first to be established. Soon after, on September 17, 1908, Olaf met with 120 other emigrants from Trøndelag in the Sons of Norway Hall in Fergus Falls, Minnesota, and founded *Det Nationale Trønderlaget i Amerika* (the National Trønderlag of America). Olaf was elected chairman the next year. The number of members had by then grown to six hundred. Olaf continued as one of its leaders for several years. Another leader was Rev. Ditlef G. Ristad from Overhalla, Norway, who had been one of Ola Five's pupils in the elementary school. Others were Peder Langback, S. O. Leirfall, Peter Lein, I. Dorrum, O. J. Fosen, and M. A. Wollan.[3]

Emigrants from Trøndelag were widely spread across the United States, and the intention of the National Trønderlag of America was to strengthen solidarity, maintain traditions from Trøndelag, and support Norwegian ventures. The organization had a drawing of the Nidaros Cathedral in Trondheim on their letterhead. Each year the local groups came together for a large celebration with over a thousand people present. Everyone showed up: farmers and city folk, lawyers and managers, pastors and professors, well-off housewives and not-so-well-off working women. Entertainment was provided by the male choruses.

The first decision the National Trønderlag of America made was to promote fund-raising for the centennial of the Norwegian constitution in 1914. They set an ambitious goal for this gift to Norway. Trønder-lag of America members wanted to use the money to help restore the Nidaros Cathedral in Trondheim, "for one of the larger stained glass windows on the western nave." But others presented different plans, including raising capital to build and run a new school at Eidsvoll, where the constitution had been signed in 1814, fund a gigantic tree-planting program, build headquarters for the Norse Federation in Kristiania, or establish a fund to fight tuberculosis.[4]

To start with, the Norwegian American newspapers were full of assurances that there was wide support, and they constantly presented new suggestions for the gift. None of them gained much enthusiasm, however. The first gift committee disbanded, and a new meeting was arranged in Minneapolis in the summer of 1909, which Olaf and other representatives from all over the United States attended. State senator L. O. Thorpe from Wilmar, Minnesota, was elected chairman for this 1914 gift committee, with editor Nicolai A. Grevstad from Chicago as vice chairman. Soon after, Grevstad was appointed US consul in Uruguay and Paraguay, and Olaf took his seat on the committee.

The heated discussion around all the gift suggestions discouraged people from donating money to this cause, and fund-raising went slowly. Olaf managed, however, to persuade members of the National Trønderlag of America to sponsor publication of two folktale books written by the folklore collector Karl Braset in Sparbu, Nord-Trøndelag. The books were called *Øventyr og sagn* (Stories and Legends) and *Hollraøventyra* (The Hollra Stories) and were illustrated by Einar Øfsti, known as the portrayer of Trøndelag nature. Olaf thought, as did P. C. Asbjørnsen, the folklore collector and landscape architect of the Sundnes estate, that by taking care of the folktales one also took care of the Norwegian soul. The foreword to Braset's collection begins, "The folk tale collector is Karl Braset, Sparbu, and it is he who has written the book. O. M. Oleson, Fort Dodge, Iowa and The National Trønderlag of America, Fergus Falls, Minnesota have financed it. In Norway nobody was willing to spend the money."[5]

The National Trønderlag of America sponsored the project with $100, which represented about one-third of the group's total spending for 1911. The Trønderlag yearbook for 1912 has the following information: "Karl Braset's Folk Tale Collection. Old Tales in Spabu dialect is now available from the secretary of The National Trønderlag of America, Fergus Falls, Minn. The collection comprises two books and costs $2.50 in elegant original binding or $2.00 in paperback. Two hundred and thirty sets have been sent to The National Trønderlag of America and for as long as this edition lasts, those who buy it will also receive a map of their home district in Norway. These maps are highly detailed and very accurate and show every farm, house, creek, road etc."[6]

Olaf Marries the Richest Girl in Town

Not long after Lucy died, Olaf found love again, and in 1907 he married Julie Haskell. He was fifty-eight years old, she thirty-eight and the daughter of the richest man in town, Aden Enos Haskell and his wife, Martha Gardner. Haskell had come from Massachusetts and was one of the earliest residents in Fort Dodge. He built up a chain of stagecoach stops and obtained a federal contract for transportation of mail, goods, and people westward, all the way to Sioux City and Council Bluffs on the Nebraska border. Haskell's company, Western Stages, had at its peak six hundred stagecoaches and three thousand horses and employed fifteen hundred people. As the railroad was extended further west, the stagecoach era ended and he and his family moved to Santa Barbara, California, where he ran a telegraph company. After a few years he sold the company, made a fortune, and moved back to Fort Dodge, where, among other things, he established Fort Dodge National Bank. Haskell died just a couple of years before Julie married Olaf. It is believed that she brought a substantial amount of money into the marriage, more than Olaf had already made for himself.[1]

Together they moved to a new house in what was becoming the most fashionable area of the city, the Oak Hill District, which stretched from Eighth to Twelfth Street and from Second to Third Avenue South, just outside the lively business district. The house was known as the O. M. Oleson House at 1020 Third Avenue South. It is an elegant three-story building made of red brick with green roof tiles, built in a modified Prairie style.[2]

Olaf is supposed to have designed the house himself, planning the interior down to the smallest detail. The walls in the entryway were covered with beautiful green wallpaper from England, probably a Morris design with branches and flowers. In the living room there was a fireplace and a door leading to a spacious veranda. The dining room was lit by thirty small spotlights mounted in the ceiling plus a large chandelier designed by Julie. It was made of bronze and had pieces of stained glass with acorns and oak leaves—a sign of happiness. There was a music room with a pipe organ, an unusual luxury in a private home. Olaf played the organ frequently. There was a large kitchen with a separate pantry. The bathroom was equipped with running water, still an uncommon feature in those days. The second floor had two bathrooms, one master bedroom with a fireplace, and four other bedrooms, including one for the maid. She had her own staircase leading down to the kitchen, and she could be summoned both from the master bedroom and the dining room at the press of a button. The third floor had a spare room and attics. The house was heated by hot water radiators from a furnace installed in the basement.

Outside the main entrance there was space for a horse and carriage. Olaf also planned the garden. Around several large oak trees he made a lawn with steps, paths, and lots of flowers, among them peonies and four hundered different sorts of irises. He had no gardener. Working in the garden was his way to relax.

Olaf married Julie
Haskell in 1907.
Private collection

Olaf and Julie's home at 1020 Third Avenue South, in the Oak Hill District, Fort Dodge.
Private collection

What was it like to live in this large house with all its rooms and without the sound of children? What was it like to enjoy the garden without children playing and laughing? Both Olaf's first and his second marriage were childless. Olaf may have thought often of his brother Ola, who had six children. For every new child, Ola proclaimed that a new heir was born. Olaf knew that the children had brought Ola a lot of joy but also much sorrow. Five of the six children died of various diseases. Only one, Olaf Wergeland, grew to adulthood. Olaf developed a good relationship with his nephew in Norway, almost as good as the relationship he had with Helen, his niece in America.

Despite the fact that the couple did not have any children, Olaf and Julie's marriage was a happy and rewarding one for both. In her earlier years Julie had run businesses with her mother. Now she had time to devote to drawing and watercolors, hobbies she had pursued from childhood. Over time Olaf withdrew from the daily management of the

Oleson Drug Store and turned over the duties to his trusted colleague and good friend Thorvold Larsen. Olaf wanted to devote more time to his hobby, botany. An appreciation for nature was something that Olaf and Julie shared. They also shared the joy of helping others. Both had a caring nature and more time and money than they needed for themselves. They let the surplus benefit their local society. They chose to support private persons, charity organizations, institutions, schools, and businesses, preferably without any publicity. Both Julie and Olaf were private by nature. They were sociable and well thought of, but not many knew them intimately. They rarely accepted interviews and only a few published pictures of them exist despite their prominent positions.[3]

It had become a tradition, both in Norway and America, that wealthy people supported artists or contributed to education, just as Olaf's first employer, Herman Løchen at the Sundnes estate, had done. In America philanthropy was also regarded as an efficient way of accelerating development and change in society without having to work through the government. At the same time, the government could let rich people carry some of the responsibility for the poor. Philanthropists in return gained a certain status. Olaf, however, did not want publicity around his charitable works.

Julie had a sister, Emma Rose, married to the lawyer Archibald Cattell. They had two daughters that Julie and Olaf were close to. Olaf also maintained a good relationship with his niece, Helen, and when she married, it was Olaf who walked her down the aisle in her wedding to Edward A. Welch. The bridal bouquet was composed of lilies from Olaf's garden, and Helen wore a gift from Olaf, a necklace of diamonds and pearls in the shape of rays of the sun. The local newspaper called this occasion a prominent society wedding. Ed Welch, son of one of the city's earliest inhabitants, had a large shoe store and was, together with Olaf, a member of the local mercantile association. Olaf offered the newly married couple a lot on Crawford Avenue on the outskirts of the city. Helen designed the house herself, an extraordinary structure inspired by the childhood home of Shakespeare's wife in Stratford-upon-Avon, England. Helen's house was covered with cedar shakes and was awarded a prize for good architectural style.[4]

Olaf's creative power and zest for life is best documented through the business projects he was involved in:

The Oleson Drug Store, Fort Dodge: founder and president
Fort Dodge Telephone Company: cofounder and president
The Oleson Land Company, Fort Dodge: cofounder and
   president
Fort Dodge Gas and Electric Company: cofounder
Fort Dodge Loan and Trust: management position
Fort Dodge Building and Loan Association: president
Fort Dodge Manufacturing Company: president
Fort Dodge Hotel Company: president
Wahkonsa Hotel, Fort Dodge: helped finance construction;
   shareholder
The Fort Dodge Serum Company: main investor
Iowa Trust Livestock Company: president
The State Bank, Fort Dodge: vice president
Commercial Club of Fort Dodge: cofounder and president
Den norske Amerikalinje (the Norwegian America Line): large
   shareholder; council member

In addition, he owned several farms and hired people to run them.
And he was a member of, engaged in, or a financial donor to the following organizations. This list is incomplete, as it does not include private
loans and gifts.[5]

Webster County Historical Society: cofounder and board
   member
Iowa Academy of Science: member
Santa Barbara Natural History Society: member
San Diego Natural History Society: member
The Norwegian Singers' Association of America: cofounder;
   treasurer; honorary president
Grieg Mandskor, Fort Dodge: founder; director
The National Trønderlag of America: cofounder; treasurer
Norwegian-American Historical Association (NAHA):
   cofounder; treasurer
Nordmanns-Forbundet: lifelong member
Fort Dodge Rotary Club: member
Fort Dodge Botanical Club: cofounder; president

St. Olaf Norwegian Church in Fort Dodge: helped finance construction; donated a pipe organ; treasurer; board member
First Congregational Church, Fort Dodge: helped finance con-
struction; donated a pipe organ
St. Joseph's Mercy Hospital, Fort Dodge: helped finance con-
struction; board member
Lutheran Hospital, Fort Dodge: helped finance construction;
board member
Young Men's Christian Association (YMCA), Fort Dodge:
donated land
Young Women's Christian Association (YWCA), Fort Dodge:
donated land
Friendship Haven, Fort Dodge: helped finance construction
Oleson Park, Fort Dodge: bought the land and donated the park
to the city
Leif Erickson Park, Fort Dodge: bought the land and donated
the park to the city
Haskell Park, Fort Dodge: bought the land and donated the park
to the city
Det norske Selskab i Amerika (the Norwegian Society in
America): yearly donations to the "best literary work"
Blanden Museum, Fort Dodge: financial gifts
Tobin College, Fort Dodge: helped finance construction; part-
time lecturer
The 1914 Gift to Norway: committee vice chairman; main donor
Fort Dodge Arsenal: helped finance construction
Fort Dodge Public Library: donated land
Commission of Pharmacy, Iowa: cofounder; board member
Iowa State Senate: first Scandinavian member; represented the
Democrats, 1892–96
"A Flora of Webster County, Iowa" 1906: co-author, with M. P.
Somes
Iowa State University: part-time lecturer in botany

Like Olaf, Julie was proud of her political and social heritage. Her
grandfather was among the first to be killed in the fight against slavery.
He was shot down in the streets of Newport News, Virginia, because he

had published his opinions. Julie chose art to express herself. She had attended Grinnell College in Iowa and the San Diego Academy of Arts in California. One of her professors was Robert Henri, who was part of the Ashcan School movement, in which artists portrayed scenes from everyday life in New York's poor neighborhoods. Julie was a member of the Iowa Artists Club, Iowa Art Salon, and San Diego Art Guild, she was president of the Fort Dodge Art Guild, and a member of the building committee for the Blanden Memorial Art Gallery in Fort Dodge. Even in her later years she exhibited her art at many galleries and shows, such as the Fine Arts Gallery and La Jolla Art Gallery in San Diego, Santa Barbara Art Gallery, Chicago Art Institute Watercolor Show, Art Institute in Chicago, Iowa Art Salon, Iowa Artist Club Exhibition, All Iowa Exhibit, and Iowa Art Show in Sioux City. She received several awards, among them the Harvey Ingham Prize for meritorious work in watercolor.[6]

Olaf and Julie donated the Leif Erickson Park and the Haskell Park, with playground facilities, to the city. Olaf believed the city's children needed easy access to nature and fresh air. The need for a special place for children to play was a new idea. These two parks were smaller than Oleson Park, but they were large enough for children to have fun. The smallest, Leif Erickson Park, is located on a hilltop on the western side of the Des Moines River, in an area where most of the Scandinavians lived.

Haskell Park was donated in memory of Julie's father. It was located in a small wooded area close to where Haskell in earlier days had head-quartered his stagecoach business. The park included Soldier Creek, which wound down the valley just north of First Avenue North and stretched to Seventh Street. Here children could wade and splash; nearby, a nice picnic spot was located. A couple of the old stagecoaches, in which Julie had played as a child, were still there.

The Wahkonsa Hotel

Julie and Olaf started spending the winters in Santa Barbara, California, where Julie had lived as a child. She couldn't handle the harsh winters in Fort Dodge anymore. The cold did not bother Olaf, but he enjoyed the mild climate in California and the opportunity to wander in the exotic botanical gardens. He got acquainted with local biologists and spent much time collecting and identifying plants from the region. Their home, however, was still Fort Dodge.

Olaf was described as "high thinking—plain living." People must have gotten the impression of a simple lifestyle despite the wealth and luxury that surrounded him. Some of that wealth he shared with the city, for instance by building the Oleson Block, donating the parks, and helping to finance the modern Wahkonsa Hotel. He thought Fort Dodge needed these modern facilities. By 1910 the city had reached a population of about fifteen thousand and had become known for its cultural and leisure activities and as a place offering educational opportunities. The city was still a walking town and the number of cars

The Wahkonsa Hotel, designed by architects Liebbe, Nourse and Rasmussen of Des Moines, Iowa, opened in 1910. *Private collection*

Fort Dodge in 1907, showing the Oleson Drug Company. *Webster County Historical Society*

could be counted on one hand. Julie drove one of them. Olaf still used his own horse to get around, which was also considered a luxury. It was, however, possible to rent horses several places in the city—at the railway station, at some stores, and at a few small hotels.[1]

Tourists coming to Fort Dodge met a white city. Though a Native American boy, Wahkonsa, was a well-known and well-liked figure in the town, there were not many other Native Americans, and the few African Americans who lived in Fort Dodge had the least desirable jobs.

As the city had a lot of visitors, Olaf established the Fort Dodge Hotel Company in order to build and run the finest hotel in the city. The Wahkonsa Hotel was finished and ready to open in 1910. The five-story Renaissance-style "skyscraper" was named for Wahkonsa, who used to run errands in the city and play with the mayor's son. The hotel had suites, an exclusive restaurant with a dance hall, a barber and a beauty shop, a tobacconist and a haberdashery. The furniture, the decor, and the entire interior were state of the art. The stairs and the floor in the lobby were made of gray and green marble mosaic. It is said to have been the largest fireproof hotel in the United States at the time. The hotel manager was "the most genial, thorough-going and aggressive hotel man in the west," and the Wahkonsa Hotel soon became the "in place" to go after the theater or to celebrate birthdays or other events. The city and the hotel also became a popular place to spend a honeymoon.

About the time the hotel opened, Olaf received news from Philadelphia that John Wanamaker, Olaf's inspiration in the retail business, had opened his new department store, a twelve-story granite building housing a huge concert hall where the world's largest organ had been installed. The organ was originally constructed for the world exposition in St. Louis in 1904, but the project ran into financial difficulties and the organ changed owners several times before Wanamaker bought it. Not only a palace of consumption, the Wanamaker Building also became a center for cultural activities.

The Norwegian America Line

The waves of Norwegian emigrants heading for America continued into the twentieth century, and the transportation of emigrants was a lucrative business, but so far Norwegian companies had not gotten their fair share in this trade. A Norwegian company, *Det Norsk-Amerikanske Dampskipsselskap* (the Norwegian-American Steamship Company), owned by one of the most prominent persons in Bergen, had ships crossing the Atlantic in the 1870s. These ships were named for the old saga kings, like *St. Olaf, Harald Haarfagre,* and *Kong Sverre.* However, they had stopped transporting emigrants to the United States before emigration reached its peak. *Kong Sverre,* for instance, was rerouted to transport pilgrims between India and Mecca's seaport.

It was not until 1910 that *Den Norske Amerikalinje* (the Norwegian America Line), or NAL, was established. It had been a long time coming. Serious planning had started in 1902 and intensified in 1904, when a Danish emigrant ship was lost at sea and 629 people died, among them 184 Norwegians. People demanded that the Norwegian authorities oversee ships carrying Norwegian emigrants. John Lund, a Liberal member of Parliament, pointed out to the government that "We are close to 2 million Norwegians in this country, and about 1½ million over there. Should there not be a connection, a line of communication between us.... Public and private should go hand in hand."[1]

The ties between Norway and the United States grew stronger as the situation in 1905 developed, and within both countries there was support for a regularly scheduled shipping line between Norway and New York for transportation of passengers, mail, and goods. A Norwegian committee was formed and it concluded that an America Line should be established with a capital of 10 million Norwegian kroner.

It would turn out to be a difficult process, with long discussions of questions such as which harbors to use in Norway, whether to purchase existing vessels or build new ones, and what to name the ships.

Advertisement for the Norwegian America Line. *Den Norske Amerika Linje, Norwegian-American Collection, National Library of Norway*

First and foremost, however, they needed to decide how to obtain the necessary capital.

Those who had taken the initiative to form the line lacked financial backing. They planned, instead, a nationwide subscription of shares and thus made the enterprise something for the whole nation to own. This proposal created much distrust among people within trade and industry and especially among the ship owners, who initially had been counted on as prime investors. Public ownership of this sort was a break with Norwegian traditions. Norwegian shipping had gradually gained its position, but now there was an attempt to form a large corporation in one go, organized in a way that Norwegians had little experience with.

A committee was elected to start the project, and in 1909 invitations to buy shares were distributed by 178 distinguished people, Bjørnstjerne Bjørnson among them, who sent inquiries to other prominent people in various fields. No invitation was sent across the Atlantic, however. The Norwegian newspaper *Verdens Gang* suggested that the 1914 gift the Norwegian Americans were planning should go to NAL. The Norwegian business magazine *Farmand*, on the contrary, advised strongly against spending money on "such a poorly planned enterprise, which never would be profitable." And it added some bitter words about Norwegian America being "a nice illusion, but nothing more." *Farmand* refused point-blank to accept the possibility of obtaining any share capital from the other side of the ocean.

The face value of the shares was 200 Norwegian kroner. It was also possible to obtain half shares. Normal face value for shares in shipping companies was between 500 and 2,500 Norwegian kroner in those days. When 50 percent of the share capital goal of 10 million kroner was achieved, the company would be organized. But the sale of shares progressed slowly. Finally, the committee decided to approach key Norwegians in America with a request for support. Soon, the commitment of Norwegians on the other side of the Atlantic made the project a reality. The negative prophecies of *Farmand* were proved wrong. With the help of Olaf's close friend Birger Osland, a businessman in Chicago, and other agents across the United States, Norwegian Americans responded quickly, subscribing for ten thousand shares.

Many potential shareholders in Norway were waiting for the government to grant money, but there was no sign of that happening. It was therefore decided to reduce the share capital needed to organize the company. Many Norwegians lost faith in the project and withdrew, while many new shareholders came forward in America. The Americans were impatient, unaccustomed to processes taking such a long time. Norwegian Americans demanded that the line be established and that more and larger ships than the one planned be built, even though that one was 7,700 tons.

"We will provide the money, build *two* ships" was the message from America. This declaration brought the Norwegians back into the game. On August 27, 1910, the NAL was established. By then shares equal to 2.7 million kroner had been sold. About 2,400 shareholders lived in America and 1,050 in Norway. The next year Olaf was listed with fifty shares. More money had been invested by people in America than in Norway. Since NAL no longer was a solely Norwegian company, as was the original plan, it was decided that the board of directors should have seven members of which one should be an American resident and the company council should have at least six American members.[2]

Two ships were contracted for, each registering twelve thousand tons. Then the naming conflict started. A name suggested quite early was *Leif Eirikson*, as a reminder of the time when Norwegians had been a major seagoing people. Many thought this would strengthen Norwegians' self confidence and demonstrate their historical right to a share of the Atlantic shipping business. Other names were suggested as well. *Dagbladet* and *Den 17. Mai*, which Ola Five had cofounded and which for many years was the second-largest paper in Norway after *Aftenposten*, took part enthusiastically. They wanted names connected with Norwegian history. The debate ended with the first ship being named *Kristianiafjord*, and other fjord names followed.

With a combination of financing from Norwegian banks, Norwegian and American shareholders, and the Norwegian government the threshold for capital was achieved in 1913, and *Kristianiafjord* was launched on November 23 of that year. Soon after followed *Bergensfjord* and *Trondheimsfjord*, the flagships of the Norwegian America Line.

By 1915 more than a third of the capital for the NAL had come from the United States. This proved there was more substance in the Norwegian Americans' "sentimental talk about the old motherland" than *Farmand* and others gave them credit for. At this time Olaf had acquired a total of 741 shares and had been elected a member of the company council. He held 3.1 percent of the American shares and 1.2 percent of the total.

The value of the NAL shares increased enormously in the first years. No dividend was paid the first three years, though, and in 1913 it was only 2.5 percent. The real growth in earnings started during the First World War when NAL obtained a monopoly in transporting goods between the United States and Norway. The shipping of grain and machinery became a gold mine for the company. In 1914 Olaf and the other shareholders received a dividend of 6 percent and 10 percent the year after. For the period 1916–18 this figure doubled to 20 percent, quite an unusual feat for such a young company. A record dividend of 30 percent was paid in 1919.

But NAL also had its setbacks. *Trondheimsfjord* was sunk by the Germans in 1914, and *Kristianiafjord* was lost at sea outside Cape Race in Canada in 1917. The company soon contracted for a new ship, *Stavangerfjord*, which became the queen of the Atlantic. It sailed continuously until 1964, when it was scrapped. In 1923 NAL could dispatch nineteen ships.

Earlier, however, in 1919, Olaf and three thousand other Norwegian American shareholders were close to losing their right to vote for a substantial part of their shares. Norwegian speculators tried to squeeze them out. The company had built up large capital reserves during the war. After the war, when the bonanza on the stock exchanges started to develop, NAL became a tempting target. Prior to the general assembly in 1919, a consortium was formed with the intention to take control of the company. A change in the Norwegian Maritime Companies Act, not communicated to the United States, implied that no shareholder could vote for more than one hundred shares. This rule, combined with an increase of the share capital and the distribution of free shares, could make a coup possible.

The consortium presented the suggestion during the general assembly in 1919, which led to a heated debate. The atmosphere was close to exploding. Many of the Norwegians present thought it would be unwise for the business to weaken the financial capacity which the

American shares represented as one should not disregard the possible need to increase the share capital in the future.

The debate ended with the managing director announcing that he would withdraw from his position if the suggestion was voted in and the consortium became represented on the board of directors. The general assembly was then delayed until the autumn. The case was brought to the Norwegian Parliament, where a question of how to avoid speculation around the NAL shares was sent to the minister of justice. When the general assembly was finally held in the autumn, the consortium had withdrawn their suggestion and NAL was no longer subject to speculation.

NAL management thought the company would continue to grow after the war and bought eleven new ships the following year, doubling its tonnage. They did not foresee the depression in the 1930s and that immigration from Norway would almost cease. In 1922 the dividend reached a temporary bottom of 5 percent. NAL tried to find a position in the exclusive cruise market, but this venture did not add positively to the bottom line. Finally it was only the cargo ships that carried the company. Other ship owners started contracting for modern ships in the 1930s, but NAL did not have the financial strength to follow up.

Sanger-Hilsen, the Singers' Periodical

In 1910, the same year the Norwegian America Line was founded and the Wahkonsa Hotel opened in Fort Dodge, the Norwegian singers in America thought they had enough members and were rich enough to start arranging festivals for just their own Norwegian choruses. These were called *Sangerfest.* The Norwegian Singers' Association of America had by then thirty-six organizations scattered all over the United States. The first fully Norwegian festival was held in Sioux Falls, South Dakota. Olaf left an imprint on the festivals, according to the 1910 yearbook of the Norse Federation: "Among the people who throughout the years have contributed to the well-being of the Singers' Association, we need to mention our popular treasurer, the pharmacist O. M. Oleson. Whenever Norwegian music is mentioned, Oleson is there. Already several days ahead of our festivals, Oleson pops up on the horizon. Everything needs to be prepared and smoothed out. A *Sangerfest* without Oleson is unthinkable."

Some thought there was too much partying and too little singing at the festivals. But this tendency was probably part of their Norwegian heritage. The rifle club gatherings arranged by Olaf's brother Ola also included parties with speeches, dancing, good food, and beverages.

The Norwegian Singers' Association of America started its own periodical, *Sanger-Hilsen* (Singer's Greeting), published once a month to start with, later twice a month. Olaf was asked if he was willing to support the magazine until it became financially stable. He accepted, and he also made it possible for people back home in Norway to keep up with what was happening with the Norwegian singing societies in America. He paid the subscription for the director of the Norwegian Student Choral Society, O. A. Grøndahl, for his two brothers Ola and Eilert, and for Lars Ranes, who had been a singer in *Grieg Mandskor* and Olaf's colleague at Oleson Drug Store. Ranes had returned to

The magazine *Sanger-Hilsen* was published by the Norwegian Singers' Association of America. *Norwegian-American Collection, National Library of Norway*

Norway and started a knitwear shop in the city of Ålesund. Olaf also paid for the subscription for the University Library in Kristiania (now the National Library of Norway) for as long as he lived.

Around 1912 there were five Norwegian choruses in Iowa. In addition to *Grieg Mandskor*, there were *Luren, Gauken*, and Echo Glee Club in Decorah and the *Nordmennenes Sangforening* in Sioux City. *Grieg Mandskor* had twenty-five members, but it was only Olaf who represented them later on their trip to Norway.[1]

During the *Sangerfest* in Fargo, North Dakota, in 1912, about a thousand singers formed one chorus (see pages iv–v). At this time Olaf and the rest of the association's leadership started planning their big tour to Norway in conjunction with the centennial of the Norwegian constitution in 1914. There were long discussions about whether to send an elite chorus with only the best singers or a larger chorus of good singers. The latter was chosen.

The association's main director was Emil Biørn in Chicago. Nine additional directors were selected for the tour, among them Olaf. These ten directors picked out a chorus of 182 men from Minnesota, North Dakota, South Dakota, Iowa, Illinois, Wisconsin, New York, New Jer-

GRIEG MANDSKOR, Fort Dodge, Iowa

Grieg Mandskor, Fort Dodge, Iowa, 1912. First row from left: Selmer Johanson, A. A. Fremming, O. T. Peterson, John Sortland, Ed. Ultang, Elmer Hovey, George Halverson, and Einar Fremming. Second row from left: Bjorn Olson, Arthur Fremming, Cyril Hovey, Carl O. Haugen, O. M. Oleson, M. M. Dahl, Helge H. Haugen, Harold Haugen, and Raymond Hovey. Third row from left: John Kulild, Chester Johnson, John Foss, A. J. Moe, Oliver Vevle, Jack Johnson, C. B. Gaard, and Karl Kallansrud. (The names were recorded in 1954, courtesy of the Webster County Historical Society.) *Program for the Sangerfest 1914, Norwegian-American Collection, National Library of Norway*

sey, Washington, Oregon, and California plus Winnipeg in Canada. The singers were told to acquire a tail coat or dark suit, white shirt, white tie, and the obligatory white cap.

The repertoire was chosen and rehearsals started. A tour committee of forty members was formed with subcommittees covering finance and transportation, in addition to an exhibit committee of which Olaf was a member. As a testimony to all that Norwegians in America had done in the area of singing, he had collected programs from the *Sangerfest*s, photographs, and lists of names of singing societies and directors. The gold, silver, and bronze *Sangerfest* participation medals would also be on display. In addition to the capital, they planned to give concerts in the cities of Bergen, Stavanger, Hamar, and Trondheim. In the meantime the singers had rehearsals and concerts around the United States.

In the summer of 1912 the *Sangerfest* was held in Fargo, North Dakota. *Photo detail: Norwegian Singers' Association of America, Norwegian-American Collection, National Library of Norway*

Repertoire of the "Norway Tour Chorus":

G. B. Lully	*Kongesangen*
	The Star-Spangled Banner
Edv. Grieg	*Fædrelandssalme*
N. Tjernagel	*Op mod de høie Fjeld i Nord*
Oscar Borg	*Gud signe Norigs Land*
Alfred Paulsen	*Naar Fjordene blaaner*
Tischendorff	*Jeg vil verge mit land*
F. A. Reissiger	*I Guds fri Natur*
Ole Olsen	*I Jotunheimen*
Halfdan Kjerulf	*Norges Fjelde*
Johannes Haarklou	*Varde*

Alfred Paulsen	*Sangen har Lysning*
Rudolph Møller	*Vikingsønner*
Kr. Wendelborg	*Norge, Norge*
Ole Olsen	*Fanevagt*
Edv. Grieg	*Den store hvide Flok*
R. Nordraak	*Ja, vi elsker*
F. A. Reissiger	*Nordhavet*
Iver Holter	*Eidsvold*
Johan Selmer	*Norge, Norge*

Soloists:
Ms. Inga Ørner, New York
Henry Andersen, Chicago
Alb. Siversten, Minneapolis
Anton Wetlesen, Brooklyn[2]

Prior to their big trip, Olaf dedicated much of his time to his work as treasurer of the association. He made lists ranking the choruses according to how well they met their duties and how often they participated in rehearsals and concerts. Olaf's own chorus, *Grieg Mandskor*, always topped the lists. He also made sure that each singer received his part of the profit from the concerts while also scolding those who failed to pay their subscription for the *Sanger-Hilsen*. He complained that he had to spend time on sending collection letters: "Each and every one has to do his duty! Our periodical is especially important now that we are approaching the centennial celebration!" He suggested that the traditional picnic during the festivals should be replaced by outdoor concerts. This would earn more money for the association and would in addition motivate people to get out of their homes on Sundays, Olaf thought.[3]

A debate about what language to use was developing in *Sanger-Hilsen* in those days. Younger members of the Norwegian Singers' Association of America wanted to have the Norwegian songs translated. The older members considered this to be blasphemy and thought in addition that it would make life too easy for young ones. Others thought it too much to require an American to learn Norwegian. They also wanted to share Nordic song literature with other Americans and pointed out that Norwegian was no longer spoken in America. It was decided that Norwegian songs were still to be sung in Norwegian.

While planning the journey to Norway, Olaf still paid close attention to what was happening in Fort Dodge. He was a supporter of several new businesses, and in 1912 he invested in what would later turn out to be the most successful project he ever engaged in. The project was based on a recently developed vaccine which had the potential to stop epidemic cholera among pigs, a disease that caused one of the largest economic losses in Iowa. The vaccine was the result of a government research project. The veterinarian Daniel E. Baughman patented the vaccine and started production through his Ames Vaccine Company. It was struggling financially, however. Olaf, who had taken an active role in the search for remedies that could cure or, even better, prevent epidemic diseases, had observed the progress of this research and was convinced that the Ames Vaccine Company would develop into a gold mine. Olaf talked Baughman into moving his laboratories to Fort Dodge. Together with other local wealthy men, he invested in the company. The name was changed to Fort Dodge Serum Company, and in the years to come it put on the market a wide spectrum of medicines and vaccines for farm animals and pets, even birds, both domesticated and wild. Olaf chose to keep his 296 shares and within just a few years the value had increased to about $20,000. That this company would become an international

The oldest house in Fort Dodge, a log cabin from 1850, was moved close to the children's playground in Oleson Park. *Private collection*

industrial giant, and what this would mean to Olaf's family, did not become evident until twenty years after his death.[4]

In 1912, Olaf and the Fort Dodge chapter of the Daughters of the American Revolution, of which Olaf's first wife, Lucy, had been a member, took the initiative to preserve what was believed to be the oldest house in Fort Dodge. It was built in 1850 to serve as headquarters for the officers at the fort. Later, a school was planned where the old fort had been located, and Olaf had the house moved to Oleson Park.

Olaf finally had to accept that the committee for the 1914 gift to Norway, which he served as vice chairman, had failed to reach its goal. The total was not enough to cover a stained glass window for the cathedral in Trondheim. Olaf and the rest of the committee brought a much smaller amount with them over the Atlantic. Olaf was, according to several sources, one of the main donors. The gift was given in the form of a foundation, and the Norwegian Parliament established an executive committee to manage it. The statutes stated that the original fund should never be touched. When the fund had doubled in size, every year on July 4, the foundation was to donate a part of its income "to help in situations of undeserved need and distress, especially in situations caused by disasters where neither the state, the local authorities nor the general community step up, and further to support useful public undertakings . . . a sure and always available help to ease sorrow and the hardship."[5]

Rather than joining in on this diffuse gift, many of the Norwegian regional societies in America chose to donate money directly to their native districts in Norway. The total donations from America for this occasion thus came close to 500,000 Norwegian kroner (about 25 million kroner today, or about $3.5 million). On top of this came money from Norwegian Americans in North Dakota intended for a sculpture of Abraham Lincoln to be erected in Kristiania.[6]

Olaf's substantial personal gift to his home region was spent on establishing Kvam Old People's Home. Olaf thought that old people without any relatives they could live with should be spared the humiliation of having to move from farm to farm. Olaf also sent a check for $250 to Julius Jæger, the president of the Norwegian Singers' Association in America, to be used to support the Norway tour. Vice president at the time was A. C. Floan, St. Paul, while T. F. Hamann, Minneapolis, was secretary and Olaf served as treasurer.[7]

The Singers' Tour to Norway

In the high-spirited atmosphere around the centennial of the Norwegian constitution, Norwegians were not paying much attention to the dark clouds building up over Europe, where a large-scale rearmament was taking place. The Norwegian capital was hosting the 1914 Jubilee Exhibition, the Norwegian Singers' Convention, and the Norwegian Marksmen's Convention, of which Olaf's brother Ola was president. About twenty thousand Norwegian Americans, most of them farmers, had arrived on the Norwegian America Line to participate in the celebration. Forty-four years after Olaf left for America, he again set foot on Norwegian soil, confident that "Norwegian male singing in America has been and still is one of the most distinguished elements in the service of preserving Norwegianness. Every city with a Norwegian population of some size, has established a singers' group, around which everyone with a sincere interest for Norway has gathered," as it was said in one of the festival pamphlets.[1]

"The Singers' Army Is Coming!" trumpeted the newspapers. The Norwegian Americans brought with them bands from St. Olaf College and Luther College with their leader, professor Carlo A. Sperati, who also led the *Luren* chorus in Decorah. The Norwegian American singers were received with exultation, banquets, and lots of music performances. A number of concerts were arranged. Twenty-eight hundred singers attended the Norwegian Singers' Convention—the largest festival ever arranged in Norway. With the king and queen leading the way, an audience of ten thousand showed up outside the Akershus Fortress to listen to a concert. The Norwegian American chorus—in Norway simply called the America Chorus—received positive reviews. One could see "these men from all classes—manual workers side by side with clerks and distinguished businessmen—blending their voices in such a way that inspired admiration for their choral singing, here in Norway."[2]

The volunteer rifle clubs gathered at Grefsen, just north of the center of Kristiania, where about two thousand members participated. They represented the Association of Volunteer Marksmen, which had a total of 57,900 members organized nationwide in 1,575 clubs. Olaf had the pleasure of seeing his brother proudly receive the Royal Order of Merit in gold for his contribution in building up the organization. Ola was proud despite the fact that he, as a radical, presumably did not think much of medals and royal finery. However, medals of various values were frequently used to honor persons both in the Association of Volunteer Marksmen in Norway and in the Norwegian Singers' Association of America.

Frogner Park, the large park in the center of Kristiania where the 1914 Jubilee Exposition was arranged, was all sunshine and festivities. A fifty-square-foot map was erected to show where every Norwegian ship across the world was located. Norwegian industry and craftsmanship were represented. So were young Norwegian athletes. Each day a competition was arranged: gymnastics, wrestling, tennis, riding, soccer, and swimming. Norwegian emigrants had their own pavilion, featuring an exhibit showing all that Norwegians had accomplished in America. The jubilee drew 1.5 million visitors.

The America Gift was handed over on July 4, American Independence Day. The streets in the capital were decorated with Norwegian and American flags. A procession marched down the main street, Karl Johansgate, to the Parliament, led by the Luther College Band. The Norwegian national anthem, *Ja, vi elsker*, and "The Star-Spangled Banner" were played and sung with gusto. Olaf and the rest of the committee for the 1914 gift followed. In front of the Parliament Prime Minister Gunnar Knudsen, president of the Parliament Jørgen Løvland, and all the members of Parliament had taken up their positions to receive the gift. The gifts from the various Norwegian American district organizations, however, received the greatest applause. They were given one by one, and politicians representing the respective district offered enthusiastic thanks.[3]

The procession continued to Frogner Park, where the sculpture of Abraham Lincoln was unveiled. Made by the sculptor Paul Fjelde, it was a gift in return for the Wergeland statue the Norwegian Americans had received from Norway two years earlier. The many

speeches that followed emphasized that Henrik Wergeland had agitated strongly against slavery and that many Norwegian pioneers
had fought under Abraham Lincoln and died in the struggle to preserve the union and abolish slavery. Thus this became an important
part of Norwegian history as well. Abraham Lincoln was addition-
ally hailed as an embodiment of the democratic ideal. The America
Chorus and Luther College Band were responsible for the artistic part
of the program. To enormous applause they ended the program with
Naar fjordene blaaner. Mixed with all this praise, however, there
were many Norwegians who looked down on the Americans, thinking they were just showing off.

From Kristiania the America Chorus went to the city of Hamar
and then further to Trondheim, where the chorus disbanded and Olaf
went home. As a parting gift from his brother Ola, Olaf received a set
of books, *Wergelands Samlede Skrifter* (a nine-volume collection of all
of Henrik Wergeland's writings).

Meanwhile, in America the men at Eidsvoll who had provided Norway with its constitution in 1814 were celebrated. All the regional societies and the Norwegian American choruses gathered in St. Paul,
Minnesota, on May 17, 1914, for a festival for those who had not traveled
to Norway. Invitations to participate were sent to "young and old, men
and women, children and the elderly. Blooming young girls and some-
what older bachelors. Merry young people and sober old maids. Widows
and orphans. The Synod and the Unitarians and the secret societies. The
educated and the uneducated, the lame and the blind. Sad and happy
citizens. Loudmouths, farmers and businessmen. Pastors and professors, craftsmen and laborers. Lawyers and other stubborn coots."[4]

It was said that the *Norrøna* people would sweep over the city like
a giant wave. And so they did. About fifty thousand found their way to
the city, and all the Norwegian American singers who did not make the
journey to Norway had their *Sangerfest* in Chicago later in the summer.

Adjusting to everyday life again after the centennial celebration,
Norwegians had to admit that war between the great powers of Europe could not be avoided. The shooting episode in Sarajevo on June 28
led to Austria-Hungary declaring war against Serbia, and on August
1 Germany declared war against Russia. Soon two powerful alliances
were formed: Great Britain, France, and Russia plus their allies against

Germany, Austria-Hungary, Turkey, and Bulgaria. The Great War was a fact. The Norwegian government, supported by the Parliament, decided to maintain neutrality in the conflict, and Norway and Sweden signed a declaration to that effect. However, many Norwegians sympathized with the British people, and Great Britain was a large supplier of oil and coal to Norway. The British forced Norway to stop exporting fish to Germany and regarded Norway as "the Neutral Ally." The relationship with Germany grew tense, and Norway saw half of its merchant fleet sunk by the German navy during the war.

Though the war raged through Europe, the Americans had not yet chosen to take part. In 1916 Olaf and the rest of the *Grieg Mandskor* celebrated their twenty-fifth anniversary. The conflict with the Swedes now resolved, they started singing with the Swedish chorus, *Adelphus*, again. They gathered for rehearsals in Oleson Drug Store. That summer the *Sangerfest*, arranged by the Norwegian Singers' Association of America, took place in Grand Forks, North Dakota, and the "Norway Chorus," as it was called in America, had a reunion. Olaf and forty-four of the original chorus sang *Naar Fjordene Blaaner* and *Jeg vil værge mit Land*, among other songs.[5]

Cover of the program for the 1914 *Sangerfest*, arranged in Chicago by the Norwegian Singers' Association of America. *Norwegian-American Collection, National Library of Norway*

Cover of the program for the 1916 *Sangerfest*, arranged in Grand Forks, North Dakota, by the Norwegian Singers' Association of America. *Norwegian-American Collection, National Library of Norway*

It is likely in connection with this anniversary that Olaf donated a pipe organ to both St. Olaf Norwegian Lutheran Church and Julie's church, the First Congregational Church in Fort Dodge.[6]

Another gift from the Norwegian Americans came to Norway that year, thanks to the doctor and scientist Eduard Boeckmann, who was born in Østre Toten, Norway, and who lived in St. Paul, Minnesota. There he helped establish Luther Hospital for Norwegian immigrants. In appreciation for having had the opportunity to study at the university in Kristiania, Boeckmann took the initiative to collect money for a gift to the university in connection with its centennial. The money was used to decorate the university's main hall with murals painted by Norway's most famous artist, Edvard Munch.[7]

Olaf wanted to stay updated on what was happening on the cultural scene in Norway, so his brother Ola sent him the latest books. In 1917 it was *Henrik Wergeland* by the Danish author Herluf Møller. Ola found this appropriate as Olaf had been given a collection of Wergeland's work during the celebration in 1914. In addition, Ola thought Møller's book was the best he had read about Wergeland, his favorite author.

Olaf also received the book *Norske Haver i gammel og ny tid* (Norwegian Gardens in Ancient and Modern Times), written by the art historian Carl W. Schnitler. This was the first book to present a description of Norwegian gardens. Over the years both Olaf and Ola managed to build considerable private libraries with books from all over the world, mostly dealing with scientific subjects. They often succeeded in obtaining first editions signed by the author.[8]

Olaf Becomes a Composer

Germany and Austria-Hungary were fighting against the other European powers of Great Britain, France, and Russia, in a combat that was locked in the trenches. Millions died. A poem by the Canadian military doctor John McCrae expressed what many people felt. It was written just after McCrae had seen a friend die in a battle in Flanders, Belgium, in the spring of 1915. This happened in the large fields where red poppies covered the area between the trenches, the machine gun nests, and the rolls of barbed wire. That morning a gentle east wind passed over the field and carried the red petals with it, a young soldier who had been with McCrae remembered.[1]

The poem puts words to the conflicting emotions felt by the soldiers. Titled "In Flanders Fields," it is the single best-known poem text from the war. Olaf was so moved that he sat down and composed a melody to it, the first example of Olaf being a composer. The song he created was sung at every Norwegian American *Sangerfest* for decades to come.

On April 6, 1917, the United States declared war against Germany and 4.8 million Americans were called up to military service. Olaf, now sixty-eight years old, was not among them. In America the conflict was called the Great War, as one could not imagine that a war on such a scale could ever occur again. Many even thought that it would be the end of all war.

During the war, American authorities became more and more convinced that all citizens should speak English and should not be hyphenated Americans. Many Norwegian congregations in America began to hold their services in English, but not St. Olaf church in Fort Dodge, for the time being. Members of the Norwegian Singers' Association of America that had not been called up for service contributed in their own way by singing patriotic songs translated to English. At the same time, new and heated discussions took place in *Sanger-Hilsen*: "Shall we throw our song-literature over board? As our language gradually disappears from the church, associations and choruses.... Then the songs will die with us unless immigration continues and that we do not believe."[2]

Olaf's setting of the poem "In Flanders Fields" by John McCrae. *Sanger-Hilsen 11 (1918), Norwegian-American Collection, National Library of Norway*

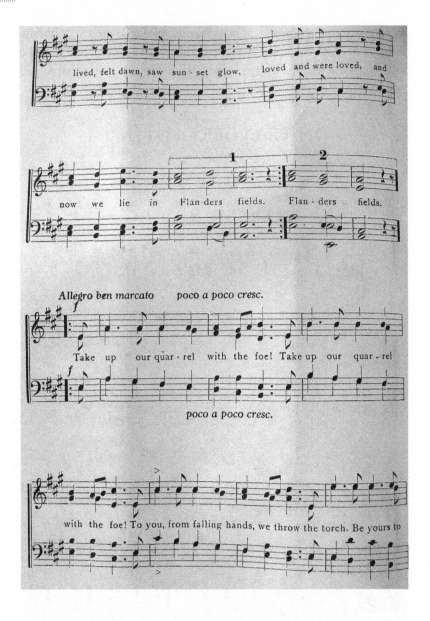

The singers accepted that it would be too much to require Americans to learn Norwegian, but to sing the Norwegian text would please both the singers and their fellow citizens, they proclaimed. A singing teacher in Sioux City argued against this: "Is it not high time that these singing societies took a wider view, erased the lines between the national groups,

became Americans, start singing all good music and do it because it is good and not just because it comes from this or that country?"[3]

The answer came from one of the Singers' Association's founders, R. F. A. Tomte in Portland, who "would protest in the strongest way against selling out our first right. Such an exchange is first of all unnatural and in addition we have a heritage that can not be thrown away just like that. . . . We are and will remain good American citizens even if we keep our songs . . . or in the end we would have to go alone to the basement or the attic with the songbook in order to have a singing lesson all by ourselves."[4]

The Americans did not want to enter a peace agreement with Germany, as shown in an August 1917 newspaper article Olaf sent to his brother Ola. The title was: "The Letter that Changed the World." It was President Woodrow Wilson's answer to a peace plan suggested by the Vatican and could be summarized in six words. "No Peace with a 'Ruthless Autocracy.'" The American press applauded: "The World Calls It 'A New Emancipation Proclamation' for 'All Mankind.'"

During the spring of 1918, the United States took an active role in the war and patriotism reached its peak. In Fort Dodge, the National Guard was called up for service and in July paraded down Central Avenue followed by volunteer organizations like the Red Cross. "United in preparedness" the banners heralded, and thousands of citizens waved at the soldiers and volunteers on their way to the front. It was thought of as the most important event in the city's history. A total of 2 million American soldiers were sent to France. These numbers changed the power balance in Europe, and Germany capitulated. On November 11, 1918, the peace treaty ending the Great War was signed. In America this day was called both Armistice Day and Victory Day, later also Veterans Day, and the poppies on the battlefields in Flander became a sign of remembrance of all victims of war. For many years Americans would attach red paper flowers to their clothes on November 11.

In 1919 Olaf was informed by the Norwegian Parliament that the value of the 1914 gift had passed its goal. The foundation was now in position to start its charitable activity by handing out a percentage of its yearly income, as intended. Among those supported were:

The District Nurse Centre in Kristiania, which was established by the Lutheran Association for District Nurses with the objective of helping sick, old, and poor people in rural areas.

The Blue Cross Rehabilitation Center at Eina Lake, Toten, about seventy miles north of Kristiania, which was run by an evangelical teetotaling organization.

Patriotiske Sange

for Mandskor

Engelsk Tekst af Siver Serumgard

1. **"The Volunteer"**
("Jeg vil værge mit Land")

2. **"Old Glory"**
("Fold dig ud vort gamle Merke")

3. **"Yanks' March"**
("Bjørneborgarnes Marsch")

4. **Columbia, Hear Us"**
("Hör oss, Svea")

❧

Disse amerikanske Sange til ovennævnte kjendte Hjemlandsmelodier, bør fra nu af findes paa vore Sangforeningers Repertoire. Foreligger samlede i et Hefte til en Pris af 15c. Løse Eksemplarer af hver Sang kan desuden faaes for 5c.

"SANGER-HILSEN"
45 Fourth St. So., Minneapolis, Minn.

Patriotic songs were translated from Norwegian to English and printed in *Sanger-Hilsen* during World War I. *Sanger-Hilsen 10 (1918), Norwegian-American Collection, National Library of Norway*

Richard Lie's Children's Home in Vadsø, Finnmark, North
Norway was an orphanage. Tuberculosis ravaged this part
of the country, and about two hundred children had lost
their parents.

Other funds were given to individuals to "help relieve need
and distress"—four of the recipients had spent several years
in America.[5]

These examples describe just a small portion of what was given
from America to Norway. During the years 1900–1914, it is estimated
that donations channeled through banks and post offices plus direct
cash payments to private persons corresponded to about a quarter of
the Norwegian national budget per year.[6]

Private individuals could send so-called Norwegian America Line
checks directly to friends and family in Norway. The checks could be
redeemed in a bank or at any of NAL's main agencies. Much money was
sent this way throughout the 1920s and '30s.[7]

Many Norwegian Americans had managed to set money aside, and
in 1919 two men came home to Norway with enough dollars to buy the
Sundnes estate at Inderøya. They were the Forberg brothers, originally
from Ytterøya, further out the Trondheimsfjord. They had to return
without success, however, as the local authorities had exercised pre-
emption rights. It was decided that the twenty-one cotters attached to
the estate should be allowed to buy the land they lived on. One can
expect that Olaf would have found this to be justified. The distillery
had been sold earlier to a consortium of farmers. The remaining 160
acres of the estate was sold to a foundation running children's homes
in 1921.[8]

The Norwegian American Composers Competition

The world war had made Olaf an American patriot, but he still felt a strong attachment to Norway. This is clearly demonstrated by the songs he wrote melodies for or arranged for choral singing. *Sanger-Hilsen* announced that, "With 'My Country 'Tis of Thee,' arranged for male chorus by Mr. Olesen, we open our periodical's musical supplement for 1919."[1]

"My Country 'Tis of Thee" was one of several American anthems for almost a century. It was written by the Baptist minister Samuel Francis Smith in 1832 and was sung to the same melody as the British national anthem, "God Save the King." In 1931 Americans chose "The Star-Spangled Banner" as their national anthem.

At the same time Olaf set music to *Norsk-Amerikansk 17.mai Sang* (Norwegian-American Song for Norway's Constitution Day) and *O' Sagaland* (O Land of the Saga). Both texts were written by Johan Selnes from Trøndelag, Norway, who had stayed some years in America. Olaf also composed "Come to Iowa" or "Iowa Song," which was the only song he arranged for a mixed chorus. Olaf had copyrighted the scores he wrote and could earn royalties on all sales, as opposed to Edvard Grieg, who had no copyright arrangement in America.

Olaf's view was that American songs should be sung in English and Norwegian songs in Norwegian. It was not just the Norwegian words he wanted to preserve. He also wanted to bring Norwegian American composers into focus. *Minneapolis Tidende* reported in 1920 that, "For the first time in Norwegian-American history a private person has on his own initiative done something to encourage Norwegian-American composers. It is almost a matter of course that this man should be Hon. O. M. Oleson from Fort Dodge, Iowa."[2]

Olaf had written to the president of the Norwegian Singers' Association of America, Birger Sande in Duluth, Minnesota, and asked him to form a committee to select three or four Norwegian American composers. They should have "written music of value for choruses, appreciated both by the singers as well as the Norwegian-American public. . . . As they will rarely achieve any financial reward for their work," the editor of *Sanger-Hilsen* wrote. Carl G. O. Hansen, Jens H. Flaaten, and J. J. Hopperstad were elected to the committee, and they had many Norwegian American composers to choose among. They found the arrangement of *Paal på Haugen* by Kristian Nilsson especially appealing.[3]

One of the committee members, Carl Gustav Otto Hansen from Trondheim, played a central role in Minneapolis. Besides being a prominent newspaper man, he was a musician and author, director of the Norwegian Glee Club in Minneapolis, and president of *Det norske Selskab*. Together with Flaaten and Hopperstad, Hansen decided on the following winners: F. Melius Christiansen, John Dahle, Rudolf H. Møller, and Alfred Paulson. Upon hearing the news, Olaf sent each of the four a check for $100.

Christiansen was a close friend of Olaf. He originated from Eidsvoll and had settled in Northfield, Minnesota, where he led the St. Olaf College Choir. John Dahle from Valdres was a professor at Luther Seminary in St. Paul. Rudolf H. Møller from Fredrikstad lived in Seattle, and Alfred Paulsen from Kristiania had his home in Chicago.

The Norwegian American composers received encouragement from another source as well. At a representatives' meeting for the Norwegian America Line in April 1919, it was decided to set aside a percentage of the profit for charitable purposes and cultural activities. The Norwegian Americans received 25,000 Norwegian kroner in all. Some of this went to Brooklyn, an area with many people in distress. The rest was spent in the Midwest. NAL's representative in Chicago, bank manager Hauman G. Haugan, who was previously a leader of *Normanna Sangkor* in La Crosse, Wisconsin, was asked to distribute the money. In a letter to Olaf, still treasurer of the Norwegian Singers' Association of America, he said he would send a check for $250 as a "modest appreciation of the association's progressive work in the service of song and music." The money was to be divided with $100 going to *Sanger-Hilsen*, $100 to the best song arranged for male chorus by a Norwegian American, and $50 to the second best. The leaders of the association were asked to set up rules for an appropriate competition and elect competent judges to evaluate the candidates.[4]

Olaf arranged "My Country 'Tis of Thee" for male chorus. *Sanger-Hilsen 1 (1919), Norwegian-American Collection, National Library of Norway*

Believed to be Olaf's original setting of "*Norsk-amerikansk 17de Maisang,*" text by Johan Selnes. "The song is supposed to be played as a brisk march." The music was found in the archives of Torvald Gjerstad, a local composer in Nord-Trøndelag, Norway. *Kvam Historielag*

Olaf responded with a letter to the NAL management and thanked them for this "unexpected but very welcome gift." He assured Hauman G. Haugan that the rules would soon be ready and that able and unbiased men would be found to act as judges. The composers had

"Come to Iowa," composed by Olaf. Author unknown. *Sanger-Hilsen (1935), Norwegian-American Collection, National Library of Norway*

only to start their work. As soon as the winners were chosen, the music would be printed so that rehearsals could start well in advance of the *Sangerfest*, which was to be arranged in Duluth that year.

The three judges were professor Carlo A. Sperati, editor Carl G. O.

Hansen, and director Olaf Halten. They received seven different anonymous compositions. The winner, *Valkyrien* with music by J. Rode Jacobsen, Chicago, and text by Helga Bekker, received $100. In second place was *Thord Foleson*, music composed by Eivind Olaf Forseth to a text by Per Sivle. Forseth was born in Trondheim, had a fine baritone, and had taught in Stockholm, Copenhagen, and Berlin. He lived in La Crosse and was a coach for the *Normanna Sangkor.*

No *Sangerfest* had been arranged during the war as many of the members had been called up for service. But in the summer of 1920 the tradition was taken up again with a festival in Duluth. This time Olaf had, as treasurer of the organization, set up an office at the hotel where he and the rest of the management stayed and here he made a roster of the members. Some of the singers tended not to show up at the rehearsals prior to the concerts. Olaf decided that each singer had to pay a dollar for each concert and those not able to document their presence at the dress rehearsal or the concert were not refunded. Olaf concluded that after this rule was introduced everybody participated. The two prize-winning songs had their premiere in Duluth. It was, however "In Flanders Fields" that received the heaviest applause and for which an encore was called. *Sanger-Hilsen* had printed a rather free translation of the poem, so that "our Singers now—with a little extra effort—may have the opportunity to sing "In Flanders Fields" in Norwegian!"[5]

According to Olaf, each and every one of the singers agreed that the *Sangerfest* in Duluth was the best arrangement ever. And he was one of a group of singers who on that occasion were awarded a gold badge by the Norwegian Singers' Association of America. The others were Oscar H. Haugan, Bernhard Svendsen, C. Parelius, F. C. Rønning, S. Huseby, and Girard A. Ellingesen, all of them living in Chicago, plus T. F. Hamann in Minneapolis.

After the turn of the century, many Norwegian immigrants moved from the prairie to larger cities like New York, Minneapolis, Seattle, and Chicago. Most of the Norwegian American singers lived in Chicago. In the 1920s the city had about fifty thousand Norwegian immigrants. Chicago could be reckoned as the third-largest "Norwegian" city, after Kristiania (renamed Oslo in 1925) and Bergen.

The Norwegian Americans in Chicago had formed more than sixty associations and clubs, among them four choruses with a total of two

Sange for Mandskor af norsk-amerikanske Komponister

Christiansen, F. Melius: **Ud, ud!** 12c
—Som Sol gaar ned i Havet 12c
—Aa hip og hoppe, Humoreske 12c
—Aa eg veit meg eit Land........... 12c
Dahle, John: **Hilsen til Vaaren** --------10c
— Fremad 5c
Erickson, Peter: **Vaarlængsel** (Har-
moniseret af J. Rode Jacobsen)..... 12c
Forseth, E. O.: **Aasgaardsreien**...... 10c
—Sneflokke ("Langt fra Hjemmet")... 5c
—Lille Karen ("Husker du i Høst")... 5c
—Thord Fo'eson (med Bas Solo)...... 10c
—I Hytte og Hal (Julesang).......... 5c
· Gregor, Johan: **Til Telemarken.** For
Mandskor. Arr. af Charles Lund.
Tekst af Per Sivle ---------------- 10c
Halten, Olaf: **Glade Jul** (med Brum-
mekor) 6c
Jacobsen, J. Rode: **Valkyrien** (præmiebe-
lønnet Komposition)............... 10c
Lund, Signe: **Du Lann** ---------------- 8c
Møller, Rudolph: **Kjærringa me Staven_** 12c
—Noraskald 12c
—Aa kjøre vatten, aa k'øre ve' 10c
—Trækfuglskare 12c
— Marsch — **Fram Sanger, nu fram** ---15c
— Paa Sangertog (med Barytonsolo) -- 20c
— V'kingsønner --------------------15c
— Kan Du glemme gamle Norge ------ 6c
—Norges udvandrede Sønner 12c

FOR BLANDET KOR.

Afholdsfolkets Flagsang _____ .15
Norges udvandrede Sønner _____ .15

FOR SOLO STEMME MED PIANO.

—Norges udvandrede Sønner 20c
— Jeg længter mod Sol og Sommer, Sang
og Piano ---------------------- 25c
Nilsson, Kr.: **Gjæsternes Indtog af Wag-
ner-Operaen** Tannhäuser, norsk Tekst 15c
— Paal paa Haugen ---------------- 15c
—Iægerkor ("Lyngen bag os staar i
Røg") 10c
—Spring Song ("Come let us sing") .. 12c
—Dixie Land (Plantation Melody).... 10c
—Old Black Joe (With Humming
Chorus) 10c
— Havet der vester.................. 10c
— I Maaneskin...................... 10c
— Solnedgang 10c
Oleson, O. M: **In Flanders Fields**........ 10c
— and My Country, 'Tis of Thee.
— Norsk-Amerikansk 17de Maisang..... 5c
—O Sagaland 5c
—Come to Iowa..................... 5c
Oulie, Erik: **Ode til Sangens Aand**
(O. M. O'eson tilegnet)........... 5c
Oven, J. W.: **Jeg spiler min Vinge**
Arr. af Rudolph Møller............. 5c

Paulsen, Alfr.: **Naar Fjordene Blaaner** _ 15c
— Kjærringa me Staven -------------- 12c
— Snorre ------------------------ 10c
— Sangen har Lysning (Bar. Solo og
Kor) -------------------------- 16c
— Giv Agt ------------------------ 10c
— Norrønamaal -------------------- 16c
— Norge, mit Norge --------------- 12c
— Ritch, ratsch, filebom, bom, bom, hu-
moristisk Sangermarsch ----------- 12c
Swenson: **Vår Gud ar oss en väldig
borg** _____ 5c
Tiernagel, N.: **Op mod de høie Fjeld i
Nord** ---------------------------- 10c
Wick, Fred.: **The Dandelion** (Comic) 12c
—Beautiful Saviour 8c
—O, Columbia, We Hail Thee (Patri-
otic) 15c
—Old Jonah Had a Whale of a Time
in a Whale........................ 15c
—Du gamla, du fria (svensk og engelsk
tekst) 15c
—Fem norske **Folkemelodier** for
Mandskor i et hefte: 1. Astri, mi
Astri. 2. Aa kjøre Vat'n, aa kjøre Ve.
3. Ola Glomstulen. 4. En liten Gut
ifra Tistedalen. 5. Bor jeg paa det
høie Fjeld 30c
—Hymn of Praise. Cantata for Thanks-
giving-Festivals and General Use.
Soprano, Tenor, Barytone Solos and
Mixed Voices. Text selected from
the Holy Scripture 60c
—Twenty-four Well-Known Hymns,
for Men's Voices 30c

"Paal paa Haugen", arr. af Kr. Nilsson er overmaade tiltrekkende

Norwegian American composers in 1914. *Sanger-Hilsen (1924), Norwegian-American Collection, National Library of Norway* hundred members. The 1926 edition of the yearbook for *Det Nationale Trønderlaget i Amerika* claimed that "In a large city like Chicago it happens quite often that a fellow countryman needs a hand, and it is then good for an Oslo-man to have an Oslo-club to fall back on, or for a *Trønder* to have a Trønderlag to turn to. If they can prevent it, the people from Trøndelag in Chicago will not let a situation develop to a point where some of their own, being in distress, have to seek assistance. They will try their best to forestall the problem and thereby demonstrate their kindheartedness."

About 30 percent of the inhabitants of Fort Dodge were at that time first-generation immigrants. Germans, English, Irish, and Swedes still dominated. In addition to the small group of Norwegians there were Czechs, Slovaks, Italians, Mexicans, Greeks, Syrians, and Jews. Each nationality had found their preferred part of the city, for example the Swedes with their Swede Town on the west side of the Des Moines River. The few Norwegians, however, did not have their own section of town.

The Ku Klux Klan, which in the 1920s had 4 million members in the United States and a strong foothold in the Midwest, generated a tense atmosphere in many places where there were a large number of nationalities. The Klan's objective was to prevent an increase in the number of Catholics, Jews, African Americans, and other immigrants to the United States. In Fort Dodge, as in many other places, most of the Lutherans avoided cooperating with Catholics. The Lutherans also declined to be treated at the hospital the Catholics had built with assistance from Olaf and the rest of the business community. This stance led to Norwegian, Danish, and Swedish congregations embarking on a money-raising campaign for a new hospital. The goal was a capacity of one hundred beds and the stipulated cost was $500,000. Initially they did not succeed, but after a few years Olaf stepped in to help.[6]

Olaf and Family Tour Europe

In the summer of 1921, Olaf, Julie, and two of her nieces traveled through Europe. Their visit started in Edinburgh, where Olaf, together with a thousand Rotary members and their families, participated in Rotary's first international congress. Olaf was a member of the Fort Dodge Rotary, where managers of various enterprises met in a spirit of fellowship to support and learn from each other, to help young people acquire an education, and to start local projects of social value for the community. In Edinburgh Olaf also found time to indulge in his favorite sport, golf.

Olaf and his companions reached Belgium in mid-July. They drove through Flanders Fields six years after John McCrae had written his poem in remembrance of the friend who had died there. The war had left the area almost without trees or bushes, but the poppies had survived and the fields were all covered in red. In a letter sent back to *Sanger-Hilsen* Olaf wrote, "The crimson colored poppy-fields were a wonderful sight. And so were the grain fields. But the farmers do not think as highly of the poppies as the tourist do as they are invading the fields intended for the grain."[1]

A few days later they arrived in Copenhagen, Denmark, where they listened to a concert in *Kongens Have* (the King's Garden), visited art galleries, and spent an afternoon in Tivoli:

> Yesterday evening we went to the famous Tivoli. One has to seek high and low to find a place that compares with this one. We had our dinner at Restaurant Nimb, and the rest of the evening we spent at this Nordic wonder of entertainment. There were thousands of people but everyone seemed to behave as one expects of real ladies and gentlemen. There was no lack of variety in the entertainment, so even the most fastidious person could find something interesting that would lift the spirits.

All the grand cities we have been to, like Edinborough, London, Liverpool, Paris, Brussels, Cologne and Berlin have their special attractions, and that goes for Copenhagen as well. . . . The citizens know how to enjoy themselves. It seemed like everyone was off on a picnic. The bicycle is a highly valued means of transportation here. I have never seen such an army of bicycles—with riders of both genders. . . . People here seem to be light-hearted; they treasure good music. This I could personally observe at the concert yesterday. The crowd was enormous, and they were all *standing* through the concert, from beginning to end, waiting for more.[2]

Driving through Copenhagen, Olaf visited many garden clubs, where "people could quench their thirst with something which for the time being is not allowed in the US. All around us people seemed to have a really nice time. . . . We have become used to high prices during most of our journey. As we knew about this beforehands we did not bat an eye. . . . They were all in need of American dollars so we should be happy to provide a bit of help. . . . Tomorrow we will be sailing with *Maud* to Kristiania."[3]

In Kristiania Olaf was met by Ola's son, Olaf Wergeland Five, who was given a lesson in the mission of the Rotary movement. And, on Olaf's initiative, his nephew Olaf and some friends established the first Nordic Rotary club, the Kristiania Rotary Club.

"In the area of music there is not much to report about," Olaf wrote. He was very disappointed in not having met any members of the student chorus in Kristiania. "They must have been on vacation, all of them," he sighed.

We made a three-week trip to Vestlandet (the south-western part of Norway) from the city of Skien and northwards. We travelled by steamship over the lakes and fjords and by car over the mountains. When the roads were too steep for the car, we had to walk, of course.

At Olden I had my first meeting with a student singer, Dr. E. Solem from Aalesund, who was staying in this beautiful place for a few days with his wife and three children. He invited us (Mr. and Mrs. Oleson and our two nieces from Chicago) to dinner at his home, when we came to Aalesund some days later. I had planned to visit a dear old friend in Aalesund, Mr. Lars Ranes, a treasured member of *Grieg Mandskor* in Fort Dodge some 20 years ago. He was accountant at The Oleson Drug Co. for two years. Unfortunately, he was not at home. He was having a three-week vacation. . . .

In Olden I also met Mr. P. Rosenkrantz Johnsen, editor, author and poet (among other things of the text to the popular song *Ulabrand* which has been on the concert program of the Norwegian Singers' Association many times). He had visited America once, and was overwhelmed by the pleasure and joy this visit had given him. . . .

When we arrived in Aalesund, we were received by Dr. Solem who took us on a sightseeing tour through the city in his nice car. It is a magnificent city, quite modern, as it was totally ruined by a terrible fire just a few years ago. Afterwards we were treated to a marvelous dinner, appreciated by everyone. Dr. Solem and his nephew sang several songs for us, which proved that the Doctor had not lost his singing voice. He was also a clever accompanist on the piano, and everything was very festive.[4]

The journey then continued over the Dovre mountains to the city of Steinkjer, where Olaf met his two brothers Ola and Eilert, his sister Karoline, and many other relatives. "Here joyful gatherings filled every day, until we had to leave, which came all too soon," Olaf recalled later.

"The rich uncle in America" had become even richer since the last time he visited Norway, and Olaf handed out gifts generously during a family dinner he hosted in Steinkjer. There were many, however, who thought of the gifts as just an advance on what was to be inherited at a later stage. After Olaf's departure, his relatives started wondering about inheritance taxes. How much would they be? An increasing number of relatives and friends came forward with requests for support for projects of all sizes. Olaf, who to this point had been generous, got tired of all the pestering. His brother Ola, who managed Olaf's assets in Norway, had to start rejecting requests for financial aid. The tap was not totally turned off, however. The two-volume edition of local history, *Stod i fortid og nutid,* written by Ola's close friend O. Norgaard, received financial support from Olaf.[5]

During his stay in Nord-Trøndelag, Olaf most likely visited the Sundnes estate at Inderøya, where he had been a gardener as a young man. The garden had fallen to rack and ruin and the interior of the main house was totally rearranged as it recently had been taken into use as a children's home. The old Sakshaug church was undergoing restoration under the direction of the Association for Historical Monuments.

Later that year another emigrant from Nord-Trøndelag returned to Inderøya. The twenty-year-old farmer Nils J. Aune had left Inderøya in 1910 and settled in North Dakota. On his return he stayed for six months before going back to America to continue farming the area he had bought in 1919. He could not have foreseen that twenty-nine years later he would come back and buy the Sundnes estate.[6]

In August 1921, Olaf and Julie visited Kvam, his homeplace in Nord-Trøndelag, where this family picture was taken. First row, from left: Ola Five, Olaf Martin Olesen, Eilert Five, Karoline (Five) Langhammer, Gine Schei, Signe Five. Second row, from left: Charlotte Five (Ola's wife), Julie Haskell (Olaf's wife), Ingeborg Henrikka Five (Eilert's wife), Helga Schive, Ragna Marksten. Third Row, from left: Aksel Schive, Kristoffer Elden (Charlotte and Ingeborg Henrikka's brother), Ole Langhammer, Bertinus Schei, Magnus Langhammer, Nils Langhammer. *Private collection*

Two brothers: the Marksman General Ola Five (left) and the Singers' president Olaf Martin Oleson, 1921. *Private collection*

Not long after Olaf's stay in Nord-Trøndelag King Haakon VII of Norway visited the Sundnes estate to attend the opening of the new children's home. The next year the estate was designated as a historical monument, thus ensuring that it would be preserved. This designation included not only the buildings but also the garden, which was quite unusual. Could it be that Olaf, through his brother Ola, had put some pressure on the decision to include the garden? Ola Five was active in preserving memories of the past and had just recently founded *Nord-Trøndelag Historielag* (the Nord-Trøndelag Historical Association). He corresponded with Harry Fett, head of the National Directorate for Cultural Heritage.

In the middle of the summer of 1921, Olaf left his childhood home of Kvam to go to Kristiania. There he finally met two of his old friends from the 1905 Norwegian singers' tour of America. Olaf had very

The main building of the Sundnes estate, Inderøya, Nord-Trøndelag, 2011.
Private collection

pleasant meetings with both the lawyer Trygve Wegge and Dr. Einar
Onsum. In the capital he also met several other people:

> At the offices of The Norse Federation I met Dr. Gade, a most
> amiable person. He told me he was planning a trip to America
> in the coming autumn. I also met Mr. Heitmann from Winni-
> peg, Canada, a member of the Norwegian Chorus of 1914, now
> living in Kristiania. At the offices I also saw the composer
> Mr. Kristian Wendelborg, who had not lost his warmth and
> good humor, and I had an especially good time with him. By
> chance I met Mr. Otto P. Hoff, who had previously lived in
> Grand Forks and was a member of the chorus *Bjarne*. He now
> lives in Kristiania where he holds a prominent position as man-
> ager of the American Division of the Norwegian Commercial
> Bank. I learned from the Kristiania newspapers that a previous

student singer, Director W. F. K. Christie, has formed a National Association for Singers, and that 60–70 representatives from various singer associations across the country are going to meet in the near future. An excellent undertaking.[7]

Wilhelm Christie was among those who had participated in the political singers' tour in 1905, then as a law student.

Julie had brought art supplies with her on the trip and made a painting of the Five farm plus several landscape paintings. According to Ola Five, on her return to Fort Dodge she spoke "to everyone and at all places about the absolutely wonderful journey and the overwhelming Norwegian nature." At an exhibit at the Chicago Norwegian Art Club some years later, her "Norwegian Fjord Exhibition" attracted much attention.[8]

Julie's paintings from Nord-Trøndelag may very well have contributed to the feeling of fellowship and self respect among Norwegian Americans in the same way as the National Trønderlag of America did. In the preface to the 1921 Yearbook of the National Trønderlag of America, the chairman, Professor Dorrum, wrote that "Trønderlaget's arrangements and Trøndelaget's yearbooks shall conjure up memories, but not memories to create wishful thinking. They shall inspire to power and useful activities in gratitude for the great heritage we have from our fathers, and in determination to set our stamp on all that is new, here where everything sprouts and grows."[9]

On Norway's Constitution Day in 1922, several thousand people were assembled at the Ole Bull monument in Loring Park, Minneapolis, listening to the Norwegian American Iowa chorus sing *Landkjenning*. At the *Sangerfest* arranged in Sioux City by the Norwegian Singers' Association of America that year, twenty-five Norwegian singers' associations were gathered and Olaf praised the female soloist, the soprano Mrs. Anette Yde Lake, saying she had an enchanting way of singing and that she became everyone's darling. The singers from the Norwegian Glee Club in Minneapolis put on the comedy *Tjarlie Trallerud*, which was a huge success. The composer was Rudolf H. Møller, who had recently received an award from the Norwegian America Line. In addition to familiar songs of Bjørnson, they sang "In Flanders Fields," and both Olaf and one of the other veteran singers, Erik Oulie, who

Cover of the program for the 1922 *Sangerfest*, arranged in Sioux City by the Norwegian Singers' Association of America. *Norwegian-American Collection, National Library of Norway*

had been the leader of the Norwegian Singers in Minneapolis, were acclaimed for their long service. Oulie honored Olaf with the song *Ode til Sangens Aand*.[10]

Gold medals were presented to those who had participated in fifteen festivals, silver for ten, and bronze for five. Olaf received a gold medal. It had been thirty years since his first *Sangerfest*.

At the end of the festival, Olaf and Julie went to Florida and stayed at the luxurious Hotel Urmey in Miami for some months. The exterior of the hotel resembled the Wahkonsa Hotel, while the interior displayed "elegance combined with refinement and comfort." Ola Five wrote to his friends that Olaf enjoyed himself there. Later Olaf and Julie crossed America to spend the winter on the West Coast.[11]

"Ode til Sangens Aand" was dedicated to Olaf in 1922. Text and music by Erik Oulie. *Sanger-Hilsen 1 (1922), Norwegian-American Collection, National Library of Norway*

Norwegian American singers kept memories of the Vikings alive. *Sanger-Hilsen 4 (1922), Norwegian-American Collection, National Library of Norway*

With Rotary to Hawaii

From his winter stay in Los Angeles in 1922–23, Olaf traveled to Hawaii. "It is winter and when people in the Fort Dodge area are freezing stiff in 33 below, our treasurer of the Norwegian-American Singers' Association of America, Olesen, is in Hawaii," reported *Sanger-Hilsen* on January 18, 1923. Olaf represented the Fort Dodge Rotary at a meeting there. In his cabin onboard the Admiral Line's *H. F. Alexander*, while on his way back to San Francisco, Olaf wrote an article for *Sanger-Hilsen*, noting that "the native Hawaiians are very musical":

> When we left Honolulu Sunday afternoon the 14th, a hurricane followed us for 36 hours. Most of the passengers stayed in their cabins, but now they are coming up on deck again. Our arrival at San Francisco is likely to be delayed due to the strong headwind we had the first days.
>
> Seasickness has been raging onboard, but it kindly avoided me, for which I am very grateful. My appetite is as it should be.
>
> Our stay on the Hawaiian islands has been very interesting and pleasant. The Rotarians have done their utmost to make us feel comfortable. The native Hawaiians are especially musical and they are very talented at singing and playing their various instruments. Their music has a touch of wistfulness. It seems as if the songs express their inner feelings to perfection. Their language—based on 12 letters, mostly vowels—is melodious and well suited for singing. They have exceptionally nice voices and they often sing when they play dance music.
>
> The islands are of great interest in many ways. On the island of Hawaii the fire-spewing mountains are their greatest natural phenomenon. They were visible both day and night and made a grand impression. And all around us we could see high mountains and wild waterfalls. Sugar cane and pineapples seem to be

the dominant farming products. Their quality is hard to match. There are a large number of sugar factories and pineapple canneries which are of great importance. The landscape, with its rich tropical flora and flowers in all the colors of the rainbow, is beautiful. The climate is extremely comfortable. But, for whatever reason, when one arrives at these islands one gets the feeling of being far from civilization, so it will be nice to set our feet on "terra firma" again in California.[1]

Olaf must have felt particularly far away from Norway and his old home in Kvam during his stay in Hawaii. Soon after his departure from the island, he composed a melody to the poem *O Sagaland*, written by Johan Selnes from Trøndelag. The *Washington Post* wrote that "The text praises our old fatherland and the melody brings the words to us in a folk ballad style, heartfelt and sympathetic." *Sanger-Hilsen* once again argued for taking care of the Norwegian language: "Therefore, all you young men and women, do not think you are disparaging your American citizenship by speaking and writing the language of your fathers. On the contrary, your view of life becomes wider and richer, and at the same time you pay tribute to your father and mother. . . . It should be an honorable thing to be able to understand several languages."[2]

In the summer of 1923, another chorus of Norwegian American singers traveled to Norway. It was named the Minnesota Chorus and was comprised of forty-one members from the Norwegian Glee Club in Minneapolis and the Normanna Male Chorus in Duluth. The chairman of the Minnesota Chorus was T. F. Hamann, and its two directors were Carl G. O. Hansen and I. N. Sødahl. They planned the tour together with the Norse Federation, and the repertoire included songs such as *Naar Fjordene blaaner, Norge mit Norge*, "In Flanders Fields," and folk songs like *Kjerringa med staven* and *Paal paa Haugen*.[3]

The singers arrived in Bergen with the ship *Bergensfjord*. Thousands of people showed up to welcome them. In Kristiania they were received by a large group of student singers, and together they paraded up to the university. After having paid a visit to several cities in Østfold, they went to Drammen and then north to Hamar, Gjøvik, and Lillehammer, and finally over the Dovre mountains to Trondheim. The plan was to give a concert in the cathedral, but after the church

"*O Sagaland*," music by Olaf and text by Johan Selnes. *Sanger-Hilsen 7 (1923), Norwegian-American Collection, National Library of Norway*

supervisor censored many of the songs they had rehearsed, they decided to drop the whole concert, to the great disappointment of many in the city who had looked forward to the event. The chorus traveled onward to Kristiansund, Molde, Ålesund, Geiranger, Haugesund, and Stavanger, where the whole city met them on the quay. Then they sailed to Flekkefjord, Mandal, Kristiansand, Arendal, Larvik, Sande-fjord, Skien, and Tønsberg. In every city they were welcomed by the local singers. The final concert was held in Kristiania on June 7. By then they had performed for more than seventy thousand people. Including those who had listened to their performances at the harbors, the total number was estimated to be two hundred thousand.

Olaf did not take part in this journey, but he made sure that his brother, the old Marksman General Ola Five, welcomed the choir in Trondheim, and that Ola's son, Olaf W. Five, with many of the local Rotary members, did the same in Kristiania. Many greetings were brought back to Olaf.

Fort Dodge Grows

In Fort Dodge, the Catholic St. Joseph Mercy Hospital had become too small and needed financial help to expand and to pay off old debt. A campaign was started to raise capital. At the same time the Lutheran congregations wanted to collect money for the hospital they had planned to build. Olaf and other members of the mercantile association decided that, as there already was a Catholic hospital in town, that organization should be allowed to go through with their fund-raising first. The Lutherans would wait until the year after.[1]

The Catholics succeeded in collecting the money they needed, and the Lutherans expected to be able to do the same for their hospital project. They bought a piece of land overlooking the Des Moines River, not far from Oleson Park. About eight thousand people were present at the ground breaking in 1924. At that time a railroad track was laid up to the area in order to ease transportation of building material and later coal to heat the hospital. Progress was good until one day the workers walked off the job. They had not received their wages. Olaf stepped in and paid. It took, however, nine years before the Lutheran Hospital was completed. A stock market collapse followed by an economic depression brought many projects to a halt. The economic climate does not seem to have affected Olaf too much, though. He supported the hospital with a total of $115,000. Had he not extended a helping hand, the project would have gone bankrupt. He was rewarded with a seat on the board of directors.

The United States had not yet been hit by the Depression when construction work on the hospital began. While Europe experienced political conflicts and financial crises, the United States was characterized by a robust individualism and the cities were buzzing like beehives. The country had become the world's leading industrial nation. A network of paved roads tied it together, and nine out of ten families had a car. Wages increased, and anyone could obtain financial credit. In Fort

Dodge, building construction boomed. The city had at that time more "skyscrapers" per capita than any other city in the Midwest. During these years the city earned the nickname "Little Chicago." That was not just due to the "skyscrapers"; the gangster Al Capone chose Fort Dodge as his hiding place when things got too hot back home. Capone personified the dark side of the American dream. Corruption began to flourish in the city's business life, an element that had been unheard of in earlier years.

Al Capone gained control over many influential people in Fort Dodge. And from here, in the middle of Prohibition, he ran his liquor, gambling, and prostitution businesses. It is claimed that the girls at the Chicago brothels were first tried out in Fort Dodge. Al Capone had installed his brother on the first floor in a building adjacent to the Wahkonsa Hotel. On the second floor he kept his bodyguards, while he himself occupied a penthouse on the top floor. In spite of these gangsters, there was never a single shot fired in Fort Dodge, not even when Bonnie and Clyde passed through on several occasions.[2]

Olaf and Al Capone, two of the city's powerful men, are likely to have seen each other frequently, for instance when having a nice dinner

The Lutheran Hospital in Fort Dodge, saved from bankruptcy by Olaf, finished in 1929.
Private collection

at the Wahkonsa Hotel. These two men acted out of totally different ideals. One gave; the other took.

While this gangster activity thrived, a new type of music sounded from the pavilion in Oleson Park. The city was no longer known just for its male chorus. Now one could hear marching band music with trumpet solos. Karl King, one of the leading composers of brass band music in the United States, had become director of the Fort Dodge Municipal Band, and every Sunday during the summer season the band held a free concert in the park. King, who was president of the American Bandmasters' Association, had been trained at and played with Buffalo Bill's Wild West Show, and he was known for being the composer of more than two hundred galops, military marches, and waltzes. Olaf was proud of the band and supported it financially.[3]

Olaf Is Honored

At the *Sangerfest* in St. Paul, Minnesota, in the summer 1924, Olaf was named the first honorary member of the Norwegian Singers' Association of America, and he stepped down from his job as treasurer. From then on, he added "Hon." before his name. During the festival's main concert the singers were accompanied by a thirty-man orchestra and a large organ. The main director was Fred Wick, and the soloists, Mr. Erik Bye and Mrs. Julia Claussen, received hearty and well-deserved applause after each performance, according to Olaf. In *Sanger-Hilsen* he wrote that "the *Sangerfest* in St. Paul was an outstanding success from start to end." He thought, however, that some of the songs should have been removed from the program, like those with a Swedish text and also *Kong Hakes Ligfærd* (King Hake's Funeral). "Can not quite understand why the last one mentioned was on our festival program. If funeral music was absolutely necessary on such an occasion for our edification and enjoyment, then a text with a less cruel theme should have been chosen. We should not emphasize or advertise the atrocities of our fathers—least of all during a *Sangerfest*. . . . Let us remember Henrik Wergeland's encouragement to praise the up-bringing our dear mothers gave us."[1]

One of the songs Olaf felt was missing was *Thord Foleson* by E. O. Forseth. It had been ranked second best in the competition arranged by the Norwegian America Line. Thord Foleson was a historical person and one of Olav Haraldsson's men killed during the battle at Stiklestad in 1030.

It is regrettable that "Thord Foleson" by E. O. Forseth was not sung as it is a fine song that I think most of the singers would enjoy, had they been given the chance to rehearse it well. It is not difficult, although the magnificent text by Per Sivle is written in a language they are not accustomed to—*Maalet* or *Ny-Norsk* (New Norwegian) and may seem troublesome to many of us Norwegian Americans. We should, as far as possible, try to concentrate on songs by Norwegian Americans at *Sangerfests*, that is to say when we have songs of *value*. This will encourage our poets and composers to keep up their good work.[2]

Norwegian American singers at the *Sangerfest* in St. Paul, Minnesota, June 1924. Olaf is in the first row, fifth from left. *Photo detail: Norwegian Singers' Association of America, Norwegian-American Collection, National Library of Norway*

The language Olaf thought of as a foreign language, New Norwegian, had long since become the language of his brother Ola. To Ola and many like-minded in Norway it was an important means in the struggle to get rid of the old governing class and its history, while Olaf and the other Norwegian Americans were focused on saving their identity as a minority.

The Twin Cities of St. Paul and Minneapolis, located on each side of the Mississippi River, had "quite excellent male choruses and directors" in the 1920s, according to Olaf. *Nordmennenes Sangforening* in St. Paul had professor John Dahle as director. Minneapolis had four large choruses, *Nordmennenes* with professor H. Gundersen as director, *Dovre* with Olaf Halten, *Nordkap* with H. Askeland, and the Norwegian Glee Club, the largest of the four, with director Carl G. O. Hansen. About the latter Olaf wrote: "Mr. Hansen has for many years been interested in song and music, not just as director, but also as a dependable and judicious reviewer and critic. His music columns in the newspaper *Minneapolis Tidende* are a true pleasure to those who find song and music interesting, as they provide a credible and understandable account of what is happening in this field. 'The Norwegian Glee Club' has thrived under Hansen's competent leadership and has become known as one of the best male choruses in America."[3]

The Centennial of Norwegian Emigration to America

By 1925 the immigration rush was over, but the centennial of the first organized Norwegian emigration to America called for a magnificent celebration. Despite the American patriotism that flourished during the First World War, many of the 2.5 million Norwegian Americans, born in Norway or having Norwegian parents, still had a basic sense of being Norwegian. They wanted to show the coming generations that these Norwegian Vikings, as they often called themselves, had taken part in forming the new world. They had plowed the prairie, fought in the Civil War, on Cuba, in the Philippines, and during the world war. Norwegian engineers had constructed bridges, roads, and buildings. And several Norwegians had reached prominent positions as businessmen, politicians, and journalists. Norwegians had helped establish thirty-eight colleges where 75,000 students, 40 percent of them female, had acquired their education. The Norwegian Lutheran church had ordained seventeen hundred pastors and across the United States there were thirty Norwegian singing societies. Forty-five *bygdelag*, among them Trønderlaget with ten subgroups counting a total of 2,556 members, were spread all over the United States. Like the *Sangerfest*, the festivals arranged by the *bygdelag* drew thousands of people.[1]

The Norse-American Centennial was arranged by the *bygdelag* in St. Paul and Minneapolis on June 6–9 of 1925. Olaf was Iowa's representative on the festival committee, where Gisle Bothne was president. The first guests from Norway to arrive was the Kristiania mixed student chorus with fifty female and male singers. They were met at the station by 125 Norwegian American singers in full dress. Together they paraded through the streets, four abreast. At the banquet that followed two bishops were present: the bishop of Oslo, Johan Peter Lunde, dressed in a black coat and with a gold cross on his chest, and his American colleague H. G. Stub, president of the Norwegian Lutheran

Church in America, wearing his insignia. Among the speakers was the Norwegian member of Parliament Carl Johan Hambro. The Norwegian Singers' Association of America, directed by professor F. Wick, entertained with songs including *Landkjenning, Naar Fjordene Blaaner*, "The Star-Spangled Banner," *Ja, vi elsker*, and *Solveigs Sang*. The St. Olaf College Band provided the music. King Haakon of Norway, the Norwegian Parliament and government, the Norwegian Church, the University of Oslo, the Norse Federation, the Authors' Association, the Press Organization, and the Association of Norwegian Women all sent their greetings.

The program was packed every day, with church services and exhibits where Norwegian history from the time of the Vikings and forward was presented. There were joint parties arranged by the various *bygdelag*. Altogether two hundred thousand Norwegian Americans attended. One day there were eighty-three thousand present. Never before had so many Norwegians come together outside of Norway. Even President Calvin Coolidge made an appearance, sending greetings to the Norwegian king and acknowledging Leif Eiriksson as the one who had "discovered" America. As if this recognition were not enough, the Americans had commemorative centennial medals and stamps made for the occasion. The US Congress had never before authorized the striking of a medal commemorating an event. A total of forty thousand silver and one hundred gold commemorative medals were minted. One side of the octagonal medals had a Viking ship under full sail with the inscription "A. D. 1000" underneath, in honor of Leif Eiriksson's arrival in America that year. The commemorative five-cent stamp, printed in blue and red, showed a design of the sloop *Restaurationen*.

In connection with the celebration, a competition for the best essay on the topic "Why We Celebrate" was announced. It was won by one of Olaf's friends, the newspaper man and author Waldemar Ager, who also had been one of the first to receive an award from Olaf for his literary work. In his essay Ager argued that if the United States was to become a cultural power, "the special qualities of the Norwegian Americans have to be preserved to the extent possible ... that which still may be found is the source from which the arts, and especially music, is nourished." He emphasized that the Norse-American Centennial would:

contribute to the preservation of our people's best traits and national characteristics. . . . The prevailing "melting pot idea" will only result in banality. Even if it succeeded, by artificial means, to create a uniform standardized type of citizen, that would only be possible by eliminating the strongest and best characteristics of the immigrated people. When the Irish-Americans cease to exist, then also the typical Irish humor will be gone and with it the bold Irish way of expressing oneself, a quality we find with many of our greatest speakers. When the German-American is no longer there, then we will also be missing the German industriousness, diligence and their unique love for music and flowers. . . .

The Centennial . . . will also be important for Norway. Norway is our mother. As any other mother, she is anxious to know how her children behave when among foreigners. If her upbringing of them has been good and their manners are well received, she is due her share of the honor and the pleasure it brings a mother, rich or poor. And if our struggle and work here through the past hundred years is worthy of any honor, it is equally as much to the credit of our new home country; since what has been carried out has been carried out here. . . .

The way they respect their parents they will themselves be respected. They will understand the struggle of previous generations and they will also learn to understand other people and by that reach the common understanding and respect that all nationalities owe each other and which, in the end, is the nation's only safe foundation.[2]

Oscar Arneson, head of the public relation committee, followed by praising Norwegian mythology from the saga period, arguing that it in several ways surpassed Greek mythology.

The Norwegian-American Historical Association

The Norse-American Centennial came to an end, but documentation of the history of Norwegians in America was taken care of, thanks to leading Norwegian American intellectuals. Later that autumn they met at St. Olaf College in Northfield, Minnesota, and founded the Norwegian-American Historical Association (NAHA). As the first contributor, Olaf donated the initial capital of $1,000 to the association.[1]

The first leadership of the association was Rev. Ditlef G. Ristad, who also happened to be president of the National Trønderlag of America. Laurence M. Larson, professor at the University of Illinois, became vice president; Ole E. Rølvaag, author and professor at St. Olaf College, Minnesota, was the secretary; and industrialist O. M. Oleson, Fort Dodge, Iowa, the treasurer.[2]

Olaf brought in his friend businessman Birger Osland from Chicago as assistant treasurer. Olaf nicknamed the man, twenty years his junior, "Johnnie on the spot," for his ability to represent Norwegian matters in America. Though they both were born in Norway, they wrote to each other in English—more than 150 letters in the first few years of the organization, which was a difficult period financially. Olaf and Osland had a constant struggle to keep Ditlef G. Ristad in check. Ristad had high ambitions for NAHA, and there were many activities he wanted to spend money on, such as sending delegates to international historical congresses and helping fund a Norwegian museum at Luther College in Decorah. "To me it seems almost foolish to branch out into other things before we are fairly well established," Olaf wrote to Osland. By encouraging people to sign up for life memberships and then investing the money in the stock market, Osland and Olaf little by little managed to create a fund large enough to finance the collecting and publishing of Norwegian American history. They insisted on this being done by the Norwegian Americans themselves, not, as they wrote to each other, the way it had been done a thousand years earlier, when the story about Norwegian immigration to Europe was written by "hostile monks." Norwegian American history had to be written now before it was forgotten. An editorial committee was chosen consisting of Theodore C. Blegen, professor at the University of Minnesota; J. Jørgen Thompson, professor at St. Olaf College; Knut Gjerset, professor at Luther College in Decorah, Iowa; and Kristian Prestgard, editor of *Decorah Posten*.[3]

NAHA began collecting letters that had been sent home to Norway, which were regarded as core material in the depiction of how the immigrants themselves experienced America and their meeting with the New World. Documentation supplied directly from the immigrants was collected, and the association was offered a separate room at St. Olaf College, which served as archive and library.

Olaf wrote to his brother Ola and asked for assistance. In return Ola sent, among other things, a copy of *Amerikaboken* (A True Account of America) by Ole Rynning. The old marksman general Ola Five had retired and moved back to Steinkjer, where he helped form the *Nord-Trøndelag Historielag*. Close to a hundred years after Rynning had emigrated to America from Snåsa, Ola Five arranged for his work to be printed as an addendum to the yearbook of the *Nord-Trøndelag Historielag*. He added that "The 'America Book' has today unfortunately become totally unknown to the people of Nord-Trøndelag."[4]

A True Account of America was translated into English by professor Theodore C. Blegen of the University of Minnesota and was sent to the members of NAHA. Together with Marcus Thrane's *Wisconsin Bible*, it was among the very first books in NAHA's collection. Over the years the collection grew into a large archive.[5]

Supported by NAHA and several private persons, among them Olaf, who donated $500, Professor Blegen acquired letters written by the Norwegian colonel H. C. Heg during the Civil War. Heg, who originally came from Lier in Buskerud, Norway, and died during the Civil War, headed the 15th Wisconsin Infantry Regiment, almost totally manned by Norwegian immigrants. *The Civil War Letters of Colonel Hans Christian Heg* was published as a book in 1936. Professor Knut Gjerset received funding from NAHA, the Norwegian America Line,

The Norwegian American Historical Association

Executive Board

REV. D. G. RISTAD,
President,
Manitowoc, Wis.
DR. L. M. LARSEN,
Vice President,
Urbana, Ill.
PROF. O. E. ROELVAAG,
Secretary,
Northfield, Minn.
HON. O. M. OLESON,
Treasurer,
Ft. Dodge, Iowa
MAJOR BIRGER OSLAND,
Assistant Treasurer,
184 N. La Salle St.,
Chicago, Ill.
MR. A. C. FLOAN,
442 Summit Ave.,
St. Paul, Minn.
DR. KNUT GJERSET,
Decorah, Iowa

Board of Finance

HON. O. M. OLESON,
MAJOR BIRGER OSLAND,
DR. T. STABO,
Decorah, Iowa
MR. A. C. FLOAN,
DEAN J. JOERGEN THOMPSON,
Financial Secretary,
Northfield, Minn.

Board of Editors

DR. THEO. C. BLEGEN,
Managing Editor,
Minn. State Historical Society,
St. Paul, Minn.
KRISTIAN PRESTGARD,
Editor, "Decorah Posten,"
Decorah, Iowa.
DR. KNUT GJERSET,
Decorah, Iowa.

Local Vice Presidents

DR. E. NYMAN FIGVED,
Boston, Mass.
A. N. RYGG,
Publisher, "Nordisk Tidende,"
New York City.
CONSUL M. MOE,
Philadelphia, Pa.
MRS. OAKLEY KISSAM BROWN,
Chicago, Ill.
PROF. C. MARTIN ALSAGER,
Chicago, Ill.
REE. H. J. THORPE,
Milwaukee, Wis.
COL. CHR. BRANDT,
Decorah, Iowa
DR. G. T. LEE, Editor,
"Lutheran Church Herald,"
Minneapolis, Minn.
JOHN NORNBORG,
Duluth, Minn.
REV. JOHN BROWN, President,
Concordia College,
Moorhead, Minn.
HANS USTRUD,
Baltic, S. D.
MRS. FRIDA BUE-HOMNES,
Crosby, N. D.
GUNNAR LUND, Publisher,
"Washington Posten,"
Seattle, Wash.

Leadership of the Norwegian-American Historical Association (NAHA). *Private collection*

and Olaf, who gave $500, for a book project, *The Norwegian Sailors on the Great Lakes.*[6]

Olaf was disappointed by the lack of financial support for NAHA, especially from the Norwegians in New York. However, the president of the Norwegian Chamber of Commerce, Sir Karl Knudsen, came forward with a substantial contribution by offering $5,000 for the acquisition of "America-letters" and by becoming a life member. Olaf paid $100 to cover his brother Ola's life membership. He did the same for Andrew A. Veblen, the first chairman of the *Bygdelagenes Fellesråd* (National Council of District Clubs in America). Among the people in Norway who were members of NAHA were Olaf's old colleague Lars Ranes in Ålesund and Ola Five's friend O. Nordgård, curator of the Academy of Science in Trondheim.[7]

At the same time Ola arranged for Olaf to be a lifelong member of the *Nord-Trøndelag Historielag*. D. G. Ristad, chairman both of NAHA and the National Trønderlag of America, thought that everyone from Trøndelag living in America should subscribe to the historical association's yearbooks: "It would not be out of place for us to learn a little about what our friends in Trøndelag do to understand the continuity in people's life and culture down through history. This provides an incentive for us to take care of our own experiences from the pioneer period and forward, so they can be transmitted to our descendants. It provides stimulation for the mind, it is our heritage, and it is noble."[8]

The two historical associations, one on each side of the Atlantic, sent each other manuscripts. What the National Trønderlag of America's yearbooks said about Nord-Trøndelag was usually written by Olaf's brother Ola, who was known as the National Trønderlag's good friend in Steinkjer. And vice versa, what was published in the yearbooks of the *Nord-Trøndelag Historielag* about the emigrants from Trøndelag was written by Ola's former pupil, D. G. Ristad. Olaf was also kept well informed of what was happening in Nord-Trøndelag through the newspaper *Inntrøndelagen*. Ola was editor and sent a copy of each issue to Olaf.

Olaf was asked to replace Dr. Gjerset as a member of NAHA's executive board in 1931. He declined at first, referring to his age and reduced work capacity, but he later accepted the appointment as it was said to be no burden, only an honorary position.[9]

In Caruso's Mausoleum and a Night at the Egyptian Opera

Olaf had reached the age of seventy-six in 1925, but he was still an adventurous man. After having celebrated the centennial and after helping found the Norwegian-American Historical Association, he joined Julie on a trip to the Mediterranean in the winter of 1925–26. First they visited Madeira, Gibraltar, Algeria, and Monaco before proceeding to Naples to commemorate Caruso—the poor boy from Naples who ended up being a world-famous opera singer and the leading tenor at the Metropolitan Opera in New York for seventeen years. Caruso had died in 1921, only forty-eight years old. Olaf had seen Caruso at the Metropolitan and wanted to visit his mausoleum at the Santa Maria del Pianto Cemetery.

Along with the letters that Olaf sent back to *Sanger-Hilsen*, the editor included a picture of Enrico Caruso taken when he was at the top of his career, adding the caption, "His body may now be viewed for just a few coins." Olaf described their trip and the sights they saw.

> We drove up to one of the hilltops in the city where the magnificent mausoleum lies. It is made of the finest marble, both on the inside and the outside. It is equipped with an altar with inlaid gold. The building is large enough for the whole Caruso family to be buried there, and the names are already there even for those who are still living. Up under the roof there is an ancient Madonna sculpture, bought for about one million lira, we were told.
>
> Caruso looks as if he might still be alive; dressed in the same costume one normally would see him in when he performed at the Metropolitan Opera. His color is rather grey, but they say that in ten years the true color will return to his face as his body by then will be fully "mummified."

There is a splendid mass every Monday, and everything is done to the extent his fortune allows. The tomb is constantly guarded and there are flowers in abundance.[1]

From Naples Olaf and Julie went on to the Holy Land, to the cities of Jerusalem and Bethlehem, where Julie painted several pictures. Their journey around the Mediterranean then brought them to Cairo in Egypt, where they stayed for two months. It was in Cairo that Peter Christen Asbjørnsen had acquired his ideas for the fairy-tale garden at the Sundnes estate and also the place where Ole Bull had climbed to the top of the Cheops pyramid and played *Sæterjentens Søndag* on his violin. Olaf and Julie went up the Nile, watched a performance of the opera *Aida*, and even managed to enter the tomb of Tutankhamon, which had just recently been opened. They were shown the latest work that had been done on the Sphinx.

The excursion up the Nile is planned to take seventeen days and we have now spent three days on the steamer *Daminetta*, which is most comfortable for such a journey. We are sixty passengers in the hands of Thos. Cook & Sons, which is sort of a guarantee for nice treatment. The tour has been exceptionally interesting.

When one looks over this landscape and sees all the different native people, one can almost imagine seeing Abraham, Moses, Joseph and others from the early days alive. I believe the way of life has not changed much over the thousands of years that have passed. Everything seems so old fashioned. A piece of bent wood is used as a plow, and water from the Nile is lifted up in goatskin buckets to water the fields and help the crops grow.[2]

Presumably, Olaf was given access to Tutankhamon's tomb with all its contents because he was able to pay well. The gold sarcophagus containing the embalmed body of the child king Tutankhamon, which had been sealed for more than three thousand years, had been removed from the tomb just prior to his visit. Olaf went to the Egyptian Museum in Cairo as well.[3]

Under the title "A Night at the Egyptian Opera," Olaf wrote in *Sanger-Hilsen*:

When it was announced that a grand gala performance of "Aida" was to be held on Sunday afternoon, before our departure from Cairo, we decided to attend, as we were assured that it would be a pleasant and rewarding experience.

The curtain went up at exactly 5 PM, and the performance lasted for 4 hours without any pauses. A splendid orchestra, a large group of exceptionally good singers—all star performers—made a deep impression on a very enthusiastic audience. With all the wonderful costumes in beautiful and picturesque colors the show stood out as "a sight for the gods." . . .

The interior of the opera house reminded one of the Metropolitan in New York, but more brilliantly decorated and equipped. The four levels of boxes were arranged in the shape of a horseshoe. The three boxes on each side closest to the stage are reserved for the king and his companions. The boxes highest up are used by the ladies-in-waiting. In front there is a beautifully carved wooden lattice, enabling the oriental beauties to watch and listen to what was happening both on the stage and in the audience, without being observed by infidels or Mohammedans.

The theme of "Aida" is of course centered on Egypt and the Nile as "the Nile is Egypt and Egypt is the Nile." If not for the enormous amount of water carried by the Nile, Egypt would just be an uninhabitable desert. Due to the monumental dams built by the English, this large river has been tamed to an extent that it now irrigates the fields whenever necessary. As a consequence they are able to produce 3–4 crops a year from this fertile land.

In the Nile one finds the sacred Lotus water lily and the ancient papyrus, which serves as paper. On the banks of the river the Sycamore tree grows (a kind of Ficus) along with palm trees. All these four plants were worshipped. They were also much used in architecture a thousand years ago, as the ruins of the many wonderful temples show. . . .

The Arabs who do most of the work in Egypt, may not have the greatest aptitude for music, but they sing almost constantly when they are working.

This is especially true when they are pulling together, such as when they are rowing, pulling a rope or a hawser, moving large stones etc. It is a fact that this makes the work easier and more gets done. Their scale seems to consist of only 3 or 4 tones in the minor key. It sounds rather sad and a little monotonous, but quite interesting nonetheless, especially when many are singing together.

At the excavation around the Sphinx, close to the three largest pyramids, more than 500 Arabs were working, shoveling sand with their bare hands into large baskets which they later emptied into small railway carriages. When these were full, they were pushed to a suitable place, emptied and then returned for the process to be repeated. The work was done to a rhythm set by an "orchestra" of five "musicians" who played

Grieg Mandskor, Fort Dodge, 1926. First row from left: Alf Hovey, Olaf, L. G. Dorheim, A. J. Moe, and O. T. Peterson. Second row from left: Rudolph Johnson, B. Hauge, O. R. Vevle, E. S. Hanson, M. M. Dahl, and A. A. Fremming. *Webster County Historical Society*

on strange instruments and led the singing. The workers of
both genders were poorly clad. The few rags they wore had
all kinds of colors and created a scene unlikely to be found
elsewhere. An anthill made of many colors with ants swarm-
ing around is probably the closest one comes to this strange
kaleidoscope.[4]

From Cairo, Olaf and Julie traveled on to Lake Garda in Italy and
stayed at the fashionable Grand Hotel Gordone. His brother Ola, who
had received regular letters from Olaf, became worried when the letters stopped coming. He was also concerned about the oldest brother,
Eilert. He was ill and confined to his bed, and Ola looked in on him
regularly. Eilert died later that year. Olaf had also become ill. The extraordinary cold and raw weather which they encountered in Italy gave
him painful arthritis. His fingers became stiff, and he found it difficult
to write. The journey home, which went by way of Florence, Cologne,
Paris, and Cherbourg, gave him little pleasure.[5]

Members of The Norwegian Singers' Association of America

MINNESOTA
The Norwegian Glee Club, Minneapolis.
Nordmændenes Sangforening, Minneapolis.
Nordkap Male Chorus, Minneapolis.
Dovre, Minneapolis.
Nordmændenes Sangforening, St. Paul.
Normanna, Duluth.
Odin Male Chorus, Fertile.
Brage, Thief River Falls.
Norrøna, Moorhead.

SOUTH DAKOTA
Minnehaha Mandskor, Sioux Falls.
Viking, Brookings.
Orpheus, Baltic.

WISCONSIN
Normanna Sangerkor, LaCrosse.
Nordrøn, Superior.
Nordmændenes Sangforening, Hudson.
Grieg Male Chorus, Madison.
Norwegian Glee Club, Racine, Wis.
Norsemen's Glee Club, Milwaukee.

NORTH DAKOTA
Franklin Male Chorus, Mayville.
Kjerulf, Hatton.
Norrøna, Petersburg.
Norden, Devils Lake.
Nøkken, Fort Ransom.
Orpheus, Fargo.
Bjarne, Grand Forks.

IOWA
Nordmændenes Sangforening, Sioux City.
Luren, Decorah.
Grieg Male Chorus, Fort Dodge.
Grieg Male Chorus, Decorah.

ILLINOIS
Normændenes Sangforening, Chicago.
Norwegian Glee Club, Chicago.
Bjørnson Male Chorus, Chicago.
Bjørgvin, Chicago.
Harmonien, Rockford.

CANADA
Norwegian Glee Club, Winnipeg.

Members of the Norwegian Singers' Association of America, 1926. *Norwegian-American Collection, National Library of Norway*

That summer Olaf did not attend the *Sangerfest* in Chicago. This was the first time in over thirty years that he had not participated. He also found it was time to step down as the leader of *Grieg Mandskor* and handed the position over to Andrew Moe.

When rheumatism started bothering Olaf, he found spending the winter in San Diego, California, was especially helpful. He and Julie occupied a suite at Park Manor, a brand-new seven-story building in Italian Renaissance style. They had a large balcony overlooking both Balboa Park with its zoo and art gallery and Glorietta Bay and the Pacific Ocean. In the garden surrounding the hotel were palm trees and flowers. Here Hollywood stars and distinguished guests could move around undisturbed and feel at home.

After finally having received a letter from Olaf, Ola said that "Olaf is surrounded by a large variety of cactuses. He is accompanied by several nature lovers. In a few days they are about to have a zoological excursion. He is complaining about the weather being too hot, though, so he has found it necessary to buy a light summer suit.—Ah, we should have been there."[6]

More about the Ole Bull Statue

In addition to having contributed to the collection of written documentation about the Norwegian Americans' first period as immigrants, Olaf also wanted to take care of the monuments the Norwegians had set up in America, such as the Ole Bull statue in Loring Park, Minneapolis. The spot should have a small hilltop with Norwegian trees and wild flowers "which would bloom on the 17th of May, along with a small brook; since it was at picturesque places like this that the great violinist got his inspiration," Olaf wrote in *Minneapolis Tidende* in 1926. He continued,

> This extremely lovely statue should have a far nicer background, than what it now has. Spruce, pine trees, and birch are of course on top of the list; but the modest and trusty juniper (*Juniperus Communis*) should not be forgotten, nor should the birdcherry (*Prunus Padus*), the mountain ash (*Sorbus Aucuparia*) or the aspen (*Populus tremula*) whose leaves rustle constantly making an almost sacred sound. The willow (*Salix Caprea*) from which we as children made "our real magic flutes"—in all sizes and keys and which is the reason our orchestra was always fully equipped with woodwind players should also be there.
>
> The background should also have a small mountain or hilltop, and in the crevices one should see Norwegian plants including heather (*Calluna vulgaris*), twin flower (*Linneæ borealis*), and harebell (*Campanula rotundifolia*). The latter two grow wild in Minnesota, so this should make it easy to plant them. In the crevices of the rock one should grow white anemones (*Anemone nemorosa*), as those would bloom around May 17. A version of this plant can also be found in Minnesota (*Anemone quinquefolia*), and it is hard to distinguish from the

Olaf among peonies and irises in his garden in Fort Dodge, circa 1926. *Private collection*

Norwegian one. A small running brook would also enhance the beauty of the place....

It would be gratifying if the singers' associations in the Twin Cities could support this wonderful undertaking; but if it ended up being necessary I am sure that the Norwegian-American music-loving public throughout the country would be happy to give their support. A landscape gardener, who really knows his trade and has the required sense for beauty and the ability to take a long view, could succeed in transforming the place into something that thousands of people would treasure for a long time to come.[1]

According to the Minnesota Historical Society, it seems the singers' associations did not follow up on this invitation.

The First Telephone Call to Norway and the Royal Order

Fifty-one years after the world exposition in Philadelphia, where Olaf saw a telephone in use for the first time, and forty-five years after Olaf had participated in establishing the first telephone exchange in Fort Dodge, it became possible to make a telephone call from Fort Dodge to Oslo, Norway. The telephone line went via Des Moines and Chicago to the link station Rocky Point on the coast. From there the signals were radioed across the Atlantic Ocean to Cupar in Scotland, where they were picked up by a cable and carried to the English Channel, then underwater to Germany and following the seabed further to Malmø, Sweden, and then finally on land to Oslo.

On July 6, 1928, Olaf was invited to be the first person to make a call "home" by way of the Fort Dodge Telephone Company. It required a great deal of planning, since Olaf wanted to speak with his brother Ola, who lived in Steinkjer, Nord-Trøndelag. On October 27 Ola Five was ready to take the call in Oslo. Ola had established a local telephone company forty years earlier, but the lines had no connection with the international network.[1]

In Fort Dodge, Olaf was sitting with a journalist from the local newspaper as an observer, and Ola, at the other end, was at the home of his son Olaf with a number of relatives. Everybody was anxious to see if it was possible to obtain a fully audible conversation between Fort Dodge and Oslo. The conclusion was "yes, loud and clear!" They spoke both Norwegian and English, depending on the language abilities of the one who was speaking. Everybody was pleased with this miraculous conversation.[2]

The Americans were surprised to learn that Oslo, with its 250,000 inhabitants, had 43,000 telephones. They thought of Norway as a country that was out on the fringes. But the fact was that Norway had always been at the forefront of accepting the use of the telephone, primarily due to the shipping business and its need for communication. A three-minute call from Fort Dodge to Oslo cost $58.50 at that time. That was quite expensive for a short chat, but far cheaper than a round trip on a liner just for the privilege of hearing a familiar voice. And it was more efficient than a telegram in cases of emergency, whether related to business or private matters. Everybody agreed to that.

At the time the telephone call was made, none of them knew that Olaf would be receiving "royal gewgaws," like Ola had some years earlier. On the same day the telephone call between Fort Dodge and Oslo took place, it was recorded in the Order Book of the Royal Norwegian Order of St. Olav that "The Norwegian American and Pharmacist Olaf Martin Oleson, Fort Dodge, Iowa, is, on the recommendation of several organizations, presented by Vice Consul Dr. T. Stabo, the Legation in Washington, and the Department of Foreign Affairs, dated 6th of July 1928, as a candidate for Knight of the First Class of the Royal Norwegian Order of St. Olav."

The order, which was named for the patron saint of Norway and instituted by King Oscar in 1847, was a "reward for excellent service to the fatherland and humanity," and Olaf received it for his "work for the preservation of Norwegianness in the U.S.A." The medal together with the diploma arrived at the Norwegian consulate in Washington, DC, on January 2, 1929, and Vice Consul Dr. T. Stabo wanted to hand it to Olaf personally. Olaf, however, was in San Diego, so Stabo sent the medal on to Rev. S. A. Berge at St. Olaf Norwegian Lutheran Church in Fort Dodge, where Olaf received it in the spring. In the meantime, he had collected many congratulations from friends who regarded him as "A knight without fear and without reproach." His brother Ola commented that Olaf seemed to be quite pleased with the decoration. "He should be as he was regarded as a leading citizen of Fort Dodge," Ola proudly concluded. Olaf added the medal to all the singer's medals he wore on his chest on ceremonial occasions. He did not want to use the title "knight," but he gladly put "honorary" or "hon.," a title he had received as a singer, in front of his name.[3]

Several other Norwegian Americans had received the same distinction, among them artist Ben Blessum, the author and professor O. E. Rølvaag, and Chicago businessman John W. Sinding. These men joined an exclusive club as Senator Knute Nelson, Minnesota, Hans G. Stub, and J. A. Aasgaard, both bishops in the Norwegian Lutheran Church in America, Laurits S. Swenson, US ambassador to Norway, Denmark, and other countries, and Knut Gjerset, professor at Luther College, Decorah, also received the Order of St. Olav.

In 1928 the *Sangerfest* was for the first time arranged in Canada, in the city of Winnipeg, Manitoba, where the mayor, "a jovial Scot," welcomed the seven hundred Norwegian American singers. They were lodged at the best spot in town, the Royal Alexandra Hotel, often just called the Royal Alex. Olaf, now seventy-nine and too old to be a member of the main chorus of the Norwegian Singers' Association of America, had instead established the *Veterankoret* (the Veteran Chorus). It soon grew to twenty-five members, and Olaf covered the bottom of the cash box with twenty-five dollars. He was rewarded by being elected honorary director.[4]

The Veteran Chorus was invited to sing at the festival but was not allowed to perform at the main concert. Despite this, "the *Sangerfest* in Winnipeg was excellent in every way, but two of the songs should have been omitted," Olaf commented. The two songs were "Soldiers' Chorus" from Faust and "Pilgrims' Chorus" from Tannhäuser. "We have our own pearls," he pointed out, and he wanted to hold on to those. This may very well be part of the reason he established the Veteran Chorus, as he then could take part in deciding the repertoire. To sing in a chorus was one of Olaf's great joys in life. This is surely the same feeling expressed by "A. F." in *Sanger-Hilsen* in 1928: "Through song one can forget one's self and one's surroundings and just become a part of the large instrument on which the director is playing to express the work of art . . . to feel like a fellow performer, seek the word, the sound, the thought behind the melody, seek the feeling that immediately flows from your true spirit."[5]

Others pointed to the fact that "the song was a means of gaining strength, the best exercise." And since it was believed that singing increased lung capacity, it was supposed to protect against tuberculosis. It was also said to help digestion, metabolism, and the appetite. Concerning the influence singing had on people's minds, one of the singers, Magnus A. Vevle from Milwaukee, Wisconsin, had some interesting reflections:

VETERAN-KØRET
— Stiftet 1928 —

ALFRED E. DAHL, President,
  3401 20th Avenue So., Minneapolis, Minn·
TH. F. HAMANN, Sekretær,
  4009 Harriet Avenue, Minneapolis, Minn.
MARTIN H. HANSEN, Kasserer,
  1259 Winona Street, Chicago, Ill.
OLAF M. OLESON, Æresdirigent
  Fort Dodge, Iowa
CARL A. MANNERUD, Dirigent
  Sioux Falls. S. D.

Fort Dodge, Iowa,

☆

VETERANKORETS SANG I ROCKFORD 1940
  Oscar Borg: "AFTENRØSTER"

Letterhead used by the "Veteran Chorus" in the Norwegian Singers' Association of America. *Private collection*

Much has been said and written about how singing—indirectly—has an improving effect on us; but little is mentioned about its direct control of our emotional life.

One afternoon when I was meditating about songs and singers, I suddenly realized that it would be impossible for a person to carry evil thoughts in his heart *while singing*, and I felt ashamed that so many years had to pass before this simple truth came to my mind.

That a man could be wandering around humming a tune and at the same time planning to get rid of his mother-in-law with an axe or a sledge hammer—no way!

So, we have the fact that singing eliminates evil in our soul and mind, and by sticking to that line of thinking we arrive at the logical conclusion that the more one sings, the closer one comes to perfection. What a wonderful thought! Somebody ought to write a book about the subject, and maybe call it "Singing. A Road to World Peace." What kind of opportunities does this open to us?[6]

Cover of the program for the *Sangerfest* held in Minneapolis, Minnesota, June 1930.
Norwegian-American Collection, National Library of Norway

The Gift to the Nidaros Cathedral

After America's golden years of increasing wages and generous credit, speculation on the stock exchange, and a blind faith that nothing could go wrong, the bubble burst. American banks with foreign debtors required the loans to be repaid. With that, the crash became worldwide. The crisis did not seem to affect Olaf too much, though, and many people, Americans as well as Norwegians, asked him for money. One of them was Ola Nordgård, curator of the Academy of Science and manager of the Biology Center in Trondheim. Nordgård had big plans for a modern fishery museum there. He got Ola Five to ask Olaf for a large donation. "I would have done it, if I had my brother's wallet," Ola reassured Nordgård and said he was certain that Olaf would not "end up on welfare" if he made the donation. Olaf, on the other hand, was becoming more restrictive and responded that, "No, for the time being I cannot accommodate the request for 10,000 kroner.—If the remainder of the amount Mr. Nordgård mentions is signed for and *paid*, I may be able to find the 10,000 kroner, but that is all I can promise. . . . [T]here is great need now in America."[1]

But nobody in Norway wanted to fund the fishery museum and, consequently, Olaf did not either. The Great Depression had gripped America, and Ola Five was obliged to turn down all requests to Olaf for financial help, whatever the project.

In Norway, preparations had been underway to celebrate the nine-hundredth anniversary of St. Olav in the cathedral in Trondheim, now named the Nidaros Cathedral. The event was to take place on July 28, 1930. The bishop in the Trøndelag region, Jens Gran Gleditsch, had at an early stage started a nationwide fund-raising effort for restoration of the cathedral, and his wife, Marie Gleditsch, engaged Norwegian women in collecting money for a new rose window on the cathedral's western wall. Thus all of Norway was taking part in a volunteer effort that had originally been started by people in Trøndelag more than sixty years earlier. The Nidaros Cathedral had now become a national treasure.

In the United States a campaign was also started to raise money for the Nidaros Cathedral, just as the emigrants from Trøndelag had planned in 1914. One of the initiators was Gudrun Løchen Drewsen, daughter of Olaf's earliest employer, Herman Løchen at the Sundnes estate. She had just been awarded the Royal Order of Merit for her effort for fellow countrymen in need in America. Among other things, she had done charitable work for the Norwegian children's home and hospital in Brooklyn. But most of all she was known, both in Norway and in the United States, for being an advocate for women's right to vote.

The Norwegian Americans' goal was to raise a large amount of money, and there were several suggestions as to what the gift to the cathedral should be: an organ, a stone sculpture, a marble floor, or an altar. The latter was chosen, an eight-foot-high silver crucifix mounted on an altar covered with silver reliefs, to be placed close to the western nave, making it the first thing seen when entering the cathedral from the western front. The crucifix was designed by the Norwegian sculptor Wilhelm Rasmussen and fabricated by the David Andersen company. Earlier Wilhelm Rasmussen had scared away all evil spirits with his army of grotesque stone gargoyles on the walls of the cathedral, and he had created a sculpture of Olav Tryggvason, king of Norway from 995–1000, that was mounted on a high column in the central square in Trondheim.

The president of the National Trønderlag of America, Rev. D. G. Ristad, was an active promoter of the fund-raising. He pointed out that,

> People in America of Norwegian heritage can not act otherwise than to do what is both their right and their duty and take part in the work our relatives in Norway have so eagerly begun, to raise enough money for the cathedral to be finished in 1930. For the sake of our honor, the love all of us carry for the cathedral, and for the encouragement it would be for our people in Norway, we must all participate. People from Trøndelag anywhere in America must take a leading role.[2]

The fund-raising in America progressed slowly despite numerous appeals through the Norwegian American newspapers. Ristad was deeply disappointed. The result was only half of what had been hoped for. The amount was too small to have a silver pedestal for the crucifix. Marble would have to do.[3]

"Singers! Now is the time to visit the Fatherland!" implored an ad for the Norwegian America Line printed in American papers. In Norway, the Norwegian Student Choral Society was about to celebrate the twenty-fifth anniversary of the America tour in 1905. On May 17, 1930, *Aftenposten* reminded readers of the historical importance of that tour,

> the greatest adventure in the choral society's history,—but it also had an important meaning externally. It tied together again threads between the Fatherland and its emigrated sons that had been cut,—it created sympathy and approval in America for Norway's cause during those dire spring days of 1905.
>
> *Therefore*, the influence and the efforts of the chorus were far more significant than one dared to anticipate when they left Norway.

On the day of the celebration, fifty-six members of the Student Chorus sent a telegram with greetings to Pharmacist Olesen in Fort Dodge and to other singer friends in America.

A little later that summer, eleven hundred Norwegian Americans arrived in Trondheim with the *Stavangerfjord* to take part in the nine-hundredth anniversary in honor of St. Olav. Among them were D. G. Ristad and the choir from St. Olaf College in Minnesota. Even though Olaf was still unhappy with Ristad's lack of financial acumen, he wrote to his friends in Norway and said that Ristad was "a splendid fellow in every way, and one that I treasure highly."[4]

Olaf did not come to Trondheim on this occasion. Nor did his brother Ola, who several months in advance had made sure he had tickets to the main ceremony in the Nidaros Cathedral. Ola died on April 26 that year, eighty-four years old, and thus did not live long enough to see the cathedral in its new splendor. The day he died he had been out buying a phonograph record with the song *Landkjenning* by Bjørnson and Grieg.[5]

Among the first things the visitors from America did was to arrange
a gathering at Stiklestad, where King Olav Haraldson, later St. Olav, had
been killed in battle in 1030. About five thousand people attended, and
D. G. Ristad was among the many speakers. He pointed to the work the
Bygdelag in America did to maintain ties with Norway. But Ristad, like
many other emigrated Norwegians, felt offended at not being regarded
as a real Norwegian, despite all the gifts they had brought and the love
they had shown for the old country. Now he took the opportunity to
call for mutual understanding:

> It is so pleasant to stand here and feel that you are trying to
> understand us, and we also want to understand you. That is
> one of the main tasks people of the same origin have, to come
> to a mutual understanding. Whether we live here or over there,
> there is this one thing we can agree on the importance of, the
> heritage from our fathers. We have to understand ourselves
> and our national characteristics, not just the physical ones
> but also the psychological.[6]

During a special church service in the Nidaros Cathedral on July 28,
with the king, government officials, many important citizens of
Trondheim, and several Norwegian Americans present, the nave of
the cathedral was consecrated and the crucifix from the Norwegian
Americans unveiled. Norwegian emigrants around the world had
sent their greetings. Part of the event in the cathedral was broadcast
to America. This was the first radio broadcast from Norway to America. The next day, which is St. Olav's Day, the celebration continued at
Stiklestad, where an audience of forty thousand had gathered for an
outdoor church service. St. Olav's Day was once again commemorated
as both a religious and a secular event.

Olaf chose to celebrate "The Week of St. Olav" in Minneapolis,
where an arrangement had been put together by the Norwegian Singers' Association of America and *Bygdelagenes Fellesråd*. A total of ten
thousand tickets for the concert had been sold, and *Sigurd Jorsalfar*
and *Landkjenning* were the high points.[7]

All the attention created by the activity around the Nidaros Cathedral, St. Olav, and the celebration of St. Olav's Day may have had an

impact on the congregation of St. Olaf Norwegian Lutheran Church in Fort Dodge. That same year they decided to build a new and larger church. The congregation had grown to five hundred members. Besides the Norwegians, people from Sweden, Denmark, Germany, Italy, Scotland, France, Ireland, England, and Holland had also joined the congregation. Services were now held in English, and "Norwegian" was dropped from the name. The Norwegian Lutheran church, which Olaf had helped found almost forty years earlier, was no longer Norwegian. It is not known how Olaf felt about this.[8]

In any case, Olaf was occupied with other projects. The Lutheran Hospital had finally been dedicated. And both Olaf and Julie were instrumental when Fort Dodge got its first home for the arts, the Blanden Art Museum. Charles Blanden, a former mayor of Fort Dodge, decided to give the city a museum in memory of his wife, who had recently died. Julie and Olaf had been close friends of the couple, and it was Julie who had encouraged Blanden to build the museum. Julie took a seat on the board. In the middle of the Depression, there was not enough money to hire professional managers, so it was decided to let local artists run the museum. This setup resulted in jealousy and in-fighting when exhibitions were being planned. Julie found that decisions were changed behind her back, and she withdrew from the board.[9]

In 1932 a *Sangerfest* was to be held in Madison, Wisconsin. At this twentieth festival arranged by the Norwegian Singers' Association of America, one thousand members representing thirty-four choruses attended, among them the Veteran Chorus, which sang *Norge, Norge*.[10] The management of the association that year consisted of:

Honorary President O. M. Oleson (Fort Dodge)
President Julius E. Olson (Madison)
Vice President Alfred E. Dahl (Minneapolis)
Grand Master Sig Huseby (Chicago)
Assisting Grand Master Carl O. Roskaft (Minneapolis)
Secretary T. F. Hamann (Minneapolis)
Treasurer Anton O. Satrang (Chicago)

Despite the Depression, a new international exposition was arranged in Chicago. The Chicago World's Fair in 1933 was called "A Century of

Advertisement for the Norwegian America Line. *Photo by Den Norske Amerika Linje, Norwegian-American Collection, National Library of Norway*

Progress" and symbolized hope for a brighter future. The theme of the fair was technological innovation, while at the same time the objective was to show the younger generation the strength of the nation. Norwegian Americans had not been able to provide funding for an official Norwegian exhibit this time. However, the first Norwegian training ship, the full-rigged *Sørlandet*, crossed the Atlantic and sailed into the Great Lakes to Chicago forty years after the *Viking* had sailed the same route. *Sørlandet* anchored at the harbor on June 20, 1933, and was welcomed by cheering Norwegian Americans, among them four hundred singers performing *Sæterjentens Søndag*. The Chicago World's Fair ended up being so popular that it was held again the next summer. The total number of visitors amounted to more than 40 million.

But it was not just the World's Fair in Chicago that brought optimism to the American people. The government had started several public building projects in order to create jobs. In Fort Dodge it was decided to build a large and modern music pavilion, the Oleson Park Music Pavilion, also called Oleson Park Bandshell. The old pavilion, which Olaf had provided thirty years earlier, was taken down, and work on a new one started in 1936.[11]

Olaf had now participated in twenty *Sangerfests*. The arrangements had brought together tens of thousands of people and given them the opportunity to enjoy Norwegian music. In order to keep people in Norway informed as to what was going on with Norwegian American singers, Olaf had always paid for *Sanger-Hilsen* to be sent to the University Library in Norway. He was, however, disappointed that he never received any thanks for this gesture. The editor of *Sanger-Hilsen*, T. H. Hamann, repeatedly encouraged the library to tell Olaf that they appreciated the gift.[12]

Keep Singing in Norwegian

Olaf, who had been honored for his work to preserve Norwegianness in the United States, now found that in his own church services were no longer held in Norwegian. Even *Sanger-Hilsen* articles were more and more often written in English, including occasionally Olaf's own. But he was still fighting to keep the songs in Norwegian. In 1935 he wrote in *Sanger-Hilsen* an article called "Keep hold of the Original Language":

> I have read with interest a couple of articles in *Sanger-Hilsen* about the need to have the text of our Norwegian songs translated into English.
>
> Personally I think we should not act too hastily in this matter. Unfortunately, the time is likely to come, mainly due to the limited immigration from Norway lately.
>
> It seems almost unthinkable to sing these wonderful Norwegian songs, with texts by our famous poets, in translation, as long as they can be sung in the original language. They are almost impossible to translate and still keep the meaning close to the original.
>
> Are we less valuable citizens if we love our dear old mother—(Norway)—at the same time as we love and admire our dear spouse—(The United States)?
>
> I do not think so.[1]

Olaf also strongly promoted the idea of uniting the Scandinavian singers in Iowa again. In a meeting in the Oleson Drug Store, the leaders of *Grieg Mandskor*, Norden Singers in Des Moines, *Luren* in Decorah, Swedish Glee Club in Sioux City, *Nordmennenes Sangforening* in Sioux City, and Norse Glee Club in Sioux Falls reached an agreement to establish the United Scandinavian Male Chorus of Iowa. The first Scandinavian singers' festival in Iowa was arranged in Fort Dodge in

May 1935, and a forty-man orchestra was hired for the occasion. The conductor was Luther College professor Carlo A. Sperati. In addition to "The Star-Spangled Banner" and the three Scandinavian national anthems, the audience of about thirteen hundred people could enjoy listening to Olaf's "Come to Iowa" and "In Flanders Fields" before the concert ended with *Landkjenning*. Afterward, all guests not from Fort Dodge were given a guided tour of Oleson Park and the new Lutheran Hospital. Dinner was served at the Wahkonsa Hotel, hosted and paid for by Olaf and Julie.[2]

During the dinner, the guests were given an overview of Fort Dodge, which now had twenty-seven churches, fifteen schools, and fifty factories making leather products, baked goods and confections, fireworks, tents, awnings, butter barrels, and pharmaceutical products. The city also had the world's largest gypsum factory. About the state of Iowa they were told that

> The soil of Iowa produces more prosperity than all the gold mines in the world put together.
>
> Iowa's corn is worth more than all the gold which each year is extracted from mines in the United States. And not only that, the production of corn is far beyond the amount of coal being dug out of all the mines. And, again, Iowa's corn harvest has a higher monetary value than all the wheat produced by Canada and Argentina combined.
>
> Iowa's production of wool surpasses the total amount of strawberries grown in California.
>
> The chickens in Iowa eat so much corn . . . that the production of eggs is worth more than California's total harvest of oranges, or all the metal taken out of Colorado's mines.
>
> More Percheron horses are bred in Iowa than "over there" and more Belgian horses than in Belgium.

The dinner was followed by festivities and singing led by Olaf. The dancing lasted until the lights were turned off around midnight. The next day the singers showed up at Olaf's house to express their appreciation and say farewell: "His home, which was located quite close to the business district, was one of those high quality mansions built about 40 years ago, elegant and comfortable. We admired the beautiful flora and the artistically arranged flower beds surrounding the house, which only a well trained gardener could have created. And that is exactly what Mr. Olesen is, as gardening was his first love."

To celebrate that seventy years had passed since the Norwegians had started their first male choruses in America, a chorus from Minneapolis traveled to Oslo in 1935. There they took part in a national song festival and performed in a concert together with three thousand Norwegian singers.[3]

The next year, the Norwegian Singers' Association of America held their *Sangerfest* in Duluth, Minnesota. The United Scandinavian Male Chorus of Iowa was welcomed and performed "Come to Iowa." This state song was sung in honor of O. M. Olesen, who had founded the Fort Dodge chorus half a century earlier. Olaf directed the Veteran Chorus, which had grown to sixty members, and they sang *Gud signe Norigs Land* by Oscar Borg. The *Grieg Mandskor* arranged a banquet with good food and drink, "fit for a royal Scandinavian family, hurra for Olesen." It was said that Olaf was in good health, and so he must have been as he and Julie were again preparing for a trip to Norway. Olaf was then the only one of his siblings still living, and he wanted to visit the graves of his brothers and sister. They went to New York first, however, where Julie had some of her paintings on display at the National American Exhibition.[4]

Olaf and Julie Visit Norway

In June of 1937 Olaf and Julie traveled on the *Stavangerfjord* on their final visit to Norway. Members of the family and a group of Rotarians had shown up when the ship from America docked in Oslo. Olaf and Julie checked in at the Astoria Hotel and hosted a lunch for the relatives at the capital's new and fashionable summer restaurant, *Dronningen* (the Queen), which was located on a bay in the Oslofjord.

In one of the newspapers Olaf noticed that the Norwegian opera singer Kirsten Flagstad was to hold an outdoor concert at the Frogner Stadium the next day. Two years earlier Kirsten Flagstad had made a sensational debut at the Metropolitan in New York. She had entered the stage as an unknown artist and left as a world star. Olaf wrote about the concert in Oslo in a letter to *Sanger-Hilsen*:

> At the last minute we were able to get ahold of two tickets. The stadium was filled up to the last seat—10,000 people. Outside, where one didn't have to pay, there were perhaps equally as many people. Loudspeakers had been set up and made it possible for them to listen to most of this magnificent concert, which is impossible to describe. She was called back on stage for encore after encore, and the singer was kind enough to accommodate the wishes for more songs.... Her brother conducted the large and splendid orchestra quite brilliantly. The King and Queen were there, in the first row.[1]

Soon afterward Kirsten Flagstad went back to America and became the main attraction at the Metropolitan, and thereby helped the institution avoid bankruptcy.

In Oslo, Olaf had a pleasant time with the lawyer Trygve Wegge and Dr. Einar Onsum, who both had taken part in the 1905 singers' tour of America. Olaf continued in his letter to *Sanger-Hilsen*,

From Oslo we drove northward and from Lillehammer we took a short trip to Aulestad, the old home of Bjørnstjerne Bjørnson. His son Erling and his daughter showed us the beautiful landscape and all the wonderful art objects Bjørnson and his wife had received on various occasions.

We went by train from Lillehammer to Trondhjem, where we stayed a few days to visit relatives. From there we went to Steinkjer and up to Kvam church, where I had been confirmed and where my father, my mother and three sisters are buried. Then back to Egge church, where Ola, "the king of the marksmen," is buried next to his wife. My oldest brother, Eilert, and his wife are buried in Steinkjer.

The Five farm, where I was born, is now owned by district governor Haakon Five, and he is a splendid man and an able farmer. What a wonderful view there is from the farm. One can look out over the beautiful lake Snåsavatnet and the surrounding district.

It is a sight for the gods![2]

Håkon Five was not related to Olaf. He took the name Five from the farm he lived on. In the days of Håkon Five, the farm was considered to be an estate. The old wooden red-painted Kvam church where Olaf had been confirmed had been torn down more than sixty years earlier. A stone monument had been erected where the church and an old pagan temple had stood. The new and larger Kvam church, painted white, was located a short distance away.

While he was at home at Kvam, Olaf was asked if he could help finance the building of a bridge over the lake, where the steamer *Bonden* operated as a ferry, but he declined and said that from now on he would rather spend his money in America where it had been earned.

Olaf most likely celebrated the Fourth of July in 1937 in Snåsa, a neighboring village, where the stone monument in honor of the famous emigrant and author Ole Rynning was unveiled. About three thousand people were present, many of them Norwegian Americans, and it was the largest gathering in the history of Snåsa. The Rynning monument was soon forgotten, however, "as he had been a socialist."[3]

Socialists and communists were regarded with suspicion by many,

Olaf and Julie at lake Snåsavatnet, at the Five farm, summer 1937. *Private collection*

both in Norway and in America. Home again in Fort Dodge, Olaf wrote an article for the local newspaper in which he summed up his thoughts after his political discussions with Norwegians. The situation in Europe was becoming more and more tense. Hitler had come to power in Germany, but Olaf was more concerned about the Russians. He thought the communists represented a threat both from the outside and internally in Norway, as they wanted to "transform private capital into organized capitalism and state capitalism." In Olaf's opinion there was even a risk for civil war in Norway since "the Norwegian Labor Party government was under the control of Moscow. . . . The Soviet Union had established large military garrisons in Murmansk with a train connection to Leningrad, prepared to expand towards northern Scandinavia. . . . The Soviets are working towards a world revolution."[4]

Olaf regretted that many Norwegians thought that by being un-armed, war might be avoided. "But a small country may live in peace only as long as the large neighbor allows it," Olaf pointed out, noting that the situation in 1905 had been different. At that time the whole country stood unified, ready for war, and the Swedes did not dare to attack. During the First World War, with commercial ties to both Germany and England, Norway was able to stay neutral. Now everything was different, he argued.

Not many weeks after Olaf returned to Fort Dodge, Ola's grandson Trond left Oslo to seek work in America. When he came ashore in New York, he witnessed two hundred thousand war veterans marching up Fifth Avenue, with a similar number of spectators. The veterans called on the US government not to join in a new war.

Olaf referred Trond to many of his business contacts, but in the end it turned out that the employment situation in the United States was even tougher than in Norway. To family in Norway, concerned about Olaf's own financial situation during the Depression, Trond wrote that Olaf "is about to offer in the order of $25,000 to help build a nursing home to be connected with the hospital he has contributed to earlier. So the guy is not broke." Olaf's home was in an idyllic location, Trond thought, but he complained that he found no opportunity to go ski-ing in Fort Dodge: "They need to import loads of rock from Norway to make the terrain more hilly. Now it is depressingly flat." Trond con-cluded that "America is fine in the sense that one does not feel like a foreigner—since everyone is more or less directly 'imported.'"[5]

Trond did not get any attractive job offers, so he returned to Nor-way. Not long after that, Olaf was also visited by two Norwegian grandnieces. The fact that Olaf, this much-discussed "rich uncle in America," was supposed to be so incredibly wealthy had created high expectations. But the two grandnieces received only a comb each before they returned to Norway.

In the fall, Olaf and Julie preferred the warmer climate on the West Coast to that of Fort Dodge. Thus Olaf missed the surprising event the other members of *Grieg Mandskor* experienced when their wives for the first time invited themselves to a meeting and rehearsal in Grieg Hall in the Oleson Drug Store. Nels Schreiber was the leader of the chorus and his wife had, quite unexpectedly, taken control. The ladies served good food and arranged party games, which everyone enjoyed. Olaf was not present either when *Grieg Mandskor* participated in the celebration of *Luren*'s seventieth anniversary in Decorah in March that year. But "In Flanders Fields" was sung and was "the evening's best number."[6]

The Oleson Park Music Pavilion

In 1938 Olaf had reached the age of eighty-nine and was no longer able to take care of his garden. He sold the house and together with Julie moved to a suite at the Wahkonsa Hotel. He gave his niece, Helen, and her son, Richard, some of the furniture. The nursing home at the Lutheran Hospital, which had just been finished with the help of Olaf's donation of $25,000, was pleased to receive his pipe organ.

Despite his age, Olaf's mind was still clear and he was able to write. The Norwegian-American Historical Association's board of editors, Dr. Theodore C. Blegen and Dr. Knut Gjerset, encouraged him to pen his memoirs. They wanted these to consist as much as possible of observations of people and of the conditions that impacted his life in business, church, and politics so as to preserve the impressions of an eyewitness to the many social and personal changes that had taken place over time in their society.

Olaf, however, responded by saying that he had already written a summary of his life, about half a page long. That would have to do. But he was willing to support people who wanted to write about what the Norwegians had achieved in America, for example by donating $1,000 to the Blegen Fund in NAHA so that Theodore Blegen could continue his work on the history of Norwegian immigrants, which so far ended with the Civil War. To honor Olaf, the historical association decided to hold its next meeting in Fort Dodge and at the same time to commemorate the important decision made in Norway on June 7, 1905.[1]

When the new music pavilion in Oleson Park was dedicated in the summer of 1938, Olaf was present. The pavilion was designed by the young architect Henry Kamphoefner and was described as a splendid example of Modern Movement Architecture. It was entirely cast in reinforced concrete with smooth-lined forms.[2]

All the thirty-five hundred seats were filled during the dedication, and thousands more stood on the grass or sat in their cars. About

The Oleson Park Music Pavilion, also called Oleson Park Bandshell, was dedicated on June 7, 1938. More than fifteen thousand were present at the opening concert, where Olaf directed "In Flanders Fields." The pavilion is today on the National Register of Historic Places. *Webster County Historical Society*

fifteen thousand showed up to celebrate Olaf, the donor of the park. He directed the *Grieg Mandskor* himself when they sang "In Flanders Fields." The public also celebrated the local composer and conductor of the city's orchestra, Karl L. King. Oleson Park Music Pavilion, or Oleson Park Bandshell, was from then on to be the home base of the Karl King Band. Olaf was quite proud of this, pointing to the fact that the United States had many big bands, but the Karl King Band was the one the musicians themselves prized the most. The dedication of the music pavilion was the largest celebration in the history of Fort Dodge, and the state of Iowa chose the pavilion as an example of state-of-the-art architecture for the New York World's Fair the following year.[3]

After the 1938 *Sangerfest* in Sioux Falls, South Dakota, thirty members of *Nordmennenes Sangforening* in Chicago traveled to Oslo. There they performed *Bådn-Låt*, *Gamle Norig*, and *Norge mit Norge* in the main hall of the university. Afterward, they were invited to a banquet at the *Oslo Militære Samfund* (Oslo Military Society).

The Chicago singers' visit to Norway was a reminder of the strong ties between Norway and America. At this time, the Norwegian Lutheran church in America started planning their centennial celebration. In 1843, the revivalist preacher Elling Eielsen from Voss had been ordained in Chicago as the first Norwegian pastor in America. Olaf donated $5,000 on the occasion of the anniversary, and the leader of the Norwegian Lutheran church in America, J. A. Aasgaard, wrote in *Lutheraneren* (the Lutheran Magazine) that he "hoped that other men and women of the church that are blessed with the means will be moved by the example of Mr. Oleson and offer substantial support to the centennial celebration."[4]

The goal was to collect $1 million for a centennial fund that would be used to pay off the church's debts. People supported this, and the amount was soon raised.

NORWEGIAN SINGERS' ASSOCIATION OF AMERICA

VETERAN CHORUS

The Veteran Chorus of the Norwegian Singers' Association of America during the *Sangerfest* in Sioux Falls, June 1938. Olaf in the first row, fifth from right. *Norwegian-American Collection, National Library of Norway*

The Norwegian Student Singers Visit Olaf Again

After having stayed in California during the winter, Olaf left earlier than usual in the spring of 1939. He was expecting visitors at his home in Fort Dodge. The chorus of the Norwegian Student Choral Society, which for the occasion was known as the Royal Norwegian University Chorus, was to follow the crown prince and princess on their US tour. The chorus had accepted an invitation from *Grieg Mandskor* to come to Fort Dodge, where they were going to give a concert that was not a part of the official program. Although none of the singers who had taken part in the political tour of 1905 were among this group, nevertheless, Olaf's name had an almost fairy-tale ring for the members of the current group.[1]

Europe was experiencing troubled times. Still, Crown Prince Olav and Crown Princess Märtha had decided to make this long-planned journey to the United States, and that convinced the fifty-three student singers to do the same. To create publicity for the coming event in Fort Dodge, the members of *Grieg Mandskor* gave concerts throughout Iowa, while Rev. Magnus Nordtvedt of St. Olaf Lutheran Church gave talks about the local chorus that Olaf had established half a century ago, about the *Sangerfests*, and about the cultural value of music. Even before the Norwegian student singers arrived, expectations were high and all concerts, including the one in Fort Dodge, were sold out.

Crown Prince Olav was the patron of the singers' tour, just as the Swedish crown prince had been in 1905. Carl Ludvig Bommen was president of the Norwegian Student Choral Society and Sigurd Tork- ildsen was director. Together with the royal couple, the singers arrived in New York on the *Oslofjord* on April 27, 1939. They were met by a fleet of small boats, flags and banners, brass bands, and Norwegian American choruses singing *Sønner av Norge* and *Ja, vi elsker*. The city was arranging the World's Fair with the slogan "Building the World of Tomorrow." Norway together with the Norwegian-American Historical Association had their own pavilion, and Crown Prince Olav presided over the official opening. This time the Norwegian sailing ship *Christian Radich* was featured, along with the Norwegian shipping, canning, aluminum, and hydroelectric power industries. Old architecture and Viking ships were now absent. The Norwegian student singers, bringing greetings from the thirty singers from 1905 who were still living, held a concert accompanied by the New York Philharmonic Orchestra. The repertoire included *Olav Tryggvason, Brudeferden i Hardanger, Gamle Norig*, and several Norwegian folk songs.

The Norwegian student chorus followed the royal couple to several university cities on the East Coast and on to the Midwest. In Chicago, they held a concert together with *Nordmennenes Sangforening* for an audience of thirty-six hundred people. Then they continued their journey across the prairie, with new concerts and banquets arranged by local Norwegian American choruses. Wreaths were laid at both the Wergeland Monument in Fargo and the Ole Bull Monument in Minneapolis.

Then the Norwegian student singers found time for a detour. On Sunday, May 7, at 1 o'clock the bus came to a halt outside the Wahkonsa Hotel in Fort Dodge, thirty-four years after the previous singers' tour and the student singers later wrote that

Fort Dodge, Iowa, was the only one of "our" cities which, along with the American university cities, was not included in the program of the royal couple.

Romantic reflections from the history of the town came to our minds just by the city's name. . . . But our dreams were soon swept away by a happening which was historical for the student singers. Outside the hotel stood none other than the now 89 year old O. M. Oleson together with *Grieg Mandskor*, exactly as they had welcomed the student singers 34 years earlier. Ever since that time, the name Oleson has had a certain fairytale ring to us singers. This was the man who had followed the chorus from city to city in order to be present at as many concerts as possible, and who had understood the singers so well, that when he arranged a big party for them in the "Oleson Drug Store" in Fort Dodge, he made it clear that there would be no speeches. He knew there had been enough of them.

There he was, together with *Grieg Mandskor* which he himself had established 50 years ago and which was still quite a good chorus, full of initiative. To create as much interest for our visit as possible, the chorus had been visiting cities around the area and holding concerts, which proved to be very valuable for us. At the front of the chorus stood the chairman of the committee, Amond Lyders, president Nels Schreiber and the long-time director, A. J. Moe, and they wished us welcome. The latter has played an important role among the local singers as he has also been director of the Webster Choral Union for many years, which every year performs no less than Händels Messiah. Dr. Roy M. Vieg was also there. He had been sent to Europe the previous year, where he paid a visit to Calle (Carl Ludvig Bommen) in Oslo. He thus made contact with the famous chorus and on this basis created fantastic promotional materials for the tour.

From the reception we went straight into the hotel, where we were seated around a nicely decorated table on the second floor as Mr. and Mrs. Oleson's guests. If Oleson had been a good host in 1905, he had not forgotten the art of it now, as was demonstrated by the dinner that followed. There were indeed speeches, but the whole thing was arranged so there was more pleasure in the visit itself than in what was said.

After a short welcome from Lyders, Rev. Nortvedt made a nice speech on behalf of those who had built a life for themselves out here. "Many of us are born here," he said, "but we can see you are Norwegians. You are sincerely welcome to our city and our homes."

Calle gave his thanks in English, and said that "we felt at home as soon as we arrived." And as for Olesen, whom we had heard so much about, we saw in him a good, old friend we had been away from just a few years.

And after we had done full justice to the soup, the ham and the apple pie, both we and *Grieg Mandskor* sang some songs,

among them *Den store hvide Flok* with Clausen as soloist.
From the walls of the hall the large group of singers from 1905 seemed to nod encouragingly to this reunion.[2]

The concert was held in the high school auditorium with an audience of twelve hundred, among them twenty people who had been present at the similar concert in the city in 1905 and who never tired of telling the story. The audience was as enthusiastic this time around. The *Fort Dodge Messenger & Chronicle* reported, "Many of the folk songs were robust, earthy humor but others were shot through with a touch of melancholy of the strange land from which they came."

The paper concluded that there had never been such an enthusiastic audience to any male chorus in Iowa. They had to sing some of the songs several times over. Olaf and Julie invited the Norwegian singers to dinner at the Wahkonsa Hotel, where they continued singing and held several speeches. The dinner was followed by a drive to see various places in the city, among them the Lutheran Hospital, before they ended up at Oleson Park, where the Norwegian singers held an evening concert and Olaf was applauded up onto the stage.

Everywhere the Norwegian student singers went "the halls were crammed full and the atmosphere jubilant." The Norwegian Constitution Day, May 17, was celebrated in Duluth, and on May 23 they boarded the liner *Bergensfjord*. Three months later, the Second World War broke out.

I Made My Fortune in America

The Norwegian student singers had left, but the celebration of Olaf continued during the summer of 1939, as he turned ninety on June 29. "He is lively, joyful and full of energy," the *Fort Dodge Messenger* wrote. A reporter had interviewed him while he was walking in Oleson Park with Julie and his niece Helen. He said, "What I have, was made here. It doesn't belong entirely to me, and I want the city to benefit by it."[1]

Officially, the estimate of what Olaf had given the city up until then amounted to about $500,000. It is not known what he had given to private individuals, local projects, and institutions. It most likely adds up to several million dollars, according to local historian Bob Jacobson. Olaf donated money to children, school projects, and people with limited means, and he offered loans which were never paid back. He donated large sums to Tobin College and the Young Men's Christian Association (YMCA). He did not deny that he made such donations, but he seldom told how much.[2]

Olaf had lived in Fort Dodge for seventy years, and he had seen the landscape change from prairie to farmland. The village of Fort Dodge had grown into a bustling city of about twenty-three thousand people, and Olaf was the last of the original Euro-American immigrants still alive. In interviews he said he believed in working hard but at the same time taking care of your health, and always looking on the bright side of things—never for problems. Once when asked to give advice to the younger generation, he said with a twinkle in his eye, "It doesn't do any good to offer advice. All the youngsters will grow up and take care of themselves."[3]

In earlier interviews he told the story about how sorry he was that he had to get rid of the nice green tie he had bought in Chicago before getting on the train to Fort Dodge for the first time. After that interview, many green ties were sent to him, and that pleased him.

One of Olaf's grandnephews, Ronald Fieve, remembered Olaf's

birthday party, which was held at the Wahkonsa Hotel with his family. It was obvious that age was taking its toll, as Olaf sat quietly most of the time. Julie was the one who kept the conversations going and made sure everybody had a good time.

The management at the Lutheran Hospital and the local Rotary club wanted to honor Olaf and threw a party where they praised him for his lifelong service in so many fields and for always following the motto of Rotary, "Service before Self." For his birthday the club gave him a newly published book, *The World Was My Garden: Travels of a Plant Explorer* by David G. Fairchild, an American botanist who, among other things, had introduced tropical plants into the United States. The hospital manager, Alvin Langehaug, handed Olaf a well-equipped travel bag— as they expected him to be out traveling again soon. Entertainment came in the form of music and singing and the pupils from the city's school for blind children demonstrated how to read and write by use of Braille. Perhaps Olaf's eyes were not so sharp anymore, either.

That year Olaf offered his collection of books on scientific topics, 230 volumes, to the Iowa State College of Agriculture and Mechanic Arts (now Iowa State University). And when the birthday celebration was over, Olaf sat down and wrote his will.

His niece Helen Oleson Welch was to get $10,000. Her brother, Oliver, was not mentioned in the will. It seemed as if Olaf did not have much faith in him. His nephews Bjarne and Torleif Fieve, who also had immigrated to America and were the sons of Olaf's oldest brother Eilert, were to get $5,000 each. Julie's sister, Rose Haskell Cattell, and her husband were to inherit the Oak Hill Farm, covering about 215 acres. The mortgage deeds to the Lutheran Hospital and YMCA were to be returned to the two institutions, respectively.[4]

The rest of his fortune was to be inherited by Julie, and she was free to do what she wanted with it. But if Julie died before him, then St. Olaf Lutheran Church would get $5,000. The remaining would go to Olaf's niece, Helen, "but, without any legal strings attached, I do hope she will spend some of it on educational or humanitarian institutions of her own choosing." The relatives in Norway were not mentioned in his will at all. Olaf had, however, just sent $1,500 to his grandnephew Trond, Ola Five's only grandchild.

Olaf had a large portfolio of shares in various companies. He owned

296 Fort Dodge Serum Company shares, which he had bought between 1912 and 1917. He had helped the founder of the company, the veterinarian D. E. Baughman, avoid going bankrupt and arranged for the laboratory to be moved to Fort Dodge. His shares in this company had at the time he wrote his will a value of $29,600 and constituted just a small part of his fortune. This would soon change, however.

During his winter stay in the Park Manor Hotel in San Diego, California, Olaf received word that the Germans had invaded Norway on April 9, 1940. The city of Steinkjer in Nord-Trøndelag was bombed, and a great part of it was turned to ashes, including the building called *Fivegården*, where his brother Eilert had lived the last years of his life. Among the many things lost was Eilert's diary, which he had written in for many years.

At the Norwegian Constitution Day celebration on May 17, 1940, Olaf was back in Fort Dodge and "In Flanders Fields" resounded over the city when he directed the Norwegian Singers' Association in Iowa during an outdoor concert. The song about the red poppies that blew between the trenches would soon resume its relevance for the Americans. In spite of the war, celebrations continued and the Norwegian American singers arranged their *Sangerfest* in Rockford, Illinois, in the summer of 1940. Olaf was there, "standing tall and proud among the second-basses" in the Veteran Chorus, now numbering eighty men. By acclamation it was decided that the chorus should be allowed to perform during the main concert, not just at the party afterward. Olaf said in his good-bye that "The songs were a joy and a pleasure to listen to. A sincere 'thank you' to the singers' association and to each and every one of the singers. Long may it live! The Norwegian Singers' Association!"[5]

This was to be the last *Sangerfest* Olaf took part in. He was not present at the fiftieth anniversary, which took place in Minneapolis in 1942. The celebration was presumably much reduced as the United States had by then begun playing an active role in the war.

The previous year, 1941, however, brought with it much festivity for Olaf. Helen's son, Richard, married Eloise Hurst, and as a wedding gift Olaf gave them a house. Olaf was also present at the fiftieth anniversary celebration for St. Olaf Lutheran Church. But in a way this anniversary became also the beginning of the end of the old church building. The congregation had grown to about seven hundred, and

Grieg Mandskor celebrating its fiftieth anniversary in 1941. First row from left: Amund Lyders, unknown, Ingebregt Dorheim, Olaf, unknown, Nels Schreiber, and Roy Vieg. Second row from left: unknown, unknown, unknown, unknown, Vevle, Moe, Fred Dorheim, unknown, Marvin Vieg, unknown, and unknown. *Webster County Historical Society*

they had purchased land for a new and larger church at the corner of Eleventh Street and Third Ave North. A few years later the old building was sold to the Calvary Baptist Group. The steeple was taken down, while the altar piece and the pipe organ, which Olaf had donated, were moved to the new, larger St. Olaf Lutheran Church.[6]

The *Grieg Mandskor* celebrated its fiftieth anniversary in 1941, and many representatives from the Norwegian Singers' Association of America came to take part. The grand master, Hjalmar Hansen, said in his speech during dinner that "The chorus provides companionship and education. It provides a practical lesson in democracy, for no matter how prominent or how lowly the individual members are, they are all brothers in the chorus. . . . It teaches you harmony not only in music but in life as well."[7]

On July 4, 1941, President Franklin Roosevelt spoke on the radio and said that this date should represent a lighthouse for the world in its fight for freedom. Little did he know that just a few months later, on December 7, Japan would bomb Pearl Harbor and the nation would be part of the war. A new generation of Americans would have their soldiers killed on the battlefield. Helen's son, Richard, was called up and fought in Africa and Europe. He was not wounded, but he did not return home until after the war. While he was away, Helen, her daughter-in-law Eloise, and her granddaughter Linda had eaten dinner every Sunday together with Olaf and Julie at the Wahkonsa Hotel.

Olaf and Julie in their living room. Probably the last picture taken of Olaf. *Private collection*

The *Stavangerfjord*, one of the Norwegian America Line's ships, was captured by the Germans and put to service on their side. The *Oslofjord* hit a mine off the English coast, while the *Bergensfjord* carried troops for the Allies all over the globe. It transported about 16,500 soldiers between America, Africa, India, and Europe.

Olaf's old business partner Thorvold S. Larsen died in a car accident during the war, at the age of seventy-one. He had been the manager of Oleson Drug Store and was highly respected in Fort Dodge. It was said that he ran the business the "old way." He did not want to sell things people did not need. He left behind his wife and five sons. The oldest son took over as manager of the company.[8]

A Monument to Olaf

Olaf did not live to see the coming of peace. He died on February 8, 1944, at the age of ninety-four, at the Lutheran Hospital in Fort Dodge. One of the men carrying the coffin out of the hospital to a simple, private ceremony was Olaf's old friend and political opponent, the lawyer Jonathan P. Dolliver, who had said that "Iowa will go Democratic when Hell goes Methodist." The funeral was conducted by the minister of Julie's congregation, the First Congregational Church. That the pastor from the St. Olaf Lutheran Church was not chosen for this occasion may indicate that Olaf no longer had a strong connection to this church. He was not buried in the St. Olaf Cemetery or the Oleson and Deming plot at the Oakland Cemetery, where his first wife, Lucy, and her parents lay. He had asked to be cremated, and the closest crematorium was in Des Moines.

Being cremated was highly unusual in the United States. The church was against it, regarding it as a pagan tradition and finding it inconsistent with the resurrection of the body. The right to cremation was, however, one of the things many of the Liberals in Norway had fought for and obtained in 1898. Julie brought Olaf's ashes back to Fort Dodge and spread them in Oleson Park, where spring would soon arrive, with white anemones carpeting the ground, just as they used to do back in Kvam at the same time of the year. Later there was to be a memorial service for Olaf. This did not happen for some time, however, as Julie wanted a special monument set up. She started to work on sketches immediately.

The year after Olaf died, his fortune was inventoried. It amounted to $630,376 and included two farms covering 371 acres, $526,564 worth of shares and bonds, plus other personal property valued at $33,105. Julie inherited all of this except what, according to his will, was to go to Helen, Torleif, and Bjarne, $20,000 altogether, one farm of about two hundred acres intended for Julie's sister, and the mortgage deeds of $24,512 in the Lutheran Hospital and $1,560 in the YMCA, which would go to the two institutions.[1]

The shares and the bonds Julie received were for the most part US bonds plus shares and bonds in Fort Dodge Telephone Company, Fort Dodge Hotel Company, the State Bank in Fort Dodge, Mitchell Investment Company, the Norwegian America Line, Rodenborn Manufacturing Company, and Renwick Savings Bank. None of these would increase in value like the 296 shares in the Fort Dodge Serum Company, which at that time were valued at $32,526. These were simply mentioned together with other minor investments Olaf had made in the Karl King Band, the Oston Fund, the Canadian Investment Company, the United Light and Railway Company, and Union Pacific Rail and the little he still held in the Oleson Drug Store.[2]

Even though Olaf's relatives in Norway were not mentioned in the will, Julie sent money to those she knew had fled to Sweden during the German invasion. And when the war was over, others were helped financially as well. Among them was Ola Five's grandson, Trond, who received in excess of $3,000 to establish his own engineering company. And Julie sent forty shares in the Norwegian America Line to each of Olaf's Norwegian nieces and nephews and a smaller number to each of their children. With these stock certificates in their hands, the Norwegian relatives were allowed to freely board the liners when they were docked. They were given guided tours and offered champagne.[3]

That same year the Fort Dodge Serum Company, which Olaf had always had such great faith in, became part of the international holding company American Home Products, which in turn owned the Wyeth pharmaceutical company. This is how Wyeth was introduced to veterinary medicine. The Fort Dodge Serum Company changed its name to Fort Dodge Laboratories, Inc., and each of the 296 shares was converted to 4½ shares in American Home Products. The value of the shares grew formidably, and Julie became an extremely wealthy woman. The expectations for a nice inheritance grew similarly among both her and Olaf's relatives.

On Sunday, September 5, 1948, a public memorial service for Olaf was arranged in Fort Dodge. Four years had passed since he died, and few people in the city actually remembered him. Most of his friends and business connections had been gone a long time. But the local newspaper referred to him as "The most public spirited citizen in Fort Dodge's long history," and his monument was unveiled in Oleson Park. It was designed by Julie, made by the local sculptor Clifton Adams, and cast by Olaf's friend A. M. Endahl.[4]

The monument, about eleven and a half feet high and ten feet wide, has on it a series of reliefs cast in concrete with light-colored sand showing six scenes from Olaf's life. They depict Olaf as a boy in Norway, as a young man driving oxen at the farm outside Fort Dodge, as a pharmacist, among his flowers, with his fellow singers, and as an old man with his books. A metal plaque tells what the reliefs depict. The monument also says "1849–1944 Olaf Martin Oleson donor of this park." The monument, surrounded by mature trees, is located in the southeastern part of the park, close to the large music pavilion.

Many representatives from the leadership of the Norwegian Singers' Association of America were present at the unveiling of the Oleson memorial monument, among them Erling Stone and Chris Christenson. The lawyer, Democrat, and Rotary member Seth Thomas from Fort Dodge gave the main speech, in which he emphasized Olaf's kindness. The *Grieg Mandskor* sang "In Flanders Fields," and the ceremony was followed by a dinner held at the Wahkonsa Hotel.

In Norway, Olaf's brother Ola had also been honored with a monument. In 1932 the Five monument had been erected on the Steinkjer parade ground in Nord-Trøndelag. The well-known Norwegian sculptor Dyre Vaa had made a portrait medallion for the installation. The monument was later moved to the rifle range at Steinkjer. Both brothers had roads named after them, Oleson Park Avenue in Fort Dodge and *Ola Fives veg* in Steinkjer.[5]

Julie Haskell Oleson lived for twenty-one years after Olaf died. During that time she kept in close contact with Olaf's relatives both in America and in Norway, and she continued to bequeath portions of her large fortune. One relative, for instance, had help in paying for his education at Harvard. But many of Olaf's Norwegian relatives were still waiting for the great American inheritance. Julie died on December 12, 1965, at the age of ninety-six. She had asked to be cremated and her ashes spread in Oleson Park, as had been done for Olaf.

Julie left a fortune of more than $2.7 million. There were $2.5 million in shares, of which American Home Products constituted about

The Oleson Memorial, designed by Julie and constructed by Clifton Adams. Located in Oleson Park, beside the bandshell. *Private collection*

$2.1 million. After Olaf died, the value of his investment in the veterinary pharmaceutical laboratory had increased 6,030 percent (before adjustment for inflation).[6]

In addition to Rolf N. Larsen, who had run the Oleson Drug Company after his father Harold Larsen died, Julie included both her and Olaf's relatives in her will. But she left the major part of her fortune, $2.1 million, to the Lutheran Hospital, which by then had changed its name to Bethesda General Hospital. The donation came as a total surprise to the hospital's management.[7]

Many of Olaf's relatives, both in America and in Norway, were shocked and angry. They felt cheated by Julie. Some of them excused her by saying that she did not understand the size of her fortune, as she had been suffering from dementia in the final years of her life. But though she had been generous to Olaf's relatives both during her life with him and in all the years afterward, she had decided to follow what she felt had been Olaf's spirit. Her donation was for the best of the people in the Fort Dodge area, eventually uniting them regardless of religious differences. Some years after Julie's death, the Oleson Foundation was established to administer the money given by Olaf and Julie for the benefit of the patients and the hospital's employees. The foundation later decided that patients at the St. Mercy Catholic hospital in Fort Dodge were also to be included among the beneficiaries. This generosity led to a closer cooperation between the management of the two hospitals and finally resulted in Trinity Hospital, one large hospital that replaced the two. It was finished eighty years after Olaf had cut through political and religious conflicts in Fort Dodge and made the citizens agree to build a new hospital, even though it was run by Catholic nuns.

Some of the revenue from the foundation is still used to buy up-to-date equipment to make life easier for patients and to further educate employees. Now, however, one of the main uses for the funds is running a hospice, where patients in their last phase of life can live together with their families.

Olaf Leaves a Legacy

Olaf's life and achievements were just the start of a story with important aftereffects. The value of what he and Julie donated, both when they lived and through their wills, is one thing. Of more obvious value to us is the use of these donations over time. Their generosity supported hospitals, parks, pharmaceutical development, veterinary medicine, the collection and preservation of the history of Norwegian emigration to America, cultural connections to Norway, and the joy of singing.

The Norwegian Singers' Association of America is still keeping up the tradition with a three-day *Sangerfest* every other year. The concerts are hosted in turn by cities in the Midwest. Large concert halls are filled to the brim, and soloists and local symphony orchestras are hired for the occasion.

The 2010 festival was arranged in Madison, Wisconsin, on June 24–26, with the concert held in the Overture Hall in the Overture Center for the Arts, equipped with a ten-thousand-pipe organ. Prior to the main concert there was a remembrance of those members who had passed away since the previous festival. The participants sang *Den Store, Hvide Flok* by Grieg.

Later each chorus came on stage, one by one, and gave a performance. These included the Edvard Grieg Chorus from Madison, Bjornson Male Chorus from Chicago, Minnehaha Mandskor from Sioux Falls, *Grieg Mandskor* from Canton, Nordic Male Chorus from Sioux City, Luren Singing Society from Decorah, Nordmennenes Singing Society from Chicago, Norwegian Glee Club from Minneapolis, Harmony Singing Society from Rockford, Norse Glee Club from Sioux Falls, and the Veteran Chorus. They were accompanied by a pianist dressed in a Norwegian national costume. The audience could hear, among other songs, *Held dig, Norge vort fædreland, Husker du den gang i måne-*

skinn, Jeg lagde meg så silde, Å bære vatn og bære ved, and *La oss leve for hverandre.*

For the main concert, the Wisconsin Chamber Orchestra and soloists were hired to participate. The joint chorus, numbering one hundred men, started with *Ja, vi elsker* and "The Star-Spangled Banner," followed by several American and Norwegian songs. Among the Norwegian songs were *Vårt fødeland* arranged by Ann Kilstofte, *So skal jenta have det* by Arne Eggen, *Vuggesang i mørketid* by Christian Sinding, and *Våren, Anitras dans, Solveigs sang, Norsk dans*, and *Bådn-Låt* by Edvard Grieg. Then *Vi er sangere* by Finn Skotter and Reidar Rinnan. As usual, the concert ended with Grieg and Bjørnson's *Landkjenning*. At the reception the members of the Luren Singing Society received wild applause when singing the folk song *Kjerringa med staven*. The next day there was a banquet plus various activities for the singers at different locations in the city.

The Norwegian Singers' Association of America visited Norway in 2005 in order to participate in the centennial of the dissolution of the union with Sweden. They gave an outdoor concert at Akershus Fortress in Oslo and toured to Lillehammer, Flåm, Sognefjord, Haugesund, Stavanger, and Trondheim.

In 2012 the *Sangerfest* was held in St. Charles, Illinois, in 2014 in Minneapolis, Minnesota, and in 2016 in Sioux Falls, South Dakota.

Both the Lutheran Hospital (later called Bethesda General Hospital), which Olaf had saved from bankruptcy during the Depression, and the Catholic Mercy Hospital, which also received help from Olaf, benefited financially from the Oleson Foundation. This connection finally led to one joint hospital, the Trinity Regional Hospital, which today serves the entire area. The Oleson Foundation constitutes the main part of what is called the Trinity Health Foundation, while all the others who support the foundation become members of the Oleson Society.

The Oleson Block, where the Oleson Drug Store was located, no longer exists. The building was demolished in 1971 to make way for a parking lot. The pharmacy was sold out of the Larsen family, but pharmaceutics remained one of the largest industries in Fort Dodge.

Banners decorated the stage during the
Sangerfest in Madison, Wisconsin, 2010.
Private collection

The St. Olaf Norwegian Lutheran Church building, which Olaf was instrumental in financing in Fort Dodge, was later replaced by a larger church building, the St. Olaf Lutheran Church. Even though the congregation is no longer Norwegian, each autumn a festival takes place where Norwegian traditions are featured. Norwegian food, handmade products, books, and cards are sold and a meatball dinner is served. There are a number of churches, chapels, and altars around the world that are named for the patron saint of Norway, but most of them are Catholic. Today there are several St. Olaf churches in the United States, among them the church in Fort Dodge and one in Austin, Minnesota. The building which used to be St. Olaf Norwegian Lutheran Church in Fort Dodge is today called Coppin Chapel and belongs to the African Methodist Episcopal Church.

Olaf's large herbarium, his plant library, the Oleson Collection, comprising twenty-three thousand species he had collected through the Fort Dodge Botanical Club, was given in 1948 to the Ada Hayden Herbarium at Iowa State University.

Olaf's collection of books, numbering about 230 volumes, mainly on scientific topics and most of them first editions, was given to Iowa State University in 1939.

The tradition of singing is still strong along the shore of the lake Snåsavatnet, much as it used to be 160 years ago. There are both male and mixed choruses.

Kvam's home for old people has moved to a new building. The original, which Olaf helped fund, now houses the *Kvam Historielag*.

The Ole Rynning Monument, which was erected in Snåsa in 1937 to honor the author of the *True Account of America*, was soon forgotten. In 1982 it was rediscovered by local historian Joralf Gjerstad, who is well known in Norway as a clairvoyant and for having healing hands.

The Sundnes estate at Inderøya, which many believe to be the oldest and most beautiful farm in Nord-Trøndelag and worthy of being listed as a historical site, is again in private hands. The Norwegian Nils J. Aune from Nord-Trøndelag came home from America in 1950 with his wife and daughter after having farmed in North Dakota for forty years. He bought the farm when the children's home, which had been located there, was closed down, and the family started restoring the old buildings and the garden.

Øventyr og sagn and *Hollraøventyra* were published in 1910 with the support of Olaf and the American *Trønderlaget*. The stories were collected by Karl Braset from Sparbu and illustrated by Einar Øfsti. Ninety years later they were mentioned in the yearbook of *Nord-Trøndelag Historielag*:

> If Oleson and Trønderlaget had not taken this step, both Trøndelag and Norway would have been much poorer. For, as the previous leader of the Nordic Institute of Folklore at Åbo University in Finland, Reimund Kvideland, wrote in a letter to *Sparbu Historielag* in 1966, "Braset is today thought to be the best and the most accurate collector of folk tales in the country. Just after the books were published the farmhouse at the Braset farm burned down, and the original manuscripts and most of the 1000 copies which had been printed were lost. This makes the remaining copies very rare. There are probably more available in the United States than in Norway."

The National Trønderlag of America was originally an organization of fifteen local clubs. In 1966 there were so few present at the gatherings that they decided to end its existence. In 1992, however, a group of people in Dawson, Minnesota, found that it was time to reestablish the organization. The name was changed to Trønderlaget of America in 1999.

The O. M. Oleson House, the home of Olaf and Julie on Third Avenue South, is still a private residence. It is one of fourteen houses in the Oak Hill Historic District of Fort Dodge, an area stretching from Eighth Street to Twelfth Street and from Second Avenue South to Third Avenue South. The area is listed on the National Register of Historic Places.

The gardens do not have as many flowers as in Olaf's day. But there are still flower beds, steps, paths, stone sculptures, and trees planted by Olaf, which now seem to be standing guard over the house and land with their large trunks and wide branches.

The Wahkonsa Hotel is also listed on the National Register of Historic Places. The building is no longer a hotel, but is divided into luxurious apartments for seniors. Much of the interior in the large lobby is as it was originally. Several old photographs and menus decorate the walls in one of the lounges.

The Norwegian-American Historical Association, NAHA, is located at St. Olaf College in Northfield, Minnesota. The association's large archives contain an extensive manuscript collection as well as many photographs and other resources related to the history of Norwegians in America. NAHA has an active publication program, with more than one hundred books to its credit. An independent organization in Norway which cooperates with NAHA in the United States, *NAHA-Norge,* arranges seminars and publishes their proceedings. A joint seminar was arranged for the first time during the summer of 2011 at Luther College in connection with the college's celebration of 150 years since its founding.

The Fort Dodge Serum Company, later called Fort Dodge Laboratories, became part of Wyeth and American Home Products in 1945. Due to lack of good air transportation, the headquarters was moved to Kansas in 1995, but the laboratories, which then had about 750 employees, stayed in Fort Dodge. It was the city's largest employer and one of the world's largest suppliers of medicine and vaccines for animals. Several changes in ownership and organization have taken place. Pfizer owns the laboratory today, and plans to close it even though it has been one of the most important businesses in the city for around a hundred years.

The foundation *Minnegaven til Norge 1914 fra det norske utflytterfolk i Nord-Amerika* was dissolved in 2001. In the period between 1920 and 2000, more than 1.9 million kroner was offered to people who were in undeserved distress. The board's representatives from the Norwegian government decided to donate the remainder of the foundation's capital to the Migration Museum near Hamar, seventy miles north of Oslo. This was done even though Olaf and the donors had insisted on statutes saying that the basic capital should never be touched. The Migration Museum spent much of the donation on building and restoring an immigrant church. The church was originally built by the Norwegian Ole Haraldsen on a hill just outside the city of Houston, Minnesota. The Oak Ridge congregation was dissolved in 1967 and the church was given to the Migration Museum. It was consecrated in 2002 as the Norwegian Emigrant Memorial Church.

The Oleson-Deming family plot at Oakland Cemetery also serves as a grave site for Olaf's nephew Oliver Oleson and his wife, Ida, as it had for Olaf's first wife, Lucy, her parents, and others of the Deming family. The Oakland Cemetery is listed on the National Register of Historic Places.

Olaf owned several farms, among them Oak Hill Farm. It covered forty acres planted to corn and soybeans. In 1997 the farm was sold by descendants of Olaf's niece, Helen.

Leif Erickson Park is still a popular playground for children, while there is not much left of what was once Haskell Park.

Oleson Park includes a large grassy area where the Oleson Park Bandshell is located, as well as a playground, a small zoo, a picnic area, woods with large old trees, paths, flat areas, wildflowers, and a valley with the remains of an old concrete bridge. Deer, rabbits, and cardinals may be seen there. The nursery, where people could buy flowers to plant in the park, is gone.

Grieg Mandskor has been dissolved, but music may still be heard from the Oleson Park Bandshell.

The Oleson Park Bandshell is listed on the National Register of Historic Places. Every Sunday afternoon in the summer the city band, the Karl King Band, gives a free outdoor concert.

At the concert on Sunday, June 20, 2010, people came in great numbers, as usual. Some sat down on the grass, others brought folding chairs, as my third cousin Barbara Welch Peterson and I had done. The old concrete benches, which had been there during our great-granduncle's days, had been removed. Other listeners sat in their cars. A charitable organization sold cakes and ice cream, and children ran around and played. The conductor welcomed everyone to Oleson Park before the orchestra started to play. When the applause after the last piece had faded away and the sun was about to disappear, an eagle could be seen floating above the top of the old trees in Olaf's park.

Acknowledgments

Many have helped me in my work with this book project. I especially want to thank Dina Horneman Tolfsby, who until retirement in 2013 was head of the Norwegian-American Collection at the National Library of Norway. She was the one who encouraged me to write this book. She also provided much of the source material and has been an inspiring conversational partner throughout the project. In the United States, the late Robert Allen (Bob) Jacobson at the Webster County Historical Society collected local information for me to use. He also guided me to the historical sites in Fort Dodge in June 2010. My third cousin Barbara Welch Peterson and her mother, Eloise Hurst Welch, received me with open arms and supplied me with narrative information in addition to family photographs and old newspaper articles. Roger B. Natte, director of the Webster County Historical Society, has been a key person in establishing contacts. In Norway, Knut Djupedal, director of the Migration Museum (earlier the Norwegian Emigrant Museum), has been my professional historical adviser, as he also was with my previous book *Kavaleristen* (The Cavalryman), about another Norwegian who immigrated to the United States. I owe Carol and Leif Tronstad at the Sundnes estate, Inderøya, many thanks for their hospitality and for all the information they gave me about the farm and its history.

While doing research I made contact with many of my distant relatives, including Aase Marksten, Gudrun Lise Larsen, Ingrid Langhammer Pettersen, and Ole Øyen in Norway and Ronald Fieve in New York. Other helpful contacts have been Roger Lyngstad, previously head of *Kvam Historielag* and now leader of the chorus *Kor Som É*; Marit Danielsen, landscape architect in Nord-Trøndelag; Yngve Torud, head of *Norsk Farmasihistorisk Selskap*; Annegreth Dietze-Schirdewahn, senior scientific officer at the *Institutt for landskapsplanlegging* at the University of Life Sciences in Ås; Richard Leake, recording secretary at the Norwegian Singers' Association of America; Rolf Valle, contact

person at *Den norske Studentersangforening*; and Anne Jorunn Kydland, research manager at the National Library of Norway, who found
many exciting old newspaper articles from the student singers' America tours.

Especially warm thanks go to my family, my daughter, Monica, who
has been a helpful listener and has made many enriching suggestions;
my daughter-in-law, Anette, for thoughtful evaluation of the manuscript; my son, Marius, for invaluable technical help in the editing
phase; my son-in-law, Lars, for designing the cover of the Norwegian
edition and for creating the layout of my home page; and Roald, my
beloved husband, for having accompanied me both to the Five farm
and the Sundnes estate in Nord-Trøndelag, to Fort Dodge where my
great-granduncle, O. M. Oleson, lived for more than seventy years, and
to Madison, Wisconsin, where the Norwegian Singers' Association of
America arranged their *Sangerfest* in June 2010.

And finally I thank professor emeritus Odd Lovoll at St. Olaf College, Northfield, Minnesota, for encouraging me to have the book published in the United States. He guided me to the Minnesota Historical
Society Press, where I was welcomed.

Notes

Epigraph: Cai, "Iowa Impromptu," 176.

Notes to "Radicals"

1. Den norske Studentersangforening, *Vestover igjen*. Regarding the Five farm and the family: Five, "Fiveslekta fra omkring år 1500 til omkring 1900"; Nordgård, *Stod i fortid og nutid*; Aarset, *Skyttergeneralen*.
2. Sandnes, ed., *Snåsavatnet, natur, kultur, historie*.
3. Memories from the childhood at the Five farm: Five, "Dagligt liv i Stod ikring midten av fyrre hundreåret. Eit yversyn," Nord-Trøndelag Historielag, *Årbok*, 1925; Aarset, *Skyttergeneralen*.
4. Nelson, ed., *History of the Scandinavians*, 266.

Notes to "From Inderøya to the Palace"

1. Aarset, *Skyttergeneralen*.
2. Regarding gardening in Norway: Foss, ed., *Nord Trøndelag Landbruksselskap*; Dietze, "Garden Art and the Bourgeoisie"; Annegreth Dietze, e-mails and conversations, 2009; Marit Danielsen, landscape architect in Nord-Trøndelag, e-mails, 2009; Åsen, "Tusenårshagen."
3. Foss, ed., *Nord-Trøndelag Landbruksselskap*, 62. Most of the information about the Sundnes estate I have received through conversations with Carol and Leif Tronstad, Sundnes, 2011.
4. Most of the information about Peter Lorange I have received through an interview with Benedicte Lorange, Store Stabekk, 1980.

Notes to "Ole Rynning's *True Account of America*"

1. Hanssen, *Bli med en tur over 'dammen.'*
2. Neuman, "Hyrdebrev med varselord til utvandringslystne bønder i Bergen stift."

Notes to "Establishing Fort Dodge"

1. *Norsk biografisk leksikon* (The Norwegian Biographic Dictionary).
2. Natte, *Fort Dodge, 1850–1970*.
3. Bob Jacobson, e-mail, 2010.
4. Brown, *Begrav mitt hjerte ved Wounded Knee*.

Notes to "Churches, Choruses, and Homes"

1. The writer's name was Iversen: Knudsen, "The Norwegian Male Chorus Movement," 51.
2. Knudsen, "The Norwegian Male Chorus Movement," 175.
3. Regarding the Norwegian singers' first years in America: *Biographical History of La Crosse*; Hansen, "Det Norske Foreningsliv i America"; Knudsen, "The Norwegian Male Chorus Movement."
4. Jacobson, "St. Olaf Church," in "Olaf Martin Oleson."

Notes to "Only a Dollar in His Pocket"

1. Riksarkivet (Norwegian Historical Data Centre), emigrant lists.
2. Regarding Olaf's first years in Fort Dodge: "Reminiscences," *Fort Dodge Messenger*, February 10, 1944; Hayden, "Olaf Martin Oleson"; "An Iowa Philanthropist," *Fort Dodge Messenger*, 1939; Natte, *Fort Dodge, 1850–1970*.

Notes to "The Singers' Associations"

1. Regarding the Norwegian singers' first years in America: Chicago foreign language press survey, Norwegian (microform), online; Hansen, "Det Norske Foreningsliv i America"; Knudsen, "Utklippssamling—Musikk."
2. Oleson, "Den første norske Mandskvartet i Fort Dodge, Iowa," *Sanger-Hilsen*, 25th Anniversary (1934).
3. Regarding Ola Five and "Folkevæpningen" (People's Arms Association): Aarset, *Skyttergeneralen*.

Notes to "Get Rich with Pharmacy"

1. Regarding Norwegian and American pharmacy history: Yngve Torud, head of Norsk Farmasihistorisk Selskap, e-mails, 2009.
2. Regarding Olaf's time as student at Philadelphia College: *Journal of the American Pharmaceutical Association* 17.3 (March 1929): 207–10; Nelson, ed., *History of the Scandinavians*, 265–66; Nordmanns-Forbundet, *Årbok*, 1927.

Notes to "Omaha and Leadville"

1. Jacobson, "The Drugstore Job that Changed His Life," in "Olaf Martin Oleson"; *Sanger-Hilsen* (1936).
2. "Commissioner of Pharmacy," State Institutions, Iowa Official Register (1882), 49.

Note to "Old Remedies"

1. Sunde, "Agerbrugsbog."

Notes to "Bjørnstjerne Bjørnson and Kristofer Janson in the Midwest"

1. Kaartvedt, "Kampen mot parlamentarismen"; Aarset, *Skyttergeneralen.*
2. Regarding Kristofer Janson: Draxten, *Kristofer Janson in America.*
3. Bj. Bjørnson to Karoline, St. Paul, January 17, 1881.
4. Bj. Bjørnson to Karoline, Fort Dodge, March 19, 1881. 1 speciedaler is equal to 0.5 US dollar today.
5. Oleson to Waldemar Ager, November 25, 1919.
6. Draxten, *Kristofer Janson in America.*
7. Aarset, *Skyttergeneralen*; Bj. Bjørnson to Ola Five, April 3, 1890; "Skytternes Marseillaise"— "Opsang til norske skytterlag," published in Norway October 15, 1881.

Notes to "Uproar from Norway Reaches across the Atlantic"

1. Aarset, *Skyttergeneralen.*
2. *Budstikken*, December 1, 1883.
3. Kaartvedt, "Kampen mot parlamentarismen," refers to *Morgenbladet*, January 28, 1883, 27A; Aarset, *Skyttergeneralen.*
4. *Budstikken*, May 30, 1883.
5. Hansen, "Det Norske Foreningsliv i Amerika," 276; *Folkebladet* 187 (1883); *Skandinaven*, January 8, 1884.

Notes to "The Norwegian-American Liberal Society"

1. *Budstikken*, January 7 and February 12, 1884
2. *Budstikken*, January 22, 1884.
3. *Budstikken*, February 19, 1884.
4. Lovoll, "1905 og norsk-amerikanerne."
5. *Budstikken*, February 19, 1884.
6. Aarset, *Skyttergeneralen.*
7. *Budstikken*, February 19 and May 13, 1884.
8. Nordgård, *Stod i fortid og nutid.*
9. Wist, ed., *Norsk-Amerikanernes Festskrift*; Hansen, "Det Norske Foreningsliv i Amerika."
10. Mjeldheim, *Folkerørsla som vart parti.*
11. Mjeldheim, *Folkerørsla som vart parti.*
12. Brøndal, *Ethnic Leadership and Midwestern Politics*, 111.

Notes to "Music Rings Out in Chicago"

1. *Budstikken*, January 1886.
2. The essential parts about the Scandinavian and Norwegian Singers in America, here and in the next chapter, are taken from "Sangerfest" programs and the magazine *Sanger-Hilsen*. Permission to use these two sources is granted by the Norwegian Singers Association of America. Hansen, "Norsk Musik i Amerika" (1907); Hansen, "Norsk musikk i Amerika" (1903); Knudsen, "The Norwegian

Male Chorus Movement"; Knudsen, "Utklippssamling—Musikk"; Ulvestad, ed., *Nordmændene i Amerika*; Wist, ed., *Norsk-Amerikanernes Festskrift*; Hansen, "Det Norske Foreningsliv i Amerika"; Berg, "Sang og Musikkliv."

Notes to "More Male Choruses Are Formed"

1. *Sanger-Hilsen* 6 (1936).
2. *Sanger-Hilsen* 7 (1923).

Notes to "Olaf Helps Establish a Church"

1. Tomlinson, ed., *A Century of Blessings*; "Norwegian Lutherans Build New Church," *Fort Dodge Messenger*, June 20–26, 1894; Jacobson, "St. Olaf Church," in "Olaf Martin Oleson."
2. Jacobson, "The Drugstore Job that Changed His Life," in "Olaf Martin Oleson."
3. Jacobson, "Olaf Martin Oleson."
4. Nøvik, *Iakttagelser i Amerikas Havebrug.*
5. The stave church, called Thams Pavilion, was built by the Norwegian company Thams & Co. The private owner decided to sell the church and in 2015 the project *Heimatt* ("Returning Home") was established by Norwegian enthusiasts to bring the church back to Orkanger, Sør-Trøndelag, the hometown of Thams, where it originally was constructed.
6. Semmingsen, "Amerikapenger," *Veien mot Vest*, 2:455; *Morgenbladet*, January 31, 1904, and January 22, 1908; *Aftenposten*, February 25 and April 21, 1906; *Dagbladet*, January 17, 1913; "Utvandringskomiteens innstiling II," appendix 4; *Bergens Annoncetidende*, February 26, 1916; *Poststatistikken 1925* (Nordmanns-Forbundet, *Årbok*, 1925).

Notes to "Olaf Declines to Run for Congress"

1. Nelson, ed., *History of the Scandinavians*, 265–66.
2. Olaf was elected again in 1932 from the Webster and Calhoun district as the only Democrat. He did not seek the office. "An Iowa Philanthropist."
3. Brøndal, *Ethnic Leadership and Midwestern Politics*; regarding no Norwegian-born Democrats in the US Congress, main sources for this conclusion are Lovoll, *Det løfterike landetd*; US Congress, online; Wist, ed., *Norsk-Amerikanernes Festskrift*; Wong, ed., *Norske Utvandrere og Forretningsdrivende i Amerika.*

Notes to "Department Store, Church, and Matrimony"

1. Regarding the St. Olaf Lutheran Church: Tomlinson, ed., *A Century of Blessings*; St. Olaf Lutheran Church, "The Golden Jubilee"; Jacobson, "St. Olaf Church," in "Olaf Martin Oleson."
2. "The Oleson Drug Company," *Fort Dodge Messenger*, August 26, 1971.
3. Jacobson, "Lucy Deming Merrit," in "Olaf Martin Oleson;" obituaries in local newspapers, August 1904.

Notes to "Olaf Contacts Bjørnson and Grieg"

1. Oleson to Bj. Bjørnson, February 14, 1896.
2. Cai, "Iowa Impromptu," 167, 168.
3. Nordmanns-Forbundet, *Årbok*, 1927. Regarding Oleson, Bjørnson, and Grieg: Cai, "A Missed Opportunity for Grieg"; Cai, "Iowa Impromptu," 150–76; Fog, Grinde, and Norheim, *Edvard Grieg*, 453; Arvid O. Vollsnes, ed., *Studia Musicologica Norvegica* 25 (1999): 226–35; Norsk Musikkhistorisk arkiv, Edward Grieg, National Library of Norway.
4. Cai, "Iowa Impromptu," 176.
5. Hummeland, "The Norwegian National League."
6. *Sanger-Hilsen* 8 (1927).

Notes to "War Drums Beat"

1. Aarset, *Skyttergeneralen*.
2. Cursin, "Centennial of the Spanish-American War"; Aarset, *Kavaleristen*.
3. Hurley, "Swish of the Kris"; Aarset, *Kavaleristen*.
4. *New York World*, October 6, 1900; Aarset, *Kavaleristen*.

Notes to "Olaf's American Landscape Park"

1. Oleson and Somes, "A Flora of Webster County."
2. Jacobson, "Olaf Oleson the Botanist," in "Olaf Martin Oleson."
3. "Fort Dodge Gets Park Thru Generosity of Citizen," *Fort Dodge Messenger*, March 2, 1905; "Take a Trip to Oleson Park," *Fort Dodge Messenger*, April 20, 1905; Jacobson, "Olaf Oleson the Botanist," in "Olaf Martin Oleson."

Notes to "Olaf Supports Norwegian American Writers"

1. Oleson to W. Ager, November 20 and December 2, 1912.
2. Oleson to W. Ager, November 20 and December 2, 1912, February 5, 1918, November 24, 1919, December 27, 1931, and December 17, 1936.

Note to "Lucy Dies"

1. Regarding the hospital: Trinity Regional Medical Center, "A Legacy of Caring"; Natte, *Fort Dodge, 1850–1970*; Jacobson, "Hospitals of Fort Dodge," in "Olaf Martin Oleson."

Note to "The Norwegian Student Choral Society Tours America"

1. The essential details about the Norwegian Singers tour are taken from Den norske Studentersangforening, *Den norske Studentersangforenings koncerttourné* and *Utklippsbind fra Den norske Studentersangforenings*. Permission to use these two sources is granted by Den norske Studentersangforening.

Note to "Norwegian Independence Celebrated at the Oleson Drug Store"

1. *Den norske Studentersangforenings koncerttourné.*

Notes to "A Tribute to Norway"

1. *Den norske Studentersangforenings koncerttourné.*
2. *Verdens Gang* 173 (June 23, 1905).
3. Hummeland, "The Norwegian National League"; Lovoll, "1905 og norsk-amerikanerne."

Notes to "The Norwegian Chorus Meets President Roosevelt"

1. Oleson to the Norwegian Singers, telegram, May 6, 2005; "Utklippsbind fra den norske Studenterforenings"; *Fort Dodge Messenger,* 1948.
2. *Den norske Studentersangforenings koncerttourné.*
3. Hagtvedt, "Unionsoppløsningen i 1905"; Aarset, *Skyttergeneralen.*
4. Hummeland, "The Norwegian National League."
5. Semmingsen, "Amerikapenger," *Veien mot Vest,* 454–59; *Morgenbladet,* January 31, 1904, and January 22, 1908; *Aftenposten,* February 25 and April 21, 1906; *Dagbladet,* January 17, 1913; "Utvandringskomiteens innstiling II, bilag 4," *Bergens Annoncetidende,* February 26, 1916; *Poststatistikken 1925* (Nordmanns-Forbundet, *Årbok,* 1925).
6. Lovoll, "1905 og norsk-amerikanerne."
7. Den norske Gleeklub, "Minnesota-Korets Norgesfærd 1923."

Notes to "The National Trønderlag of America"

1. Tolfsby, "Nordmanns-Forbundet feirer sitt 100-års jubileum."
2. Oleson to Birger Osland, March 2, 1927.
3. Regarding the first years of the National Trønderlag of Amerika (*Det Nationale Trønderlaget i Amerika*), the National Trønderlag of Amerika, *Årbok,* 1909, 1910. Nord-Trøndelag Historielag, *Årbok,* 2000.
4. Sartz, "Fra Amerikas Nordmænd."
5. Bjerkrem, "Trønderlaget i Amerika"; Tømmerås, "Øventur, Sagn av Karl Braset."
6. Nord-Trøndelag Historielag, *Årbok,* 1912.

Notes to "Olaf Marries the Richest Girl in Town"

1. Jacobson, "Julie Haskell Oleson," in "Olaf Martin Oleson."
2. Jacobson, "The Oleson Home," in "Olaf Martin Oleson"; Marie H. Grunwald, "The O. M. Oleson Home," *Fort Dodge Today,* Historical Sites, Fort Dodge Public Library; "Noted Philanthropist and Pioneer Pharmacist Lived in this F.D. Home," *Fort Dodge Today,* December 30, 1972, Historical Sites, Fort Dodge Public Library.

3. Jacobson, "Julie Haskell Oleson," in "Olaf Martin Oleson"; "Work of Art Guild Members Receives Wide Recognition," January 27, 1940; "In Art Circles Here During Past Summer," October 28, 1933; "Local Artist in Iowa Art Show in Sioux City"; "Local Artists' Exhibit Merits Much Praise," in Julie Haskell Oleson collection, Webster County Historical Society.
4. Article supplied by Eloise H. Welch; Eloise H. Welch, communication, 2010.
5. Most of the information comes from Jacobson, "A Man of Business," in "Olaf Martin Oleson."
6. Jacobson, "Julie Haskell Oleson," in "Olaf Martin Oleson."

Note to "The Wahkonsa Hotel"

1. Jacobson, "Olaf Martin Oleson."

Notes to "The Norwegian America Line"

1. Most of the information about Den Norske Amerikalinje: Hambro, *Amerikaferd*; Vea, Schreiner, and Seland, *Den Norske Amerikalinje*.
2. Oleson to Osland, September 25, 1936.

Notes to "*Sanger-Hilsen*, the Singers' Periodical"

1. *Sanger-Hilsen* 15 (1912); Knudsen, "The Norwegian Male Chorus Movement."
2. Knudsen, "The Norwegian Male Chorus Movement."
3. *Sanger-Hilsen* 15 and 22 (1912).
4. Jacobson, "The Fort Dodge Serum Company," in "Olaf Martin Oleson."
5. *Minneapolis Tidende*, November 25, 1928; Norsk apotekerforenings tidsskrift, 1929; "Mindegaven til Norge 1914 fra det norske Utflytterfolk i Nord-Amerika," Nordmanns-Forbundet, *Årbok*, 1920.
6. *Dagbladet*, June 5, 1914.
7. Lyngstad; Kvam Historielag; *Sanger-Hilsen* (n.d.).

Notes to "The Singers' Tour to Norway"

1. Wist, ed., *Norsk-Amerikanernes Festskrift*; Hansen, "Det Norske Foreningsliv i Amerika."
2. *Sanger-Hilsen* (1919).
3. "Mindegaven til Norge 1914 fra det norske Utflytterfolk i Nord-Amerika," Nordmanns-Forbundet, *Årbok*, 1920.
4. Source unknown.
5. "Sangerfest" program, Grand Forks, ND, 1916, Norwegian-American Collection, National Library of Norway.
6. Jacobson, "Olaf Martin Oleson."
7. Anker and Berman, eds., *Edvard Munchs aulamalerier*.
8. Ola Five, account book, 1916, private collection.

Notes to "Olaf Becomes a Composer"

1. "In Flanders Fields," Arlington National Cemetery website, November 12, 2008.
2. *Sanger-Hilsen* 8 (n.d.).
3. *Sanger-Hilsen* 11 (1917).
4. *Sanger-Hilsen* 11 (1917).
5. "Mindegaven til Norge 1914 fra det norske Utflytterfolk i Nord-Amerika," Nordmanns-Forbundet, *Årbok*, 1920.
6. Mørkhagen, *Farvel Norge*.
7. "N.A.L. post," July-August 1956, Norwegian-American Collection, National Library of Norway.
8. Carol Tronstad and Leif Tronstad, Sundnes.

Notes to "The Norwegian American Composers Competition"

1. *Sanger-Hilsen* 1 (1919).
2. *Minneapolis Tidende*, 1920; Sartz, "Fra Amerikas Nordmænd."
3. *Sanger-Hilsen* 2 (1920).
4. *Sanger-Hilsen* 6 (1919).
5. *Sanger-Hilsen* 5 (1919) and 7 (1920).
6. Trinity Regional Medical Center, "A Legacy of Caring"; Jacobson, "Hospitals of Fort Dodge," in "Olaf Martin Oleson."

Notes to "Olaf and Family Tour Europe"

1. *Sanger-Hilsen* 7 (1921).
2. *Sanger-Hilsen* 9 (1921).
3. *Sanger-Hilsen* 9 (1921).
4. *Sanger-Hilsen* 10 (1921).
5. Nordgård, *Stod i fortid og nutid.*
6. Carol Tronstad and Leif Tronstad, Sundnes.
7. *Sanger-Hilsen* 10 (1921).
8. Ola Five to O. Nordgård, n.d.
9. Nord-Trøndelag Historielag, *Årbok*, 1921.
10. *Sanger-Hilsen* 6 (1921) and 7 and 8 (1922).
11. Ola Five to O. Nordgård, February 3, 1922.

Notes to "With Rotary to Hawaii"

1. *Sanger-Hilsen* 2 (1922).
2. *Sanger-Hilsen* 1 (1923).
3. Den norske Gleeklub, "Minnesota-Korets Norgesfærd 1923."

Notes to "Fort Dodge Grows"

1. Regarding the hospitals: Trinity Regional Medical Center, "A Legacy of Caring"; Fort Dodge Telephone Company, Iowa, 1923, online; Jacobson, "Hospitals of Fort Dodge," in "Olaf Martin Oleson."
2. Jacobson, "Olaf Martin Oleson."
3. Natte, *Fort Dodge, 1850–1970.*

Notes to "Olaf Is Honored"

1. *Sanger-Hilsen* 7 (1924).
2. *Sanger-Hilsen* 7 (1924).
3. *Sanger-Hilsen* 7 (1924).

Notes to "The Centennial of Norwegian Emigration to America"

1. Regarding the centennial: "Norse-American 1825 Centennial 1925. Souvenir Edition."
2. Ager, "Why We Celebrate," "Norse-American 1825 Centennial 1925. Souvenir Edition."

Notes to "The Norwegian-American Historical Association"

1. Oleson to Osland, October 1, 1935, and January 14, 1936; Osland to Oleson, January 17, 1936, and April 5, 1940.
2. Nelson, *Det norsk-amerikanske historielag gjennom 40 år.*
3. Oleson from/to Osland, W. Ager, C. G. O. Hansen, K. Gjerset, O. E. Rølvaag, D. G. Ristad, J. Thompson, K. Prestgard, J. H. Blegen, and M. Swenson are filed at the Norwegian-American Historical Association. Oleson to Osland, May 6, October 23, November 5, and December 1, 1926, June 17, 1927, October 11, 1937, January 11, 1938, and September 14, 1939; Osland to Oleson, November 5 and December 17, 1926, June 16, July 16 and 21, and August 2, 1927, August 9, 1929, and April 30, 1930; Oleson to Ristad, December 18, 1927.
4. Nord-Trøndelag Historielag, *Årbok*, 1929.
5. "Comments by Birger Osland on certain proposals, contained in letter to Mr. Prestgard from Dr. Blegen dated November 1, 1926, and other papers, attached hereto, which are all forwarded to Mr. O. M. Oleson with request that he comment on same and forward to Professor J. Jörgen Thompson," November 8, 1926.
6. Oleson to Osland, September 1, 1926; Osland to Oleson, April 27, 1927, December 6, 1930, and January 17, 1936.
7. Oleson to Osland, August 9, 1929; Osland to Oleson, August 22, 1927; Oleson to Ristad, May 20, 1926.
8. Nord-Trøndelag Historielag, *Årbok*, 1929.
9. Osland to Oleson, copy Magnus Swenson, O. E. Rølvaag, January 29, 1931; Osland to Oleson, March 2 and 12, 1931; Knut Gjerset to Osland, January 30, 1931; O. E. Rølvaag to Osland, February 3, 1931; Oleson to Osland, February 2 and March 8, 1931.

Notes to "In Caruso's Mausoleum and a Night at the Egyptian Opera"

1. *Sanger-Hilsen* 2 (1926).
2. *Sanger-Hilsen* 2 (1926).
3. Oleson to Osland, January 15, 1926.
4. *Sanger-Hilsen* 5 (1926).
5. Ola Five to Nordgård, March 5, 1926.
6. Ola Five to Nordgård, December 16, 1927.

Note to "More about the Ole Bull Statue"

1. *Minneapolis Tidende*, October 14, 1926.

Notes to "The First Telephone Call to Norway and the Royal Order"

1. Natte, *Fort Dodge, 1850–1970*; "O. M. Oleson Telephones to Oslo, Norway," local newspaper, October 27, 1929, Norwegian-American Historical Association.
2. Ola Five to Nordgård, 1928.
3. Regarding the St. Olav's Order: *Minneapolis Tidende*, November 25, 1928; "Fortjent Udmerkelse," *Decorah-Posten*, 1928; Jacobson, "Olaf Martin Oleson"; "Senator Oleson Is Made a Knight," 1928, and "O. M. Oleson Knighted by King of Norway," November 23, 1928, local newspapers; Ola Five to Nordgård, December 15, 1928.
4. *Sanger-Hilsen* 9 (1935).
5. *Sanger-Hilsen* 7 and 11 (1928).
6. *Sanger-Hilsen*, 25th Anniversary (1934).

Notes to "The Gift to the Nidaros Cathedral"

1. Ola Five to Nordgård, April 24, 1928, April 26, 1928/9?, May 23 and June 25, 1929.
2. Det Nationale Trønderlaget i Amerika, *Årbok*, 1927.
3. Kolsrud, *Nidaros og Stiklestad*.
4. *Nidaros*, July 8, 1930; Oleson to O. Nordgård, August 16, 1930.
5. Aarset, *Skyttergeneralen*.
6. "Norskamerikanarane på Stiklestad. Ei vellukka stemne igår. Talar av prost Hole, fru Betzy Kjeldsberg og pastor Ristad," "N.-am Utklippsbind/Avi," "Norsk-amerikanere besøker Norge, 1930," local newspaper, 1930, and *Adresseavisen*, July 17, 1930, Norwegian-American Collection, National Library of Norway.
7. Knudsen, "Utklippssamling—Musikk."
8. Tomlinson, ed., *A Century of Blessings*; St. Olaf Lutheran Church, "The Golden Jubilee."
9. Jacobson, "Olaf Martin Oleson."
10. *Sanger-Hilsen* 6 (1933).

11. Bandshell Restoration Project, online photo archive, 73; "Bandshell Ground-breaking Is Monday," *Fort Dodge Messenger*, September 5, 2004.
12. *Sanger-Hilsen* (1934, 1935).

Notes to "Keep Singing in Norwegian"

1. *Sanger-Hilsen* 1 (1935).
2. *Sanger-Hilsen* 7 (1935).
3. *Sanger-Hilsen* 9 and 11 (1935).
4. *Sanger-Hilsen* 1 and 4 (1936).

Notes to "Olaf and Julie Visit Norway"

1. *Sanger-Hilsen* 10 (1937).
2. *Sanger-Hilsen* 10 (1937).
3. Gjerstad, *Snåsninger og andre nordmenn i Vesterled.*
4. "Peaceful Norway Has Its Troubles, O. M. Oleson Finds," local newspaper, 1937.
5. Trond Five to his mother, 1937, private collection.
6. *Sanger-Hilsen* 3 (1938).

Notes to "The Oleson Park Music Pavilion"

1. Oleson to Osland, April 2, 1937, and January 21, 1938; Osland to Oleson, April 6 and March 30, 1937, January 19 and 27, 1938, and August 1, 1939.
2. *Sanger-Hilsen* 5 (1938).
3. Berglund, "Preserving the Past."
4. *Sanger-Hilsen* 10 (1938); *Decorah-Posten*, June 14, 1938; Nordmanns-Forbundet, *Årbok*, 1943. J. A. Aasgaard was president of the Norwegian Lutheran Church of America.

Notes to "The Norwegian Student Singers Visit Olaf Again"

1. The essential part about the Norwegian Singers tour is taken from Den norske Studentersangforening, *Vestover igjen.*
2. Freely translated from the source: Den norske Studentersangforening, *Vestover igjen.*

Notes to "I Made My Fortune in America"

1. "An Iowa Philanthropist," *Fort Dodge Messenger*, 1939.
2. Jacobson, "Olaf Martin Oleson."
3. "An Iowa Philanthropist," *Fort Dodge Messenger*, 1939.
4. Jacobson, "Olaf Martin Oleson."
5. *Sanger-Hilsen* 6 (1940).
6. Tomlinson, ed., *A Century of Blessings*; St. Olaf Lutheran Church, "The Golden Jubilee."

7. Cai, "Iowa Impromptu," 150–76.

8. Jacobson, "T. S. Larsen," in "Olaf Martin Oleson."

Notes to "A Monument to Olaf"

1. Oleson, "Last Will and Testament."
2. "In 21 Years 63-fold Gain in AHP Stock Values," local newspaper, 1965.
3. Julie Oleson to Trond Five, private collection.
4. "Oleson Building Dates to 1894. Old Landmark to Disappear from Downtown," *Fort Dodge Messenger*, August 7, 1971.
5. Aarset, *Skyttergeneralen*.
6. "J. Oleson Estate: $2,640,840," *Fort Dodge Messenger*, January 27, 1966.
7. Trinity Regional Medical Center, "A Legacy of Caring."

Sources

In addition to narrative information from members of the family in Norway and the United States and information available at the digital archive at the Norwegian National Archive and at Ancestry.com, I have used the following sources:

Aarset, Ane-Charlotte Five. *Kavaleristen.* 2007.
———. *Skyttergeneralen.* 2005.
———. *Utvandreren.* 2012.
Anker, Peder, and Patricia G. Berman, eds. *Edvard Munchs aulamalerier. Fra kontroversieltprosjekt til nasjonalskatt.* 2011.
Åsen, Per Arvid. "Tusenårshagen." Agder Naturmuseum og Botaniske hages tusenårsprosjekt, 1999–2002. Museumsnett.
Baughman, Kenneth. "Daniel E. Baughman, D.V.M., Founder of Fort Dodge Laboratories: A Pioneer in Veterinary Medicine." Internet.
Benestad, Finn, ed. *Edvard Grieg. Brev i utvalg 1826–1907.* Vol. I. 1998.
Berg, Martin. "Sang og Musikkliv paa Østkysten." Nordmanns-Forbundet, *Årbok,* 1925.
Berglund, Lori. "Preserving the Past: A Look Back at the History of Fort Dodge." *Fort Dodge Living,* June 2010.
Biographical History of La Crosse, Monroe and Juneau Counties, Wisconsin. 1892. Murphy Library, University of Wisconsin–La Crosse. Internet.
Bjerkrem, Johan Einar. "Trønderlaget i Amerika." Nord-Trøndelag Historielag, *Årbok,* 2000.
Bjørnson, Bjørnstjerne. Letters to Karoline from America-journey 1881. www .dokpro.uio.no/litteratur/bjoernson/bbka1.txt.
———. Letter to Ola Five, April 3, 1890. Manuscript Collection, National Library of Norway.
Brøndal, Jørn. *Ethnic Leadership and Midwestern Politics: Scandinavian-Americans and the Progressive Movement in Wisconsin, 1890–1914.* Urbana: University of Illinois Press, 2005.
Brown, Dee. *Begrav mitt hjerte ved Wounded Knee.* 1974.
Cai, Camilla Haugen. "Iowa Impromptu: Norwegian Immigrant O. M. Oleson Seeks Music from Bjørnson and Grieg." *Iowa Heritage Illustrated* 82, no. 4 (Winter 2001): 150–76.
———. "A Missed Opportunity for Grieg: Olaf Martin Oleson the Emigrant." *Studia Musicologica Norvegica* 25 (1999): 226–35. Norsk Musikkhistorisk arkiv, Edward Grieg, National Library of Norway.
Chicago Foreign Language Press Survey: Norwegian. Microform. Internet.
Cursin, Lincoln. "Centennial of the Spanish-American War 1898–1998." Internet.

Danielsen, Marit. *Landlige hager—hagekultur i Trøndelag.* 2006.

———. E-mail correspondence. 2009.

Den norske Gleeklubb og Normanna Mandskor, Duluth. "Minnesota-Korets Norgesfærd 1923." 1923.

Den norske Studentersangforening. *Den norske Studentersangforenings koncert-tourné gjennom det norske Amerika i mai og juni 1905. II. Forbunds-Historier.* 1906.

———. *Utklippsbind fra Den norske Studentersangforenings reise til USA i 1905.* Norsk musikksamling, National Library of Norway.

———. *Vestover igjen. Den norske Studentersangforenings ferd i USA 1939.* 1949.

Det Nationale Trønderlaget i Amerika. Yearbooks.

Det Norske Sangerforbund i Amerika. "Sangerfærden til Norge i 1914." 1915.

Dietze, Annegreth. "Garden Art and the Bourgeoisie, 1750–1850: Social, Political and Economic Aspects of Garden Art in the South of Norway with Focus on Plant Import." PhD thesis, University of Life Sciences, Ås, Norway, 2006.

Draxten, Nina. *Kristofer Janson in America.* Northfield, MN: Norwegian-American Historical Association, 1976.

Five, Ola. Letters to O. Nordgård. Gunnerus Library, NTNU, Trondheim, Norway.

Five, Olaf Wergeland. "Fiveslekta fra omkring år 1600 til omkring 1900." Private collection.

Fog, Dag, Kirsti Grinde, and Øyvind Norheim. *Edvard Grieg—Thematisch-Bibliographisches Werkverzeichnis.* 2008.

Fort Dodge Historic Preservation Commission. "A Capsule History of Fort Dodge." Internet.

Foss, Olaf. *Nord-Trøndelag Landbruksselskap.* 1930.

Gjerstad, Joralf. *Snåsninger og andre nordmenn i Vesterled.* 1998.

Grieg, Edvard. "Impromptu til Griegs Manndskor i Fort Dodge, Iowa, U.S. of. A." Grieg Archives, Bergen Public Library.

Guhnfeldt, Cato. "Fant hedensk helligdom uten sidestykke." *Aftenposten,* December 23, 2011.

Hagtvedt, Arne O. "Unionsoppløsningen i 1905—Forsvarets rolle." *Folk og Forsvar.* 2005.

Hambro, C. J. *Amerikaferd; av emigrasjonens historie. Til den Norske Amerika-linjes 25-års jubleum.* 1935.

Hansen, Carl G. O. "Det Norske Foreningsliv i Amerika." In Johannes B. Wist, ed., *Norsk-Amerikanernes Festskrift 1914.* Decorah, IA, 266–91.

———. "Norsk musikk i Amerika." In Martin Ulvestad, ed., *Nordmændene i Amerika, deres historie og rekord.* Det norske Selskabs Aarbok 1903, Vol. I.

Hanssen, Inger Marie. *Bli med en tur over 'dammen': Utvandring til Amerika fra Namdalseid, Malm, Beitstad.* 2000.

Hayden, Ada. "Olaf Martin Oleson." Memorial. 1944. Ada Hayden Papers, Iowa State University.

"History of Fort Dodge and Webster County, Iowa." Internet.

Holck, Per. *Merkedager og gamle skikker.* 1993.

Hummeland, Andrew. "The Norwegian National League. What Was the Norwegian National League Doing 100 Years Ago?" Internet.

Hurley, Vic. "Swish of the Kris: The Story of the Moros, Kris versus Krag." 1936. Internet.

Jacobson, Robert Allen (Bob). "Olaf Martin Oleson." 2009.

Joranger, Terje Mikael Hasle. "Identitet blant norske immigranter i Amerika: regionalisme eller nasjonalisme." Lecture, 2008.

Journal of the American Pharmaceutical Association 18 no. 3 (1929): 207–10. Internet.

Kaartvedt, Alf. "Kampen mot parlamentarismen. Den konservative politikken under vetostriden." PhD thesis, 1956.

Knudsen, Alf Lunder. "The Norwegian Male Chorus Movement in America: A Study." PhD thesis, University of Washington, 1989.

Knudsen, Alfred. "Utklippsbind 8—Musikk." Norwegian-American Collection, National Library of Norway.

Kolsrud, Oluf, ed. *Nidaros og Stiklestad: Olavs-jubileet 1930. Minneskrift.* 1937.

Kvam Historielag. *Utvandringen til Amerika 1849—1924, fra Kvam og Følling til Stod prestegjeld.* 1984.

Larsen, Lars Frode. "Knut Hamsuns Exodus. Amerika-oppholdet 1882–1884. Bakgrunn og erfaringer." Lecture, 2000.

Lovoll, Odd S. "1905 og norsk-amerikanerne." *Dagbladet,* July 30, 2005.

———. *Det løfterike landet.* 1983.

Lyngstad, Roger. Various local historical details, Kvam, by e-mails, 2010–11.

Lysdahl, Anne Jorunn Kydland. "Sangen har lysning. Studentersang i Norge på 1800-tallet." PhD diss., University of Oslo, 1995.

Malmin, Gunnar J., trans and ed. "Bishop Jacob Neumann's Word of Admonition to the Peasants." *Studies and Records* (Norwegian-American Historical Association) 1:95.

Mjeldheim, Leiv. *Folkerørsla som vart parti. Venstre frå 1880-åra til 1905.* 1984.

Mørkhagen, Sverre. *Farvel Norge. Utvandrere til Amerika 1825–1975.* 2009.

Natte, Roger B. *Images of America: Fort Dodge, 1850–1970.* Charleston, SC: Arcadia Publishing, 2008.

Nelson, O. N., ed. *History of the Scandinavians and Successful Scandinavians in the United States.* Vol. II, Parts I and II. Minneapolis: O. N. Nelson and Co., 1897.

Nelson, Peder H. *Det norsk-amerikanske historielag gjennom 40 år.* Nordmanns-Forbundet 1966.

Neuman, J. "Hyrdebrev med varselord til utvandringslystne bønder i Bergen stift." 1937. In Norway-Heritage, "Hands Across the Sea." Internet.

Nord-Trøndelag Historielag, yearbooks.

Nordgård, O. *Stod i fortid og nutid.* Vol. 2, 1920.

Nordmanns-Forbundet, periodicals.

"Norse-American Centennial. 1825–1925. Souvenir Edition." Published by the committee, president Gisle Bothne. Norwegian-America Collection, National Library.

Norwegian Singers' Association of America. Program leaflets from *Sangerfestene,* 1904–42. Norwegian-America Collection, National Library of Norway.

Nøvik, Peter. *Iakttagelser i Amerikas Havebrug.* 1894.

Oleson, Julie, letter to Birger Osland. Norwegian-American Historical Association, Northfield, MN.

Oleson, O. M. "Last Will and Testament." District Court of Webster County, IA, Webster County Historical Society.

———. Letter to Bjørnstjerne Bjørnson. Manuscript Collection, National Library of Norway.

———. Letter to O. Nordgård. Gunnerus Library, NTNU, Trondheim, Norway.

———. Letters to Birger Osland, Waldemar Ager, and D. G. Ristad. Norwegian-American Historical Association, Northfield, MN.

Oleson, O. M., and M. P. Somes. "A Flora of Webster County, Iowa." *Proceedings of the Iowa Academy of Science* 13 (1906).

Osland, Birger. Letters to O. M. Oleson and Julie Oleson. Norwegian-American Historical Association, Northfield, MN.

Ottestad, Eldrid. "Anglofile vegger." *Aftenposten*, March 10, 2012.

Peterson, Barbara. Pictures, articles, and narrative information, 2010.

Riksarkivet (The National Archives of Norway). Emigrant lists.

Ristad, D. G. "Den norske innsats i amerikansk kulturliv." *Norsk Pedagogisk Årbok*. 1927.

Rynning, Ole. *Sandfærdig Beretning om Amerika til Oplysning og Nytte for Bonde og Menigmand, forfattet af en Norsk, som kom derover i juni Maaned 1837*. 1839.

Sandnes, Jørn, ed. *Snåsavatnet. Natur, kultur, historie*. 1994.

Sandvik, Bjørn. "Norsk-amerikansk innflytelse på kirkelivet i Norge. Et forsømt forskningsfelt." Lecture, 2005.

Sanger-Hilsen. 1912–44. Norwegian-America Collection, National Library of Norway.

Sartz, R. S. N. "Fra Amerikas Nordmænd," "Minnegavens historie og mænd." *Nordmanns-Forbundet, Årbok*. 1913 and 1920.

Selnes, Johan. "O. M. Oleson." *Nordmanns-Forbundet, Årbok*. 1927.

Semmingsen, Ingrid. *Veien mot Vest*. Vol. 2. Utvandringen fra Norge 1865–1915. 1950.

The Norwegian Singers' Association of America arranges a three-day *Sangerfest* every other year at a midwestern location. In June 1924 the festival was held in St. Paul, Minnesota. O. M. Oleson, the first honorary president, stands in the middle of the front row,

Skej, Jarle, ed. *Bygdebok for Stod, Kvam og Egge*. Vol. I and II, 2006 and 2011.

St. Olaf Lutheran Church. "The Golden Jubilee (1891–1941)." Archives of the American Lutheran Church. Luther Theological Seminary, St. Paul. MN. Norwegian-American Collection, National Library of Norway.

Stenseth, Nils Chr. and Thore Lie. "Den norske døren til Darwin." *Aftenposten*, February 12, 2012.

Strand, A. E., ed. *A History of the Norwegians of Illinois*. 1905. Internet.

Sunde, Ole Larsen. "Agerbrugsbog," handwritten, 1846– . Private collection.

Tolfsby, Dina. "Bjørnsons foredragsturné vinteren 1880–1881—en stormfull tid i det norske Amerika." National Library of Norway. Internet, 2010.

———. "Nordmanns-Forbundet feirer sitt 100-års jubileum." Lecture, 2007.

Tomlinson, Charlotte, ed. *A Century of Blessings, 1891–1991, St. Olaf Lutheran Church, Fort Dodge, Iowa*.

Tømmerås, Bodvar. "Øventyr, Sagn av Karl Braset." *Kumur* 23 (2000). Published by Snåsa Historielag.

Torud, Yngve. "Om norsk og amerikansk farmasihistorie." E-mail, 2009.

Trinity Regional Medical Center. "A Legacy of Caring: The History of Trinity Regional Medical Center. Working Together. Making a Difference." Iowa Health System, 2002.

Tronstad, Carol, and Leif Tronstad. Narrative information, pictures, and maps. The history of the Sundnes estate.

Ulvestad, Martin, ed. *Nordmændene i Amerika, deres historie og rekord*. Vol. 2, 1907.

Vea, Erik, Johan Schreiner, and Johan Seland. *Den Norske Amerikalinje, 1910–1960*. 1960.

Wananaker, John. "Who Made America? Innovators." Wikipedia. Internet.

Welch, Eloise Hurst, Fort Dodge, IA. Married to Richard Welch, son of Helen Welch, daughter of Ingebrigt (Five) Oleson. Photos, articles, and narrative information, 2010.

Wist, Johannes B., ed. *Norsk-Amerikanernes Festskrift 1914*. Decorah, IA.

Wong, Johs, ed. *Norske Utvandrere og Forretningsdrivende i Amerika. Utgitt*

just beneath the American flag. The members of the *Grieg Mandskor* stand at far left with their banner. *Photo by P. Schwang & Fenney, Norwegian Singers' Association of America, Norwegian-American Collection, National Library of Norway*

som Minde i Anledningen av Hundreåret for Den Norske Innvandringen til Amerika. New York, Oslo, 1925.

Newspapers: *Adresseavisen, Aftenposten, Bergens Anoncetidende, Budstikken* (1883–84), *Dagbladet, Decorah-Posten* (1884, January 30, 1911, and June 14, 1938), *Farmand, Folkebladet* (1883), *Fort Dodge Messenger, Lutheraneren, Minneapolis Tidende* (October 14, 1926), *Morgenbladet, New York World, Nidaros* (September 8, 1930), *Skandinaven* (1883–84), *Verdens Gang, Washington-Posten* (December 28, 1923).

Jacobson, Robert Allen (Bob), historian at Webster County Historical Society, collected local historical material for this project and referred to the following sources:

Blanden Art Museum records.
Cai, Camilla Haugen, "Iowa Impromptu."
City Directories, 1886–1944.
Dolan, Bill. "A Book of Days."
Fort Dodge Art Club files.
Fort Dodge Garden Club files.
Fort Dodge Genealogical Society.
Fort Dodge Historical Society.
Fort Dodge Messenger.
History of Iowa from Earliest Time to Beginning of 20th Century, Vol. 3 and 4.
Iowa State Gazette and Business Directory.
Oak Park Cemetery records.
Natte, Roger. *Images of America: Fort Dodge 1850–1990.*
Trinity Hospital file.
Personal visitation of parks, buildings, and places mentioned in connection with Mr. or Mrs. Oleson.
Information gained from other researchers from their knowledge about times and places.

Index

They Sang for Norway has been typeset in Karmina Serif and Sans, a typeface designed by Veronika Burian and José Scaglione and released in 2007.

Book design by Wendy Holdman.

CPSIA information can be obtained
at www.ICGtesting.com
Printed in the USA
BVOW09s0318220517
484708BV00002B/4/P